HISTORY OF PORTUGAL

VOLUME II:

FROM EMPIRE TO CORPORATE STATE

A. H. DE OLIVEIRA MARQUES

History of Portugal

VOLUME II:

FROM EMPIRE TO CORPORATE STATE

COLUMBIA UNIVERSITY PRESS

New York and London

1972

Copyright © 1972 Columbia University Press
ISBN: 0-231-08700-4
Library of Congress Catalog Card Number: 77-184748
Printed in the United States of America

*To António José Saraiva
and Vitorino Magalhães Godinho*

CONTENTS

HISTORY OF PORTUGAL

VOLUME II:

FROM EMPIRE TO CORPORATE STATE

CONSTITUTIONAL MONARCHY

OLD STRUCTURES AND NEW ORDER

The opening of Brazilian ports to all nations in 1808 and the commercial treaty with England in 1810 ruined the foundations of the Portuguese economy. In 1820 the balance of trade registered a deficit of 21 million cruzados for Portugal. When the bourgeois dreams of recovering the lost colony were over, and the total autonomy of former Portuguese America was acknowledged by the Treaty of Rio de Janeiro (1825), the shaping of a new economic physiognomy for Portugal had to be realistically envisaged.

For many, the answer lay in an upsurge of agriculture. Father Correia da Serra, expressing the physiocratic view, had stated that "the first step in any nation, to take profit of her advantages, is to know exactly the land she inhabits, what they produce in themselves, what they are capable of." Thus, to exploit the soil and to foster agriculture became for nineteenth-century Portugal the main goal. Skeptical about the possibilities of developing a new empire, both statesmen and economists attempted to look inward, to realize the country's possibilities in the fields of agriculture, stockbreeding, fishing, mining, and (somewhat later) industry. This attitude and program needs to be stressed, because it was the opposite of almost four centuries of colonial exploitation. It went against tradition and habits; in fact, it seemed revolutionary and had to be backed by many other revolutionary structures. Constitutional Portugal was indeed, or tried to be, a revolutionary new order. Starting from chaos, from the lowest point in economic decline, and from political enslavement to England, it fought bravely to raise up a new nation. The very survival of Portugal in the twentieth-century world is proof that this struggle succeeded, although not entirely in the manner desired.

No development of agriculture would be possible—so the physiocrats and the liberals contended—without complete destruction of "feudal" ties, which harassed the farmer and his activities as a producer. In Portugal, as in France during the Revolution and elsewhere in Europe, legislation was enacted for the alleged purpose of "freeing" the field worker and making possible an upsurge in agriculture. Such legislation affected both property in all its forms and rural society in many ways. The ecclesiastical tithe was abolished. The sales tax was reduced by half and maintained only on real estate. All feudal rights such as corvées; exclusives on ovens, presses, wine sales, and the like; and payments of all kinds to the lord or the king or others disappeared. Other seignorial traditions were abolished too, like the game preserves and the stud farms. The so-called Crown patrimony (Bens da Coroa) became the "Nation's patrimony" (Bens Nacionais), and all lands and rights granted to commandatories and donataries were to revert to the state as soon as their present grantees died. Entailed property was also limited to wealthy estates with more than 200,000 réis of annual liquid revenue, and several measures were adopted to ensure their elimination in the near future. The numerous duties of all sorts existing in the borough charters (forais) were also abolished, as well as many internal tolls on trade and circulation, import and export permits, and all hindrances to free commerce. Finally, lands to be cleared or recently cleared were granted freedom of taxation for a period of twenty years. All this legislation was enacted in 1821–23 (by the cortes elected in 1820 and 1821) and later, in 1832 (by Secretary Mousinho da Silveira). In between, conservatives had repealed most of the earlier acts, which had to be renewed when the liberals came to power again.

Another important act eliminated the religious orders (1834), and their property was conveyed out of mortmain and auctioned off. The government also sold much land belonging to the Crown. In this way previously wasted or improperly cultivated land now became productive, owing to the interest of the new proprietors. These lands gave excellent yields in the beginning, because they had been fallow so long. The total suppression of entailed estates in 1863 gave property in Portugal a modern structure and further helped the rise of agriculture. Rural credit was organized, a large company appearing in 1864 for that purpose (Companhia Geral do Crédito Predial Português). Last but not least, the development of transportation and communications after 1840 brought about the beginnings of an adequate substructure for the rise of agriculture.

It took some time for these and other measures to produce their effects on agriculture. The political turmoil and the civil wars of 1832–34 and 1846–47 did nothing to improve clearing of land and agricultural output. Little by little, however, agrarian conditions changed and effective development was noticeable by the second half of the century.

Imports of wheat gradually declined. From 1838 to 1855 Portugal even exported some grain to the overseas territories and to foreign countries. This was mainly a result of two protectionist laws, enacted in 1821 and 1837, which strictly controlled imports, raised the customs duties, and protected national grain production. However, when soil fertility waned, with the number of people increasing, imports became necessary once more. The law of 1837 was repealed (acts of 1856–65). Wheat imports rose from nothing to 31,000 tons (1856–57 to 1862–63), then to 67,000 (1865 to 1888), and to 134,000 (1890 to 1899). A number of agrarian studies and plans appeared, all aimed at solving this problem. They either dealt with grain alone or with the broader question of developing agriculture in general. Partly because of this, some important laws and regulations were enacted from 1889 to 1899 which had significant results for agriculture, particularly the act of 1899 (signed by Secretary Elvino de Brito). By closely controlling imports and again raising customs duties, fixing prices, and fostering grain production, this law succeeded in reducing wheat imports—to an annual average of 88,000 tons for 1899–1913. In the same period the population grew 10 per cent while the cultivated area of the country was enlarged. Indeed, the study of Portugal's empty lands throughout the nineteenth and the early twentieth century is the best proof of the country's development in agriculture and settlement. In 1819 two-thirds of the Portuguese soil lay uncultivated; this had decreased to one-half fifty years later, and to less than 40 per cent in 1902. The law of 1899 encouraged further clearing of the land up to World War I (see chapter 12).

Among the new crop cultures introduced or developed in this period, potatoes and rice were foremost, with important consequences. Potatoes replaced the extensive consumption of turnips and chestnuts in people's diets, particularly in the North and the Northeast. Vast areas of chestnut groves gradually yielded to potato plantations. In many regions of Portugal, fallowing could be partly replaced by potato fields. Rice cultivation spread in the mid-nineteenth century and imports declined. High-tariff legislation (1837) promoted rice fields all over the country. Later on, a reaction against their proliferation (to the detriment of other cultures) and their unhealthfulness prevented larger outputs for a time. At the beginning of the twentieth century, however, rice production was again intensified, gradually becoming a popular food for all Portuguese.

Cork too was extensively developed. After 1822, Catalan immigrants fostered its cultivation by using more advanced techniques for both growing and transforming cork. From 1870 to World War I, cork exports increased 100 per cent, with a corresponding increase in the area in groves. Other more traditional cultures showed a similar expansion. Vineyards, for instance, were extensively planted in Estremadura and Ribatejo. In the North, however, countless vines were destroyed by a disease, phyloxera, after 1872. Areas devoted to almond groves and carob groves increased in the Algarve. Orchards and herb gardens spread, making the general landscape more varied than before. With few exceptions all forms of agriculture made remarkable progress in yield per hectare, a result of better techniques too. In the 1860's the first agrarian machines were introduced although it took a century for them to be adopted countrywide.

To promote agriculture and its modernization, several associations developed: the Sociedades Agrícolas, officially constituted 1844–54; the Associação Central da Agricultura Portuguesa, founded 1860; the Liga Agrária do Norte, appearing in 1889. In addition, many exhibitions and congresses were held in various places.

Redistribution of property was one of the main features of nineteenth-century Portugal, with important consequences, both economic and social. During the Civil War of 1832–34, the Liberals decreed the confiscation of all property belonging to their foes, an act which they called "indemnity." Victory was still far off, but it did not matter. Land and other goods were auctioned off and promptly acquired by the wealthy victors, most of them traders or industrialists. Some months later the liberal government disbanded all religious orders and confiscated their vast property. It also decided to sell off property belonging to the Crown. Some thousands of acres changed owners and cloyed the greedy appetites of the victorious bourgeois. Up to 1836 one-fourth of the nationalized goods had been auctioned off to more than six hundred people; but it took at least a decade to complete the whole transaction, the value of which was estimated at twice the amount of the state's annual revenues. When finished, the sale revealed a new Portugal in landownership. While many estates changed hands with no significant boundary alteration, many others were either parceled off or purchased together by the same buyer. The rich Tejo and Sado meadowlands were acquired for 2,000 contos by a company (Companhia das Lezírias) with several capitalists joining. A class of landed bourgeois rose, strongly supporting the liberals and preventing the return of the old regime.

The development of industry was another feature of constitutional Portugal. Until the 1830's few changes were achieved in this field, partly because power belonged to rural landowners, traders, bureaucrats, or nobles and partly because the political struggles were not favorable to any steady growth of industrial activities. England eagerly assured the supplying of industrial items to Portugal.

After 1834 things changed; for example, a law abolished corporations and other hindrances to the free growth of trade and industry (1834). The junta for commerce, agriculture, factories, and navigation, which controlled the industrial development of the country, disappeared. Industrialists were thus given a free hand to adopt innovations, invest capital, fix prices, and exploit labor as they pleased. Then, in 1836 power was concentrated for a time in the hands of some industrialists, supported by craft workers and other townspeople. The 1837 customs tariff firmly protected existing national industry, while fostering the rise of new activities. For Portugal this marked the beginning of a new epoch.

Pre-capitalistic forms of production and industrial relationships gradually evolved toward fully capitalistic forms. It took a long time, however, for Portuguese industry to overcome the craft tradition, the female handwork at home, the lack of capital, and the scarcity of qualified labor and modern machinery. Some figures may help to show this evolution. Steam engines, for example, were nonexistent for industrial purposes before 1835. In 1840 four were already working, with a total of 79 horsepower. Ten years later almost double the number were working, with ten times more horsepower. In 1881 Portuguese industry employed a total of 9,087 horsepower, which had again increased ten times by the early twentieth century, including a very small percentage from electricity.

Such "leaps" forward, while revealing Portugal's general industrial growth, also show the weakness of its industry compared with that of other countries. Thus Belgium, half the size of Portugal, employed 720,000 horsepower in the early 1900's, against 111,000 for Portugal. Statistics for factories and human labor are also meaningful: there were less than 15,000 workers in 1,031 plants in 1822; 180,000 in 1,350 factories in 1881; some 200,000 in more than 5,000 factories on the eve of World War I. In a population of $5\frac{1}{2}$ million, the number of industrial laborers was certainly minor, particularly since statistics did not distinguish between homeworkers and plant workers. The rate of increase in the number of invention patents also shows the growing interest in industry: 5.1 in 1837–52 (annual average), 14.4 in 1863–67, 27.4 in 1873–77, 60 in 1878–82, 109.5 in 1887–92.

Which were the industries experiencing this growth? Here, too, changes had deeply affected the Portuguese tradition. Before 1820 leather led the way, followed by textiles. Together, they accounted for 80 per cent of the workers and the factories. Sixty years later the leather industry had declined to a second-class level, using no machinery at all. The textile industry had risen to first place, followed by tobacco (which employed 4,000 people and used 30 steam engines), milling, ceramics, cork, and glass. On the eve of World War I textiles accounted for one-fourth of Portuguese industry (50,000 workers). In addition to the other crafts mentioned for 1881, the processing of dairy products and sardine-canning were showing a rapid rise.

From the 1870's on the process of capital accumulation and concentration of firms speeded up. In 1881 there were already some large industrial combines, in tobacco and textile manufactures. Foreign capital (English mostly) began to enter Portugal at a quickening pace: in 1884, some 10 per cent of all the anonymous societies and companies (for both trade and industry) in Portugal were foreign, but their invested capital amounted to about 20 per cent. By 1900 foreign firms had increased to one-sixth of the total (half of them British), and their investments controlled one-fourth of Portugal's trade and industry. In 1891 the tobacco industry was converted into a monopoly, the capital of which belonged predominantly to foreigners. Yet some large Portuguese combines also appeared, the first important Portuguese industrialists or millionaires becoming apparent by the end of the century. The milling industry was one of these, with a virtual monopoly in supplying Lisbon with bread, biscuits, and pastries. In glass and ceramics similar concentrations developed. Two big names related to industry arose in the early 1900's: Narciso Ferreira (Riba d'Ave) in textiles and Alfredo da Silva in the chemical industries. They started dynasties which are still going on, more prosperous than ever.

The economic expansion of Portugal resulted largely from the governmental policy of developing transportation and communications. The building of roads, railroads, harbors, lighthouses, and telegraph connections were the goals of most Portuguese governments, particularly after 1851. Some timid measures of road development had been enacted in 1838 and 1843, when the government entrusted several companies with the building of a number of roads in the northern, central and southern regions. Those firms were authorized to set up toll stations along the new roads for a certain period. In 1844 a Company for Public Works (Companhia das Obras Públicas de Portugal) endeavored to make or repair roads all over the country. At the same time (under Costa Cabral's "strong governments," 1842–46; 1849–51) several bridges were erected—the important suspension bridge over the Douro River, for instance—while work began for the improvement of the Douro sand bar. But it was only under Secretary Fontes Pereira de Melo (Secretary of Finance, 1851–52; Secretary of Public Works, 1852–56; Prime Minister, 1871–77, 1878–79 and 1881–86) that a well-developed policy of public works became a major concern of government. Known as Fontismo (after Fontes), its aim was to modernize Portugal through a program of material improvements, emphasizing transportation and communications, i.e., the infrastructure of trade, industry, and agriculture (areas where the state intervention should be minimal according to the liberal ideology). Fontismo strove hard to give Portugal an honorable place within the civilized world, to "Europeanize" the country and pull her out of a condition of deep backwardness. By means of extensive loans, Secretary Fontes and his successors (especially Emídio Navarro, Secretary of Public Works from 1886 to 1889) could get the necessary credits for their policy of expansion.

Road building led the way: when Fontes took office as the first Secretary of Public Works, in 1852, Portugal had only 218 km. (135.5 miles) of modern, macadamized roads. Four years later, when he left office, there were 678 km. (411 miles) ready and 120 km. under construction. In 1884 such figures had increased more than tenfold (9,155 km. = 5,667 miles), and in 1900 Portugal could boast a road network of 14,230 km. (8,843 miles).

Railroad building also had a spectacular growth. Projects for endowing the country with trains had started in the 1840's, Prime Minister Costa Cabral having commissioned the Companhia das Obras Públicas de Portugal with the building of a first track from Lisbon to the Spanish border. The project failed, however, and it was Fontes who had the credit of providing the country with her first railroads: from 1851 to 1856 several contracts with Portuguese and foreign companies were signed and the first trains were in operation after 1856. The network increased twentyfold from an initial 36 km. (22.3 miles) in 1864, to more than 1,500 in the mid-1880's, 2,288 km. in 1892, 2,381 km. in 1902, 2,974 km. in 1912. In 1894 Portugal held an honorable tenth place among the countries of the world in the extent of railroads for each 100 miles of territory—ranking above Spain, Roumania, Norway, Greece, and other European countries. The situation was roughly the same twenty years later.

Along with roads and railroads went bridge building. At the end of his first term in government, Fontes claimed the construction of seventeen bridges and the beginning of twenty-eight others. The great train bridge over the Douro built by the famous French engineer Eiffel (1875–77) allowed the completion of the railroad from Lisbon to Porto. The same happened with the building of the international bridge over the Minho, which opened direct railroad communications between northern Portugal and Spanish Galicia (1886). For people and carriages a new monumental bridge over the Douro opened in 1886, replacing the suspension work of forty years before.

Gradually, all the provinces of Portugal welcomed the advantages of easy communication: departing from Lisbon by train it became possible to reach Alto Alentejo (1861); Ribatejo (1863); Beira Litoral, Douro, and Baixo Alentejo (1864); Porto and Minho (1877); Beira Alta (1882); Trás-os-Montes (1883); the Algarve (1889); and Beira Baixa (1893). In less than forty years the whole country, even the most distant towns, had been brought closer together. Connections with Spain (i.e., with Europe) started in the 1860's.

Railroads were followed by telegraph (1857), with an almost immediate connection with Spain. In 1864 more than 2,000 km. of telegraph were working, a figure which had jumped four times by World War I. Submarine cable also began in the 1850's (Lisbon-Azores). In 1870 it linked Portugal to England, then to Brazil via Madeira and Cape Verde (1871). Telephone connections entered Portugal very early: Lisbon had its first phones by 1882. Wireless telegraph arrived only at the beginning of the twentieth century.

Harbors and lighthouses were greatly improved. The government had an artificial port made at Leixões in the North, to serve Porto and its hinterland (1884–92). In the port of Lisbon, a development plan was begun in 1887. In the 1890's, efforts to give light to the Portuguese coastline (called the black coast) led to fruitful results with the building of numerous lighthouses.

The post office was thoroughly reformed and improved in the 1850's, and then, several times, up to the end of the century. Postage stamps appeared in 1853, along with a new map of postal districts. The complex and traditional system of weights and measures underwent a complete change, when the government introduced the decimal metric system, effective by 1868 (in currency the decimal system had been established in 1835). It took, of course, generations to get the public used to so different a process of accounting. Post office, telegraphs, and telephones (with the exception of those in Lisbon and Porto) were nationalized from the very beginning. Half of the railroad network belonged to the state too.

In trade, the adoption of the liberal ideology prevented government interference. In the beginning, its main goal was only free exchange inside and outside the country; hence all the measures abolishing local tolls, permits of circulation, municipal monopolies, exclusives and privileges for certain companies, sales taxes, the corporations, and the like. It was, however, possible for the state to endow commerce with a framework that could regulate, organize, and also simplify the free circulation and distribution of products. The first Portuguese code of commerce was soon enacted in 1833, revealing clearly the bourgeois features of the new administration. Its author was Ferreira Borges, one of the main leaders of the liberal revolution. The code lasted until 1888, when the tremendous development of trade, both in Portugal and abroad, required a new one, that of Veiga Beirão. Tribunals of commerce were also established (1834). Lavish legislation starting with Ferreira Borges' code created and regulated economic associations, particularly joint-stock companies, which rapidly became favorites. Quota partnerships officially appeared in 1901. Other important legislation included codes of commercial proceedings (1896, 1905) and a code of commercial failures (1899).

Private associations of all sorts for trade purposes resulted from these laws and the general economic expansion of the country. The big traders of Porto and Lisbon founded their respective commercial associations (Associação Comercial do Porto, 1834; Associação Mercantil de Lisboa, 1834). By 1875 some fifteen commercial associations existed in the main urban centers, with an important impact on the rise of trade, industry, agriculture, and overseas expansion. In 1894 the government authorized a Chamber of Commerce and Industry for Lisbon. Joint-stock companies developed, particularly after 1867, when governmental restrictions on their free constitution were lifted: in 1875, 136 existed throughout the country (29 of them foreign); in 1885, 445 including companies of trade (46 foreign); in 1900 more than six hundred (one-eighth foreign). Half of the foreign companies and capital was British. Up to the end of the nineteenth century, the overwhelming majority of joint-stock companies were in trade, a minimal number only being concerned with industry. After 1900 the proportion drastically changed in favor of industry.

Obviously, a large share of this commercial growth—which brought about the rapid development of Lisbon and Porto—derived from better transportation and communications. Railways and roads made it easier to sell the products of agriculture (and industry), and facilitated rural credit operations and property transactions.

The development of external trade began especially after 1832. Duties on national exports went down from 8 per cent to 1 per cent. The customs tariff of 1837 (Passos Manuel) registered 1,499 different items, rationalizing duties on imports and exports, and trying to protect the national interests against exploitation by foreign powers. With England, Portugal's largest commercial partner, a new treaty of commerce was signed in 1842. It reduced the privileges granted to the British in 1810 and 1831. Other treaties of commerce were later signed with different countries.

Fontism reacted against protectionism. The new customs tariff of 1852 lowered the duties on many imports, particularly raw materials, instrumental for the development of industries and communications. For forty years, and despite some later corrections of the customs tariff, general economic policy tended toward free exchange. Only in 1892, when a serious crisis threatened the country, did a new tariff go back to less liberal principles, on behalf of national and colonial products.

The balance of trade registered a permanent deficit, which substantially increased after 1899: a yearly average of 12,017 contos de réis in 1880–89, 15,244 in 1890–99, 31,033 in 1900–1909. At the beginning of the century Portugal imported (mainly from England) twice as much as she exported. The most important imports included woollen, cotton, and silk fabrics; machinery; raw cotton, wool, and silk; coal; sugar; iron; and codfish. Understandably industrial expansion created the need for more and more raw materials and consequently a worsening balance of trade. The deficit could partly be covered by the foreign exchange credits sent by Portuguese immigrants in Brazil.

The rise to power by the bourgeoisie and the economic expansion of Portugal coincided with the foundation of the first banks. Up to the early nineteenth century, the peculiar economic structure of Portugal, based upon state intervention and foreign domination, had prevented the rise of a banking system. Several attempts since 1800 had failed, except in Brazil (see chapter 9). After the liberal revolution, however, the new economic and social conditions permitted the establishment of the first Portuguese bank, the Bank of Lisbon (1821). With a capital of 5,000 contos, this Bank was granted the monopoly of banknote issues, which it kept to 1835. It was primarily a commercial bank. Up to the 1860's, growth of the banking system was minimal. Three new banks appeared, one of them devoted to the Overseas (Banco Ultramarino, 1865). The important feature of this earlier period was rather the fusion of the Bank of Lisbon with another one, the result being the much more important Bank of Portugal (1846), with a capital of 11,000 contos.

In the 1860's an economic boom stirred the country, a consequence partly of the international conjuncture and partly of the policy known as Fontismo. Transactions on the stock exchange developed and speculation reached a level disproportionate to the country's possibilities. The number of banks increased from four (1863), to twelve (1865), then twenty-six (1874), and finally fifty-one (1875). Their deposits increased from a level of 3,183 contos in 1858, to double that in 1865, again double in 1872, and double once more in 1875 (24,513 contos). But while the total amount of deposits had grown, their concentration in a few large banks very much declined: 79.4 per cent in the five main banks by 1870, 55.2 per cent five years later. When the economic crisis of 1876 shook Portugal, a good many of the smaller and local banks closed their doors. By 1880, when the crisis was over, only forty-four banks survived. The late 1880's were a similar period of expansion: forty-eight banks in 1887–88, then forty-five in 1889–90, and forty-four in 1891. Deposits, which had increased to 55,000 contos in 1889—comparable with the "high" level of 1875—went down again: 48,000 contos in 1890, 39,000 in 1891, and 33,000 in 1892. The great crisis of 1892 reduced the number of banks to less than thirty. Afterward, though deposits went up once more—in 1917 they were double the amount in 1892—banks were roughly the same in number: twenty-eight in 1910, although concentration of deposits in the five largest ones continued to increase.

The history of prices in Portugal was no different from the other countries of Europe during the same period. The long-term price trends showed a decline from about 1817 to the 1840's, then a rise to the mid-1870's, followed by another drop until 1890 and a new rise which would stop only some years after the end of World War I. These rises and falls were usually gentle and gradual, causing no great disturbances from a social standpoint (with a few exceptions) at least to the early twentieth century. In Portugal the price graph for the period 1868–1910 shows very few variations till the rise of 1890, after which there was a plateau with some slight fluctuations to 1904. Beginning with that year there was an almost continuous upward movement, which brought about widespread discontent and revolutionary tendencies.

Money followed a similar trend, with few devaluations and a general stabilizing tendency. Lack of Brazilian gold produced the first change in the value of the money after the mid-1700's: an act of 1822 raised the price of a mark (230 g.) of minted gold from 102,400 to 120,000 réis, a debasement of 17 per cent. This measure again put into practical circulation gold coins, which up to then tended to disappear and be melted. Silver experienced no change, which means that the ratio between the two rose to 1:16 instead of 1:13.5. In 1835 a full monetary reform was accomplished. Silver was debased almost 20 per cent (1 mark = 7,750 réis instead of the former 7,600) but no alteration affected gold. More important was the adoption of the decimal principle in currency: while keeping the real, the law established a new coin denomination system, based upon 1,000 réis—gold coins of 5,000 and 2,500 réis; silver coins of 1,000, 500, 200, and 100 réis; and copper coins of 20, 10, 5, and 3 réis.

In 1847–54 money suffered a new slight debasement: 7 per cent for gold (1 mark = 128,000, later 129,000 réis), 18 per cent for silver (1 mark = 9,180 réis); but up to the beginning of World War I no other important changes affected the currency. Besides the Portuguese gold coins (10,000, 5,000, 2,000 and 1,000 réis), British gold pounds fixed at 4,500 réis had legal tender in Portugal. In silver, a new 50 réis coin appeared, while the 1,000 réis ceased to be minted.

By the end of the century, the gradual disappearance of the Portuguese gold coins, which under Luis I and his successors had no longer been minted (after 1861), coinage of nickel (100 and 50 réis), and the increase in the circulation of paper money were signs of a gradual deterioration of the currency. English gold flooded the country, altogether replacing the Portuguese and being trusted much more than the national bills. Note circulation increased, despite all the efforts to hold it down.

Public finance also received the attention of the liberal governments from the very beginning. It actually became the main source of concern for most administrations throughout the nineteenth and the early twentieth century. The old system of government irresponsibility was over, and with it the confusion between king and Crown. From 1820 on, governments had a parliament to supervise them, an organ to which they periodically rendered accounts. The law of 1832 (Mousinho da Silveira) abolished the royal treasury and organized a public treasury tribunal (Tribunal do Tesouro Público), actually determined by the constitution. This tribunal was to audit all accounts throughout the country and define them as current or not. In each province a receiver-general or collector-general (recebedor geral) centralized revenues and paid expenditures. He had, as his representative in every *comarca,* a delegate *(delegado)*, and he could also name deputies wherever he thought advisable. Another body known as Junta do Crédito Público (junta for public credit) was created (later dissolved and created again) for the purpose of receiving an annual endowment fixed by the *cortes* and of spending it on public debt interest and amortization.

Later acts introduced some changes in this system. The public treasury tribunal was dissolved, then reestablished. A law of 1842 set up central coffers in each district for collecting all revenues which had no well-determined local use. According to the same law, the court would appoint a receiver or tax collector for each municipality. The civil-governors of the administrative districts were entrusted with the supervision of tax collecting and its application to the public expenditures. An act of 1849 created the court of accounts (Tribunal de Contas) in charge of fiscalizing all public revenues and expenditures. Other laws (1860, 1870, 1886, etc.) corrected and altered some minor details without essentially changing the basic principles.

No reform, however, could solve one of the major problems of parliamentary Portugal, that of the scarcity of government funds. In truth, this problem was as old as the country itself. The introduction of public control in the state finance system, however, gave wide publicity to what previously had been the concern of only a few. Moreover, the end of Brazil as a colony and the abolition of many feudal taxes reduced the revenues, while the French invasions, the revolution, the Civil wars (that of 1832–34 cost 6,000 contos), and reforms of structure hopelessly increased expenditures. Later on, the very expansion of Portugal brought about new state expenses in all areas. Public works cost money and their eventual profit took some time to be collected. Meanwhile, more expenditures arose to absorb the new revenues. Again, this was (and is) a general concern of all countries, with somewhat graver aspects in a small one, with less maneuverability. Consequently, both the budget deficit and the public debt grew larger and larger, because the increase in expenditures greatly exceeded the increase in revenues.

In 1805 the Crown received 11,200 contos (i.e., 11,200,000,000 réis) in revenue. This figure went down to an average of 5,000–7,000 contos after the French Invasions, while the figure reached almost 15,000 contos in the years of highest expenditures (1828, 1834). Public debt went up to nearly 40,000 contos (annual charge of 1,269), including interest, paper money, promissory notes, and unpaid pensions and salaries. In 1834–43, the average yearly government revenues had gone up to 8,000 contos, but expenditures reached more than 10,000 contos a year. Yet the trend in revenues pointed to better days: the 1842–43 revenues matched the level of 1805, for the first time in almost forty years.

Fontismo along with the general development of the country and the end of the revolutionary period eased the budgetary situation. In the 1850's, revenues permanently surpassed the level of 1805 and jumped forward rapidly: annual averages reached 14,527 contos in 1854–63, 18,560 in 1864–73, 30,323 in 1874–83, 41,332 in 1884–93, 54,104 in 1894–1903, and 67,090 in 1904–10. Thus, at the beginning of the twentieth century Portugal, in terms of taxation, was five times wealthier than at the apogee of her exploitation of Brazil, a clear proof that the country could survive even without colonies (in those days the colonial weight on public revenues was minimal). At the same time, expenditures grew to still higher levels: 17,520 contos (1854–63), 25,220 (1864–73), 34,108 (1874–83), 47,420 (1884–93), 57,372 (1894–1903), and 69,085 (1904–10). The history of deficit was thus the history of constitutional finance, with its most terrible years in the late 1860's and in 1888–91. Afterward, the pressure of public opinion, and particularly the republican threat, led to a more careful management of state finance, which reduced the deficit by reducing expenditures.

The growth of public debt was still more impressive. The government borrowed money from every possible source, both internally and abroad. England, of course, was its main source, and England required prompt and honest payment. Regarding other sources, the usual solution was not to pay and periodically to declare bankruptcy, in the old tradition of the Portuguese Empire. After 1851 the governments elevated the principle of non-amortization to a rule of administration, funded debt increasing to unheard-of proportions (around 38,000 contos in 1835, 93,000 in 1855, 194,000 ten years later, 573,000 in 1890, 797,000 in 1910, some 90 per cent of the total debt).

Among the structural changes which shaped a new Portugal, the reforms in administration are significant. The *cortes* began those reforms in 1822 by regulating elections at the municipal level and adopting new principles for city organization. Then the Constitution set up the bases of administrative reform and the independence of the tribunals. Portugal was thoroughly divided into districts (*distritos*), each one encompassing a number of municipalities (*concelhos*). Administrators-general (*administradores gerais*) appointed by the king represented the government in every district, while the municipalities elected their deputies to an administrative junta (*junta administrativa*), which assisted the administrators. Such principles closely followed the French law, in those days considered the most perfect one, which had a tremendous influence on many new liberal regimes of Europe. The counterrevolution of 1823 ended all that. It was only in 1826 that the liberal restoration began another plan of administrative and judicial changes by entrusting two committees with the task of studying and suggesting practical methods of reform. But again the political evolution of Portugal interrupted this until 1832. In that year, the "provisional government" active in the Azores enacted three laws reforming public finance, civil administration, and judicial administration (Secretary Mousinho da Silveira). They would become the foundations of modern Portugal.

According to the constitutional principles, administrative and judicial functions could not and should not be confused, as before. Thus, the new laws thoroughly changed most of the existing rules on administration, repealing a large part of the *Ordenações* (see chapter 7) and other legislation. Along with the Azores and Madeira Islands, Portugal was divided into provinces (*províncias*), *comarcas,* and municipalities (*concelhos*), the first headed by a prefect (*prefeito*), the second by an under-prefect (*sub-prefeito*), and the last by a purveyor (*provedor*), all appointed by the king. Each of these officials would be assisted by collective bodies, indirectly elected by the people: *junta geral de província, junta de comarca,* and *câmara municipal.* In every province a three-member court or council, of royal choice, had consultative as well as substantive powers (*conselho de prefeitura*). A high degree of centralization and extensive powers granted to the representatives of the government characterized the act of 1832.

This law was altered three years later (Rodrigo da Fonseca) although its basic provisions underwent few changes. Provinces disappeared and districts replaced the *comarcas.* Under-prefects were renamed civil-governors (*governadores civis*), and purveyors, administrators (*administradores dos concelhos*), the latter being elected by the people and then confirmed by the government. A *conselho de distrito,* with consultative powers, substituted for the *conselho de prefeitura.* Elections for the general junta (*junta geral do distrito*) and the City Council became direct. Below the municipalities the new law acknowledged the existence of parishes (*paróquias*), with their local juntas—elected by the population—and their commissioners (*comissários de paróquia*), also directly elected but confirmed by the administrator. The administrative code of 1836—the first one in Portugal—maintained the law of 1835 with minor alterations (Passos Manuel). Both acts tended to lessen centralization and increase local autonomy.

The acts of 1840–42 (administrative code of 1842—Costa Cabral) reacted against decentralization and went back to the principles of 1832. Administrators and *regedores* became once more of governmental choice. The seesaw policy between centralization and decentralization would continue to the present, according to the changes in politics. Thus, after several attempts to correct the legislation of 1840–42, the administrative code of 1878 (Rodrigues Sampaio) granted local autonomy as never before, depriving the government of most powers of inspection and supervision. The code of 1886 (with later alterations) strengthened centralization again (José Luciano de Castro). (The *juntas gerais* of the districts disappeared.) The codes of 1895 and 1896 (João Franco) went along with the same trend toward greater centralization, particularly in regard to the districts and the municipalities. The *juntas gerais* were restored for the Azores and Madeira Islands. With some minor alterations afterward, stability in administration could now be achieved, the new laws enduring for quite a long time.

The judicial organization of Portugal as enacted in 1832–35 (Mousinho da Silveira and others) besides introducing a fundamental principle, that of the jury, divided the country into judicial circles later named districts (*círculos judiciais, distritos de relação*), subdivided into *comarcas,* which encompassed *julgados,* divided in their turn into *freguesias.* In Lisbon a Supreme Court was established, with jurisdiction over all the realm. An attorney-general (*procurador geral da coroa*) assisted it. In each circle there was a court (*tribunal de segunda instância,* later called *relação),* assisted by an attorney (*procurador régio*). The *comarcas* had their own judges and jurors, assisted by an attorney-delegate (*delegado do procurador régio*). Each *julgado* had its judge and its under-delegate (*sub-delegado*). The *freguesias* also possessed their justices of the peace. Up to the *julgado* level, the magistrates were chosen by election. The higher judges were appointed by the government.

In 1836–37 and 1841 this reform underwent some alterations, although its fundamental clauses were kept unchanged. The new civil code (1867) brought about the need for more changes, particularly in proceedings. Thus, the code of civil proceeding (1876, Secretary Barjona de Freitas) simplified and shortened its forms, without jeopardizing precise and good justice. Another important body of law was the Penal Code of 1852, which would last for a long time with only minor changes. Among their achievements, the Liberals had also abolished the death penalty, a quite revolutionary measure in the world of those days (1867, Secretary Barjona de Freitas), and slavery (1869), reforms which had been under way for a long time (see chapter 11).

The most relevant step in this whole field of administration and justice was the enacting of the Civil Code (Código Civil) of 1867, prepared by the Viscount of Seabra and countersigned by the Secretary of Justice, Barjona de Freitas. Highly original in its structure and in many of its articles, this new code, which at last replaced the *Ordenações* of Philip III, introduced some principles "revolutionary" for most Catholic countries in those days, such as lay marriage for non-Catholic couples.

In government, the growing complexity of public affairs led to an increase in secretariates and internal departments. The four portfolios of the early nineteenth century (i.e., interior, foreign affairs and war, navy and overseas, and public finance) rose to six in 1821, when the secretariate of foreign affairs and war was split into two parts, and a new secretariate of ecclesiastical affairs and justice came into existence. In 1852 the secretariate of public works was established and then, for a few months only (1870), that of public instruction, reintroduced in 1890–92. To preside over the ministry there had been assistant secretaries from time to time since the reign of Maria I, yet no permanent prime minister. Maria II's first constitutional government in 1834 introduced the novelty of a president of the council of ministers or prime minister (Presidente do Conselho de Ministros), who was then the Duke of Palmela. Very often, the prime ministers were also entrusted with one or more secretariates, particularly with that of the interior. Other reforms encompassed the army and the navy, public charity, and of course the Overseas territories (see chapter 11).

Throughout Europe, the nineteenth century was one of boundless growth of population. In the towns the number of inhabitants multiplied several times in a hundred years. The countryside, too, showed an increase and a better distribution of its people. Although in a more moderate way, Portugal reflected that trend, a result of a century of peace and prosperity, featured by important achievements in the areas of health and hygiene. Population estimates, roughly to the 1860's, more precisely after 1864—when the government organized the first scientific census—clearly displayed such a growth: 3,100,000 in the 1820's, 3,500,000 in the 1850's, 3,829,618 in 1864, 4,160,315 in 1878, 4,660,095 in 1890, 5,016,267 in 1900, 5,547,708 in 1911. With the inclusion of the Azores and Madeira archipelagoes, these figures would be some 300,000 to 400,000 higher. The rate of growth was particularly impressive after 1878. In a European context Portugal's birth and

death rates at the beginning of the twentieth century were below
countries like Germany, Spain, and Italy but above Belgium, Switzerland, England, and France.

Lisbon and Porto showed some interesting and peculiar aspects.
The capital had some 200,000 people in 1820, a figure that remained
static to the 1860's. The great leap forward started then: 227,674 in
1878, 301,206 in 1890, 356,069 in 1900, and 434,436 in 1911. Thus,
Lisbon's population doubled in less than fifty years after remaining
static for the preceding fifty years. Its parishes also increased from 41
in 1833 to 48 in 1885 when a sort of "Greater Lisbon" made its appearance with the incorporation of vast suburban boroughs. In total area,
Lisbon rose from 947 hectares (early nineteenth century) to 1,208
(1852), then to 6,500 (1885), and finally to 8,244 (1895–1903). The area
devoted to housing, however, increased much less; it was perhaps twice
as great at the beginning of the present century as in 1820.

Porto jumped from 50,000 inhabitants (around 1820), to about
60,000 in 1838, 86,000 in 1864, 105,000 in 1878, 138,000 in 1890,
168,000 in 1900, and 194,000 in 1911. Up to about 1870, Porto's growth
was major, the population difference with Lisbon gradually diminish-
ing. Afterward, the trend changed, and by 1910 the capital had 8 per
cent of Metropolitan Portugal's population, as against only 6 per cent
in 1820. Figures for Porto were, respectively, 3.4 per cent and 1.6 per
cent. Together, the two great cities encompassed more than 11 per cent
of the country's population in contrast to 8 per cent ninety years
before. Such was the result of the urban movement. The other towns
registered a more modest increase. Some even declined, particularly in
the interior and in the South. The trend in the countryside toward a
continuous rise of population in the coastal North and a stagnation or
decrease in the rest of the country went on undisturbed, to the late
1800's. Only the laws on agriculture were able to change this tendency
afterward and foster a southern rise.

Another important trait of demographical evolution was the increasing emigration to America, particularly to Brazil. Emigrants came
mostly from Minho and coastal Beira—and the Azores and Madeira
Islands—all places where the number of people had become disproportionate to their conditions of survival with minimal well-being. As
in many other countries of Europe, accelerated emigration only started

after 1850. The figures for Portugal show an increase of emigrants from a possible 6,000 level in 1855 to about 10,000 in 1886, then double that annual average, to 1900, reaching almost 50,000 in 1911. Clandestine emigration would put these figures still higher. Only a small minority returned home, yet the money from Brazil and elsewhere sent by emigrants to Portugal had an impact on the Portuguese economy, helping to solve the balance of trade deficit: estimates give about 3,000 contos in the 1870's, more than 12,000 in the 1890's, and perhaps 20,000 by 1910—an amount equal to more than one-fourth of the total state revenues!

Among the fundamental changes in structure carried on by the liberal governments after 1820 the religious reform should not be omitted. It brought about serious consequences, which still affect modern Portugal. The *cortes* started by abolishing the Inquisition. This abolition of a centuries-old body with such a tremendous impact on history had undoubtedly a symbolic meaning but very few practical consequences, because the Inquisition had been slowly fading away for years. Much more important was the liberal attitude regarding the regular clergy.

The religious orders still played a significant role in the Portuguese society of that time. They partly controlled charity and education. They owned extensive property, which made them an economic power throughout the country. The religious orders influenced all social classes, especially in the lower ranks of society, and were thus political forces of importance. Under their direct command, thousands of clients lived with them, worked with them, and thoroughly depended upon them. From a strictly religious standpoint, they were soldiers of Christ everywhere, doubling or tripling the presence of the secular clergy, pervading the country in the remotest places, constantly reminding everyone everywhere of the traditional, deeply Catholic, old Portugal, intolerant and superstitious, fanatic and reactionary. The convents had moreover the dubious moral role of welcoming many young ladies whose parents did not want them to marry, and of accepting their forced vows.

Anticlerical feeling had slowly emerged in Portugal, as everywhere, a characteristic of the late eighteenth-century ideologies. The upper classes became increasingly indifferent in matters of religion, to the point of atheism. To many, the clergy was a dangerous symbol of the past, an obstacle to progress. The notorious decadence of the ecclesiastical order, both in the secular and the regular forms, did nothing to contradict this view. Priests, monks, friars, and nuns were gradually playing a less and less relevant role in the fields of education and culture in general. A lay intelligentsia had arisen, composed of nobles, bureaucrats, army and navy officers, traders, and industrialists, which had no need for clerics and often scorned them. Even in charity, state intervention had much reduced the clergy's traditional role.

Victorious Liberalism directed an offensive against the clergy, particularly the religious orders. Tithes were abolished, along with several other taxes, depriving the clerics of their most important source of revenue. Moreover, the constitutional governments imposed on Church property a new burdensome taxation, in some cases as much as 50 per cent of all revenues. Confiscations based upon several pretexts further increased ecclesiastical grievances against the new order. In the political sphere, the Constitutions of both 1822 and 1826 denied the regular clergy's right to representation in the Chambers and to voting in the elections. And it seemed obvious that a free press along with the right to free discussion, would bring about a decline in the clergy's influence on the minds of people by way of the confessionary and the pulpit.

For these and other reasons the great majority of the clergy sided with the absolutist opposition. They backed the restorations of 1823 and 1828; they supported Miguel against Pedro. Yet their integrity as a class was no longer the same during the second restoration and the Civil War. Secular clergy and regular clergy were now divided, because the Constitution of 1826 favored the former against the latter. The bishops had now been granted permanent representation in the upper Chamber, which put them on the same level with the high nobility. And paradoxically, their subordinates at the head of the parishes also started to receive some economic benefits from the triumph of the new order, based upon equality and governmental subsidies, because most of the existing revenues went to the bishops and to the regular clergy. Through this internal division the liberal governments achieved a victory over the clergy, which permitted a relatively easy, yet revolutionary, set of ecclesiastical reforms.

The fact that many monasteries actively supported the defeated side in the Civil War, while many friars and monks took up arms against the "impious and blasphemous" liberals, encouraged them to enforce measures that had been considered for a long time. To start with, the Nuncio was ordered to leave the country and diplomatic relations with Rome were broken, because the Holy See had recognized Miguel's regime. This deprived the Portuguese clergy of a powerful ally and put them at the mercy of their triumphant enemy. The Jesuits, whom the Pope had re-established and Portugal welcomed in 1829, were immediately expelled. All bishops nominated by the "usurper" king were deposed and their sees declared vacant. Ecclesiastical patronates were abolished. A good many monasteries, which their occupants had abandoned in fleeing the invasion, were considered extinct. Monks, friars, and priests suffered all kinds of persecution and discrimination, even open violence and death. A law of 1833 forbade novitiates in any monastery, thus insuring the gradual extinction of the orders. At last, Regent Pedro made up his mind and accepted Secretary Joaquim António de Aguiar's repeated proposal to abolish all monasteries and disband their male population (May 28, 1834). This act affected 401 religious houses (including colleges, hospices, and also twelve convents) all over the country and the Overseas provinces and more than 6,500 people, of whom less than half were actually friars and monks. Many of them left the country, while others retired to the homes of relatives or friends. A goodly number were still young enough to start a new life, which they did, several later rising to positions in administration, education, organized charity, and the world of letters. Many others joined the secular clergy and became priests. The law endowed every ex-monk or ex-friar with an allowance, if he could get no other source of revenue (but it excepted all those who had fought against the liberals). Convents were not dissolved, but lacking any further novitiates, they gradually closed. Property belonging to the monasteries (both male and female) was nationalized. Sacred vessels and apparel were given to the churches.

The dissolution of the religious orders brought no special harm to the country, apart from the losses in artistic monuments, books, and manuscripts which were destroyed or sacked in the confusion. On the contrary, it generally benefited agriculture and landownership, as we

have already emphasized. It also gave the nation an important share of
wealth in landed property and solid buildings. Socially, it met with
little resistance and was applauded or accepted with indifference by
most people, including the secular clergy. From a religious standpoint,
however, it contributed to a certain decline of faith among the lower
classes. And it helped prepare them to accept other influences instead.

The religious orders came back, although in a disguised form. In
1857 some French Sisters of Charity (order of St. Vincent of Paul) were
admitted to Portugal for charitable purposes. They had to leave five
years later, because of the anticlerical campaign against them which
ravaged the country. After the 1850's, Jesuits, Franciscans, Fathers of
the Holy Spirit, Benedictines, Brethren of St. John, Sisters of the
Poor, Salesians, Lazarists, and scores of others arrived with the pro-
fessed aim of establishing schools, hospices, hospitals, and the like. A
law of 1901 (Hintze Ribeiro's government) practically authorized the
coming of any religious order to Portugal provided it pursued educational or charitable goals. In the early twentieth century there were
again more than fifty religious congregations or associations in the
country with some hundreds of members. They had a growing influence, particularly among the aristocracy.

The reform of the secular clergy had a much more limited impact.
According to the Constitution, the priests became civil servants of a
sort, paid by the state to perform services for the benefit of the nation.
This put the entire clergy under the government's supervision and
converted them into docile clients of the ruling groups. Sitting in the
upper Chamber, the bishops took an active part in the political life of
the country, siding with one or another party but never posing any
threat as an ecclesiastical body. After the re-establishment of diplomatic relations with Rome (1842), an agreement signed six years later
solved some problems and paved the way to peace and harmony between Church and state (the concordats of 1857 and 1886 concerned
the Overseas only), which would last until the Republic. The gradual
decadence of the clergy, in spite of its official protection by king and
government, could not be denied, and went along with the rise of anticlericalism. The Church, as it became increasingly involved with cultural problems, displayed its reactionary tendency and its inability to
cope with the new times. The number of priests declined in propor-

tion to the rise in population. As lay schools increased, the educational role of the Church declined. Yet its seminaries continued to be nuclei of instruction throughout the country and to provide free studies to all classes.

A symbolic aspect of the decline of the Church throughout the nineteenth century was the stagnation and even decrease in the number of dioceses. Despite the fact that Portugal's population almost doubled by 1910, no administrative reform was ever accomplished by the Church; moreover, five existing bishoprics disappeared: Aveiro (1837), Castelo Branco (1831), Leiria (1873), Pinhel (1838), and Portalegre (1833, re-established 1883).

With the triumph of the new order the other pillar of absolutism, the feudal nobility, suffered much less than the clergy. In theory, the official acknowledgment of equality downgraded the aristocrats. The law abolished feudal rights and commanderies (1821–46) and also entailed property (partly in 1832, totally in 1863); deprived the nobles of their usual allowances granted by the king; nationalized Crown property; and so forth. To subsist—and many could not—the nobles had now to rely exclusively upon their own estates and their participation in trade and industry. This moved them closer to the bourgeoisie than ever before. On the other hand, the government policy of granting titles to petty aristocrats, traders, bureaucrats, and soldiers went on at a still more rapid pace. In 1821–30, title-grants had reached 51, but this was small in comparison with the inflation of later decades: 101 in 1831–40, 38 in 1841–50, 112 in 1851–60, 205 in 1861–70, 192 in 1871–80, 152 in 1881–90. Most such titles were not permanent, being granted for one or two lives only. Scores of Brazilians and other foreigners were included, which meant little else than a modern decoration. Viscounts and barons took the lead, with 81 per cent of the total. Up to about 1850, baron-grants surpassed any others, their beneficiaries having become an object of derision for all the other nobles. Partly because of this, titles of viscount went up instead and led the way to the end of the century, with of course a similar result. Besides, the policy of title-granting was so discredited by the end of Luis I's reign that his successors, Carlos I (1889–1908) and Manuel II (1908–10), reduced it to a minimum, granting nobilitation according to the ancient rules.

As a result of all this, by the end of the century the old aristocracy and constitutional aristocracy were so intermingled that it would have been difficult to make a distinction between them on other than historical grounds.

The constitutions of 1822 and 1838 did not provide for a separate representation of the nobility in the Chambers. Yet the constitutions did not endure, and precisely because of that. The landed aristocrats—and almost all the new title-bearers coming from other sources of wealth wanted to buy land—played such an important role in the economic structure of Portugal (at least in the 1870's) that leadership in public affairs naturally had to belong to them, either in part or in whole. This is why the Constitution of 1826, granting the nobility hereditary representation in the upper chamber, could triumph and subsist—despite its several changes—to the end of the monarchy.

Yet the evolution of Portuguese society was somewhat more complex. To a first phase of aristocratic rule, lasting for about half a century (if one omits the rather short periods of 1820–23 and 1836–42, of almost pure bourgeois predominance), a second phase of leadership by nontitular bankers, industrialists, and traders followed. Up to the 1870's, more than one-fourth of the cabinet ministers and 80 per cent of the prime ministers were title-bearers, all of constitutional stock. Afterward, their share of government responsibilities rapidly declined. The Duke of Ávila, Prime Minister in 1877–78, was the last title-bearer to head a government. Up to 1910 the number of cabinet ministers who were title-bearers constantly decreased: 35 per cent of the positions in 1861–70, 17 per cent in 1871–80, 3.2 per cent in 1881–90, 3.4 per cent in 1891–1900, and 2.9 per cent in 1901–10. This decrease in participation of the upper nobility in the tasks of governing was partly replaced by a rising petty aristocracy of ancient lineages but no titles, depending upon government jobs as well as their lands. The proclamation of the Republic in 1910 cut short the rise of this new nobility, without giving it time to assert itself.

The decline of the constitutional nobility after 1870 had its parallel in the legislation. With the complete abolition of entailed property, there was no place for heredity anywhere. The second amendment to the constitution (1885) abolished hereditary peers in the upper House of Parliament, reduced to a hundred the number of nobles and clerics seated there, and instituted elective peers as well. In the 1890's, however, the nobility had still enough strength to strike back and regain some of the lost positions. The third amendment (1896) suppressed elective peerage and allowed the hereditary peers existing in 1885 to go back to their seats, although on a temporary basis. Such was the situation when the Republic was proclaimed.

The bourgeoisie, which had been given a large share in government and administration since Pombal, triumphed in 1820 and then, permanently, in 1834. Few monographs exist concerning its features, evolution, and quantitative aspects. By 1820, the bourgeois groups constituted some 8 per cent of the total population, but the great majority consisted of civil servants (including army and navy officers), teachers, students, lawyers, doctors, and the like. Traders and businessmen accounted for only one-tenth. By 1867 the proportion of bourgeoisie in the country had perhaps doubled, traders and industrialists predominating over civil servants and all the others. Up to the beginning of the twentieth century, both groups continued to grow. An analysis of the general censuses based upon reliable data (from 1864 on) clearly shows the decline of that part of the population engaged in agriculture: 72 per cent in 1864, 61 per cent in 1890 and 1900, 57 per cent in 1911. As the figures for the industrial groups do not reveal more than about 100,000 real proletarians by 1910, the gap may be accounted for by the rise of a bourgeoisie, where traders and industrialists soon led the way.

Lisbon and Porto were the two cities with a particularly high percentage of burghers. In Lisbon government and central administration went hand in hand with army officers, liberal professions, bankers, traders, and a few industrialists. Many large landowners lived in the capital too. In 1880, 568 firms (of which one-sixth were foreign), 192 doctors, and 140 lawyers (including solicitors) were active in Lisbon. Porto had proportionally more trade and more industry but was obviously weaker in all the other fields. Both towns controlled banking, commerce, and industry in the country, the role of capital being successively enhanced by the rising centralization of administration and the general development of Portugal.

The bourgeoisie undoubtedly increased in class-consciousness by the second half of the century. Titles of nobility became less coveted and were even refused by some wealthy bourgeois. Allied to a petty aristocracy, the bourgeois permanently controlled government after the 1870's. No more title-bearers were appointed prime ministers. No member of the high nobility ever presided over the twenty-seven governments which ruled Portugal from 1878 to 1910, and only three or four of the heads of government could be considered nobles of ancient lineage. None of the great statesmen of that period bore a title. At last the bourgeoisie realized its own value and looked down upon nobles and titles. They preferred to become peers, to be granted the title of councillor (*conselheiro*), and to be decorated.

Among the lower groups of society, what must be stressed was the slow and gradual rise of a proletariat. Early in the nineteenth century, the craft workers who owned their shop and tools in the old style of production still made up two-thirds of the whole "industrial population." Workers and apprentices numbered about 36,000. Rural workers, however, who owned nothing, constituted some 70 per cent of the total rural population.

A century later workers in plants with more than ten people—i.e., real proletarians—were no more than 100,000, some 20 per cent of the total number of workers engaged in industry and craft activities. The great majority of the industrial population were still working in small shops with less than ten workers, in craft activities at home, and the like. Women continued to perform a large role, although the proportion in active production had been declining since the 1880's or 1890's: 34.8 per cent in 1890, 29 per cent in 1900, 28.3 per cent in 1911. Child labor was also declining. Yet the Industrial Inquiry of 1881 still showed minors (those less than sixteen years old) to be 6.6 per cent of the total industrial population, and a 1907 estimate showed 7 per cent.

General working conditions seem to have worsened during the nineteenth century. Real salaries decreased, particularly after 1880, with the increase in capital and industrial concentration. The standard of living—of nutrition, lodging, and the like—also worsened. Despite a law of 1891, the workday could not be standardized throughout the country. By 1900 the average pointed to ten hours, but there were many exceptions in excess of this. Neither the government nor the industrialists provided the workers with any legal protection or assistance against accidents, old age, and the like.

The workers responded in the two usual ways: by joining in associations and by striking. Apart from some old and insignificant associations, the first group to engage in class struggle appeared only in 1853, in Lisbon (Centro Promotor do Melhoramento da Classe Laboriosa). It was followed by many other groups with several different goals—the cooperative movement soon rose in Lisbon and Porto, for instance—the whole accompanied by propaganda and social indoctrination in newspapers, pamphlets, and books of all kinds. Mutual benefit societies of workers rose from 65 in 1876 to 590 in 1903. In 1889 the total number of workers' unions of all types reached 392, of which more than 300 were in the districts of Lisbon and Porto. Their combined membership was 138,870. Syndicalism developed from 24 associations in 1876 to 135 in 1903. A Socialist Party appeared in the 1870's.

Up until the Republican revolution, strikes were considered illegal and punishable according to the Penal Code. Nonetheless, they first occurred in the 1870's, and their role in the life of the country began to have a certain importance after the turn of the century. By 1899 more than sixty strikes had affected Portugal, but their number increased to 91 between 1900 and 1910, most of them successful. In 1903 there were three very important strikes, one in Porto (practically a general one), another in Lisbon (exceptionally violent), and the third in Coimbra (where workers and students fought together). At least 8 per cent of the proletariat was mobilized by such strikes. In the South of the country, rural strikes also played a role.

Despite these and other factors of social unrest and industrial growth, the proletariat of Portugal in the early twentieth century was far from posing any threat to the bourgeois leadership. The urban workers were few, illiterate for the most part, and easily maneuvered by bourgeois and noble politicians and philosophers. Both in the towns and in the country, proletarians generally appeared as the humble clients of traders, industrialists, and landowners, with a strong clerical influence to divert them from any widespread rebellion.

Official concern with education began in Pombal's days. The Enlightenment espoused the principle of spreading instruction to the people, but not to everyone. The law of 1772, one of the world's earliest attempts to officially organize primary lay education, led to establishment of a number of first grades by the end of the eighteenth century: 720 schools existed by 1779. But such an interesting movement was not carried on as it deserved. Many schools were closed and few new ones ever opened. Others were entrusted to the Church.

The liberal revolution fostered glamorous principles of giving education to all citizens—quite logically, because free voting depended upon it. Thus, in fourteen months, 59 primary schools were opened; there were improvements in the financial and moral situation of instructors; and freedom of teaching was proclaimed. The Constitution of 1826 established free primary instruction as a right for every citizen. The reactions of 1823–26 and 1828–34, however, closed down schools and persecuted teachers, who were supposed, and rightly so, to be sympathetic to Liberalism.

After 1834 progress in all the fields of education could be carried on without interruption. The first task was to set up schools everywhere, to prepare instructors, and to try to overcome the nearly 90 per cent illiteracy. This took time and money, which was often hard to come by. In 1841, for instance, only about half of the male children of school age attended school. Nonetheless, the number of official primary schools steadily increased: one to 120 square kilometers in 1820, one to 40 fifty years later, one to 20 in the early twentieth century. To these, private schools must be added—270 in 1845, 1,500 in 1870—although their growth never matched the rate of increase of the official schools, which constituted 74.2 per cent of all primary institutions by 1900. Girls' schools also increased, particularly after 1860. Primary instructors tripled between 1870 and 1910, hand in hand with the establishment of teachers' colleges after 1860. Accordingly, the rate of illiteracy gradually declined: 76.0 per cent for those over seven in 1890, 74.1 per cent in 1900, 69.7 per cent in 1911. These figures seemed quite high, even for late-nineteenth-century Europe, a fact which endowed Republican propaganda with one of its best weapons. Throughout the country 702 parishes (17.5 per cent of the total) still had no school. Nonetheless, considerable efforts had been undertaken by the government, especially after 1900. Primary schools included three years of compulsory attendance, plus a voluntary fourth year.

As in many aspects of administration, one of the great problems here concerned centralization or decentralization of the primary system. Should the central government direct everything or should the municipalities control schools? Governments and reforms wavered between these alternatives. In the 1820's the tendency was to centralize education from a bureaucratic standpoint; in the early 1830's decentralization prevailed. The reform of 1836 pointed again toward centralization, which was confirmed by the reform of 1844, but thoroughly changed in 1878–81. After 1890 centralization once more won out. Of course, this question went along with political ideologies, which defended full concentration of power in the hands of the government or else favored greater autonomy to the local institutions.

The ruling classes of Liberalism were actually more concerned with the two upper levels of education, which affected their own children for a long period of time, than with the creation of new primary schools or the sending of more primary teachers throughout the country. One of their major achievements was the thorough reform of secondary studies, according to the French pattern of the lycée (high school). After long planning which had started in 1821, Secretary Passos Manuel instituted a *liceu* in every district capital and two in Lisbon (1836). At the same time a full program of secondary studies was organized, including humanities (history, geography, literature), languages (French, English, and German) and sciences (chemistry, physics, algebra, geometry, natural history), besides the traditional study of classical languages, rhetoric, and philosophy. *Liceus* were thus restricted to urban centers, precisely those places where the ruling bourgeoisie dwelt.

Passos Manuel's reform was too progressive and too ambitious to endure. Thus, Secretary Costa Cabral totally eliminated scientific studies from the lycée program, while limiting the teaching of living languages to the main cities (1844). More progressively he reduced fees to one-fifth. Only in 1860 did the legislators go back to Passos' original ideas although in a moderate way: secondary studies were extended to five years, including physics, chemistry, and natural history (Secretary Fontes Pereira de Melo). Up to the end of the century, several other reforms did little to improve this state of things. They were concerned mainly with the extension of studies (five years, six years), the arrangement of disciplines per year, the examination system, and some further technical points.

In 1894–95, Secretary João Franco approved a new reform and regulation for the high school, which Professor Jaime Moniz had elaborated. It was a model reform, framed by the most advanced principles of pedagogy, insisting on the so-called "class regime" (i.e., the conforming of subjects to a common goal), adding a seventh year to secondary studies and increasing the number of disciplines. Despite some later amendments, Jaime Moniz's reform was to last for a quarter of a century.

The introduction of secondary technical studies resulted from the need to equip Portugal with experts in the industrial and commercial fields (little was achieved in the area of agriculture). Passos Manuel set up the basis for regular technical studies with his Conservatórias de Artes e Ofícios (Conservatories of Arts and Crafts) in Lisbon and Porto (1836). Fontes Pereira de Melo's new Secretariate of Public Works organized a full system of technical studies in three levels: elementary, secondary, and complementary. Industrial schools opened in the 1850's, followed by commercial ones in the 1880's. Secretary Emídio Navarro's reforms were paramount in developing technical studies, reaching much farther than ever before. Yet the proper framework for the modern technical schools resulted much more from a gradual evolution of efforts than from the achievements of a single man. Up to the proclamation of the Republic the decisive steps had been undertaken.

By comparison, the reform of the University was a poor one. Coimbra continued its theoretical monopoly of university studies, but the majority of its teachers could never cope with the tremendous progress which was taking place in the world in all the fields of knowledge. From the very beginning, the Liberals distrusted the University of Coimbra (which they considered a center of tradition and absolutism) and always fought it. The University, in its turn, always slowed down all efforts to create new centers of higher knowledge. Until 1859 Coimbra even supervised general teaching throughout the country. It had few powers to influence any reforms at primary or secondary levels, but it had powers to prevent its own reform. Indeed both Passos Manuel and Costa Cabral included the University in their legislation, yet they were unable to produce in it any revolutionary consequences. It was the teachers of the University itself who prepared the reforms, and they were too timid and too conservative to change structures. Therefore, the only significant alterations in almost a century were the fusion of the two schools of Law and Canons into one—the new School of Law—and the adding of a few scientific disciplines. In spite of some exceptionally good and up-to-date teachers, the University of Coimbra played a poor role in practically every field of knowledge to the twentieth century. Only the School of Law could boast a certain prestige—much more because of its uniqueness in the country than because of any significant advancement in the Law studies—and an always increasing enrollment. It became a real college of administration and "the school" where every noble or wealthy bourgeois wished to send his sons.

The development of upper university studies in nineteenth-century Portugal should rather be referred to the eight other schools which were gradually created in Lisbon and Porto. In 1836–37 Passos Manuel abolished the Colégio dos Nobres (see chapter 8) and the Royal Naval Academy, replacing them by the new Escola Politécnica (Polytechnical School) based upon the French *Écoles Polytechniques*. In Porto he instituted a Polytechnical Academy (Academia Politécnica). Both schools offered a plan of courses in science and prepared future officers for the Army and the Navy. (At the same time a new Military Academy—Escola do Exército—replaced the old Academy of Fortification and enlarged its plan of studies; some years later, a Naval School—Escola Naval—made its appearance too.) The existing schools of surgery in both cities were also converted into Schools of Medicine and Surgery (Escolas Médico-Cirúrgicas), with a much larger group of disciplines. The fifth upper college established by Passos Manuel was the General Conservatory of Dramatic Art (Conservatório Geral de Arte Dramática) of Lisbon which incorporated a recently created school of music with new schools for theater and dancing. Finally he established schools of Fine Arts in both Lisbon and Porto. The last important school founded in the nineteenth century (owing to the initiatives of King Pedro V) was the so-called Upper Institute of Letters (Curso Superior de Letras) for the teaching of humanities, which opened its doors in Lisbon in 1859, and was constantly improved and enlarged thereafter.

Along with several other institutions of culture, such as numerous

ABOVE: *Pedro IV, king of Portugal (Pedro I, emperor of Brazil), by Simpson, 1821–34: Museu Nacional dos Coches, Lisbon.* UPPER RIGHT: *Fontes Pereira de Melo.* BELOW: *Bourgeois architecture and decoration: the Stock Exchange Palace (Palácio da Bolsa), Oporto, 1862–80.*

museums, academies of arts and letters, the Royal Academy of Science, and private associations of all sorts, those schools could prepare a relatively rich elite that flourished in the second half of the century and gave Portugal an honorable place among the civilized countries of the world. Indeed, one of the most interesting features of nineteenth-century Portugal was her cultural development, which probably surpassed the golden age of the 1500's.

This was first of all a result of the opening up of the country. The liberal governments started by abolishing censorship of books and newspapers (1821), by proclaiming and effectively enforcing freedom of speech and press, and by stimulating discussion on all levels and on almost all subjects. As a consequence, the number of publications jumped to unsuspected levels. Newspapers, for instance, of which there were only four in all of Portugal and Brazil in 1820, rose to more than twenty a year later. The reactionary periods of 1823–26 and 1828–33 brought about censorship again and, as might be expected, a decline in publications. The following three decades showed a constant moderate growth in the number of newspapers. After 1860, however, there was a marked upward spurt. In the late 1800's and early 1900's Portugal had a very honorable ranking among nations in both the absolute and the proportionate number of newspapers of all kinds. Similarly with books and pamphlets. Despite some restrictive laws and some (moderate) persecutions of the press, freedom of publishing could be considered complete.

The large number of newspapers and magazines stimulated literary production and were, in turn, stimulated by it. Most great authors started by publishing articles or by serializing their novels in daily issues of newspapers. Freedom of speech and association led to the growth of lecturing and of cultural clubs of all kinds. Parliamentary life contributed to the development of political rhetoric, while the frequent elections favored cultivation of good speech throughout the country. The consequence of all this was a widespread cult for good writing and for lay oratory. The newspapers, magazines, and books of those days display amazingly good style and a general tendency toward rational and clear thinking, if one makes allowance for the inevitable romanticism of the epoch.

Another aspect that helps explain Portugal's cultural expansion was the improved means of communication with Europe, particularly with France. The setting up of railways and the possibility of reaching Paris directly in two or three days brought Portugal closer to the great centers of European culture than ever before. It must be recalled and again emphasized that Portugal looked upon France as her cultural model and strongly reflected every French influence. The growing imports of books and magazines by train—which made them more readily available and also much cheaper—enhanced such a cultural link from the 1870's on. But railways also linked Portugal to other countries of cultural significance, such as Spain, Germany, Belgium, Switzerland, Italy, and England. Nobles and bourgeois had their children learn foreign languages, French above all, but also German and English. Later, they began sending them abroad, to the best schools available.

From a literary and artistic standpoint, the great social, economic, and political changes of the century brought about Romanticism in Portugal as everywhere in the world. The new style exhibited its best elements in the theater and in historical fiction as well as in painting and sculpture, the genres which appealed to and could be easily understood by the bourgeoisie. The legislation of 1836–37 provided the framework for the development of a Portuguese theater, the best representative of which was Almeida Garrett. A national playhouse controlled by the government was built up in Lisbon, while many other theaters, lavishly decorated, rose all over the country to the end of the century, as symbols of the bourgeois urban culture. In a way, they replaced the traditional church and monastery building as a mark of affluence and prestige. Despite Garrett's fine play-writing (*Um Auto de Gil Vicente*, 1838; *O Alfageme de Santarém*, 1842; *Frei Luis de Sousa*, 1844), accompanied by many other Romantic authors, foreign translations soon flooded the stages and were often preferred by the public. Nonetheless, the quality of the Portuguese plays was comparable to the best abroad, particularly by the end of the nineteenth century and the beginning of the twentieth (authors Marcelino Mesquita, 1856–1919; Gervásio Lobato, 1850–1895; João da Câmara, 1852–1908; among many others). Comedies and satires displaying a fine humor—which the public welcomed and showed a preference for —led the way and revealed better talents than drama. This also explains the rise of the musical show (*operette*), where Spanish, French, and Austrian imports competed with some good Portuguese examples. A genuine national genre, the *revista* or musical satire of current events, started in the 1850's with a tremendous success. Both drama and comedy had at their service one or two generations of outstanding actors, who flourished from the 1880's on. On the other hand, a national opera could never develop despite the love for musical drama. Italian, French, and (later) German companies visited Portugal year after year and entirely fashioned the Lisbon and Porto tastes. The same happened with concert music, where the Portuguese contribution was poor.

Historical fiction developed after the publication in Portuguese translation of Walter Scott's works. A periodical magazine, the *Panorama* (first number 1837), published several historical novels serially, which influenced at least one generation of writers and readers. Alexandre Herculano, the greatest Portuguese author of the mid-1800's, was also the main representative of historical fiction, where the Middle Ages had a predominant role (*O Bobo,* 1843; *Eurico, o Presbitero,* 1844; *O Monge de Cister,* 1848). Many others followed him, such as Rebelo da Silva (1822–71), Andrade Corvo (1824–90), and Arnaldo Gama (1828–69). Historical novels continued to appeal to the bourgeois taste well into the twentieth century, with a second remarkable group of authors flourishing in the late 1800's and early 1900's (see chapter 12).

History experienced a tremendous development, with the systematic use of archival sources. When the liberal governments nationalized the monasteries, most of the ecclesiastical archives entered the official depositories, particularly the Lisbon National Archives, where organization and proper classification started. Alexandre Herculano, who had a hand in such a task, showed an incomparable talent for history, the conception of which he entirely remodeled according to the modern principles of his time. Besides many other important works, he began writing a monumental *History of Portugal* (1846–53), which only extended to the late thirteenth century. His work, his strong and austere personality, and his methodology had a formidable impact on his contemporaries and on all the following generations of historians, to the present. History, too, flourished to the beginning of the twentieth century.

The novel developed in Portugal in accordance with the new social conditions and also because of the influence of French and English authors. A first generation of Romantics (Camilo Castelo Branco, 1825–90; Júlio Dinis, 1839–71) supplied the basis for the exceptional realistic novels of Eça de Queirós (1845–1900) and some other lesser-known contemporaries of his. A diplomat, who lived most of his life abroad, Eça introduced in Portugal a sort of international taste and way of writing, although insisting on Portuguese themes and cudgeling the Portuguese bourgeois society with his satire (*O Crime do Padre Amaro*, 1876; *O Primo Basílio*, 1878; *Os Maias*, 1888).

Eça de Queirós belonged to the "generation of 1870," a remarkable group of intellectuals who were in their twenties by that time and who consequently flourished from the late 1870's to the beginning of the twentieth century. They were the result of Portugal's total opening up with the development of communications and the maturity of press freedom. They were the exponents of the new Portugal, European-minded, modern, striving to rise from industrial, commercial, and political underdevelopment to a new society based upon the industrial revolution, the bourgeois leadership, and the parliamentary system. Although these intellectuals often reacted against and strongly criticized those aspects of society, they were its best and most thoroughly integrated representatives. In foreign influences, the generation of 1870 was particularly affected by the French writers Renan (biblical criticism), Michelet ("Germanism"), Victor Hugo (struggle for freedom, progress), and Balzac; these writers, in turn, transmitted and disseminated other influences from Germany and England. The Portuguese generation of 1870 was anticlerical, rationalist, positivist (or at least strong believers in scientism) and generally antimonarchist, some of their members tending toward a Republican system, others even aiming at a vague socialism.

Most of these intellectuals studied at the University of Coimbra. There, the beginnings of their assertion started (1865) with the so-called "Coimbra question" (*questão coimbrã*), which involved two groups of opponents—a younger group of students, led by Antero de Quental, eagerly contesting the prevailing spiritual, social, and literary values of their time, and an older group of intellectuals led by the blind poet Castilho, defending them. Later on, in Lisbon, the former joined together in a private club, which organized a cycle of lectures in a

Casino, on the modern aspects of literature, history, religion, and education. These lectures (conferências do Casino) soon became a daring social and political attack on the existing order, and were cut short by the government, which forbade them (1871).

The generation of 1870 had, as its main representatives, besides Eça de Queirós, Antero de Quental (1842–92, a leading poet and social essayist); Ramalho Ortigão (1836–1915, a social critic and novelist); Teófilo Braga (1843–1924, a productive historian of literature and politician, and the future President of the Republic); Oliveira Martins (1845–95, a penetrating historian, sociologist, and politician); and Guerra Junqueiro (1850–1923, an extremely popular poet, anticlerical and antimonarchical). But it also included artists, scientists, professors, aristocrats, journalists, and many others, who helped raise the level of Portuguese culture to a remarkable height.

In the domain of science, Portugal played a much more modest role. Modern science required more extensive equipment, costly devices which the generally meager budgets of schools and governments were unable to supply. Nonetheless, countless efforts led to the opening of many scientific museums, laboratories, observatories, and botanical gardens, and to a moderate flourishing of science, which, if not inventive, at least managed to keep up with the international scientific movement. Mathematics, geology, chemistry, botany, zoology, and anthropology developed; there was special interest in the soils, the fauna, and the flora of Africa, where the Portuguese had a natural field of research. In medicine, too, the nineteenth century meant great progress for Portugal, especially in the field of tropical diseases.

The art movement is still poorly known, except in the area of painting. Classicism, neo-classicism, and neo-medieval styles (Romanesque and Gothic) had their impact on architecture, as everywhere in the world. The first half of the century saw the completion of Lisbon and the disappearance of the last earthquake ruins. Numerous churches, all alike but all relatively pure in neo-classic forms and sober in decoration, were built in the capital and in other parts of the country. Their internal decoration, particularly in regard to images and pictures, probably deserves something more than the twentieth-century disdain paid to them. More important were the countless bourgeois dwellings, both within the towns and in the countryside, displaying the increasing affluence of their owners. Theaters, statues, railroad stations, city halls, bridges, fountains, hotels, and other lay examples of architecture still await their impartial historian. There were some unique examples of tile coverage of walls and façades. The growth of Lisbon, Porto, and other towns caused widespread building activity, which covered extensive urban areas with typical Portuguese houses and improved city planning. By the end of the nineteenth century, a nationalist reaction against the use of international formulas in architecture led to a Portuguese school which flourished only in the 1900's. It struggled for a "Portuguese house" where tradition and modern conceptions would be harmoniously combined.

Sculpture and painting had some noteworthy representatives. Soares dos Reis (1847–89) was perhaps the leading sculptor of his time. The painters Silva Porto (1850–93), José Malhoa (1854–1933), and Columbano Bordalo Pinheiro (1857–1929) emerge from a large group of excellent artists, who absorbed nationalist tendencies much earlier than the other fields of culture. Most of them preferred rural themes, scorning the cities and their "corrupt" society. Despite its good quality and a certain originality in Portuguese painting, especially in the second half of the nineteenth century, one must acknowledge its inability to follow the advanced international trends of the time. Currents like impressionism, fauvism, and cubism had practically no adherents in Portugal, where conservative tendencies always played the leading role.

THE POLITICAL LIFE

As a system of political, economic, and social doctrines, Liberalism was known in Portugal beginning with the late 1700's. Among the "enlightened" authors of Pombal's and Maria's times (see chapter 8), a certain body of liberal or pre-liberal indoctrination could certainly be detected; yet Enlightenment as such should not be confused with Liberalism, which is often its most complete opposite. Indeed, the Liberals defended a political constitution set up on popular bases; a strong restriction of the royal prerogatives; freedom of religion, press, and speech; freedom of trade and industry; and many other "subversive" doctrines altogether contrary to the fundamental principles of enlightened despotism.

The American Revolution gave reality to many theories of French and English philosophers and essayists. Then, thirteen years later, the French Revolution completed and enlarged the process. By the 1780's and 1790's, to be a Liberal came to have the precise meaning of one defending doctrines which had triumphed somewhere. Consequently, most European governments became increasingly concerned with the Liberal "subversion" and began to adopt severe measures of repression.

In Portugal, Liberalism entered by way of the French and English influences. Although the former have generally deserved the main attention of historians, the English influences should not be neglected. Authors like Jeremy Bentham and Adam Smith were widely quoted and praised. The impact of the American Revolution was felt— mainly via England—but much less than that of the French Revolution.

In the spread of Liberalism, Freemasonry had a leading role. Although known in Portugal from early days, only by the time of Prince John's regency did the number and activity of the Portuguese Freemasons start to trouble the government. In 1801, there were five masonic lodges in Lisbon, with a membership that included nobles, wealthy bourgeois, and some clerics. The first Portuguese grand-master, a nobleman and top bureaucrat, was elected in 1804. Persecutions of all kinds prevented a smooth development of the Masonry. The French Invasions had a new impact, and by 1812 thirteen lodges were active in Lisbon. In Porto, several Freemasons and Masonry sympathizers founded the so-called Sinédrio (1818), a secret society which decisively contributed to subversion and actually organized the Revolution of 1820.

Other vehicles for spreading liberal thought were the exiles (mostly in London and in Paris) during John's regency. They encountered the realities of Liberalism, watched the function of parliamentary institutions, and conceived a whole program of political and economic reforms to be established in their country. Their revolutionary newspapers (*O Correio Braziliense,* London, 1808–22; *O Investigador Portuguez em Inglaterra,* London, 1811–19; *O Portuguez,* London, 1814–23; *Annaes das Sciencias, das Artes e das Letras,* Paris, 1818, among many others) and pamphlets managed to enter Portugal, despite police controls, and were widely read. Some of those exiles returned to Portugal after the Napoleonic wars and became leaders or at least influential figures among those who opposed the existing regime.

The ideology that triumphed in 1820 contained some of the international trends of Liberalism but also a good many national tendencies. It rested upon the right of individual property, from which all the liberties derived: freedom to do everything not forbidden by the law; freedom from arrest without charge or trial except according to the law; freedom to use one's property; freedom of speech and writing without previous censorship (although limited by the church in dogma and morals); equality of rights and laws for all; the end of property confiscations, legal infamy, torture, and other physical penalties; the right of all to compete for public offices; the right of protest, complaint, or petition; inviolability of the mails; abolition of feudal law and rights. It asserted the national sovereignty, the principle of the law as the citizens' will, the tripartite division of powers, and so forth. Portuguese Liberalism also stood for the union of Church and state, and for the hereditary constitutional monarchy.

More peculiar principles, a result of Portugal's own needs, were a certain defense of protectionism and high tariffs against free trade with foreign countries; the development of technology, transport and communications; and an "agrarian reform" tending to get rid of the huge *latifundia* in the hands of the Crown and the religious orders. Portuguese Liberalism also acknowledged the nation as being "the union of all Portuguese in both hemispheres" (which justified its "colonial" policies, both in 1820–25 regarding Brazil, and later on regarding Africa); all Portuguese were granted, at least in theory, equal rights and duties.

It is important to note that the basic principles of Liberalism were retained and enforced in Portugal throughout the whole monarchical period (1820–1910) and even during the Democratic Republic (1910–26). Its various political tendencies did not alter the basic fundamentals defined in 1820–22 and clearly expressed in the first constitution.

Liberalism also triumphed because it posed as a restorer of the old "liberties" of the realm. The preface to the first constitution was quite frank regarding that point. It stated that the *cortes* ". . . intimately convinced that the public disgraces, which so much have oppressed and still oppress her [the Nation], had their origin in the contempt for the citizen's rights and in the oversight of the basic laws of the monarchy; and having also considered, that only by the reestablishment of those laws, enlarged and reformed, the prosperity of the same Nation can be achieved. . . ." In this way, the Liberals altogether condemned that period of history which had preceded them—a vague period because some limited it to Maria's and John's reigns, while others traced it back to the end of the Middle Ages—and presented themselves to the nation as restorers of something destroyed and forgotten, rather than as revolutionaries. The adoption of the traditional word *cortes* was symbolic of this.

The Constitution of 1822 was a long document with 240 articles. It mainly followed the Spanish constitution of 1812, although with some changes and adaptations to the Portuguese case. After a listing of the individual rights and duties—possibly influenced by the French constitution of 1795—it went on to assert the sovereignty of the nation and admit the independence of the three powers—the legislative, the executive, and the judicial. The first belonged to the *cortes* (with one chamber directly elected by all the literate males—friars, servants, and some others being excepted); the second to the king and the government (composed of secretaries of state appointed by him); and the third to the judges. On law-making the king had only the right of "suspensive veto," i.e., the right to return to the *cortes* once any law he did not agree with, explaining the reasons for his discordance. The government was responsible to the *cortes* and could be called by them for explanations or information. The constitution also adopted a sort of federal system for Portugal and Brazil (according to John's decision in 1815), creating a five-member regency and a three-member government to act in Rio de Janeiro. There was still a Council of State, composed of thirteen counselors, of which six were for Portugal, six for the Overseas, and one for both.

This constitution did not endure (see part 3 of this chapter). It was too progressive and too democratic for its time. Suffrage for all male literates might be dangerous for the interests of landowners and big businessmen. It did not satisfy the nobility, or the clergy (neither were given any special prerogatives), or the king, whose powers were reduced to almost nothing. No wonder, then, that it lasted for less than two years in its first phase (October 1822 to June 1824), and then, on a provisional and theoretical basis, from September 1836 to April 1838.

The second Portuguese Constitution bore the name of "Constitutional Charter" (Carta Constitucional) and was generally known as "The Charter." Its name followed the French examples (1814), copied elsewhere in the world (South Germany, Poland, Brazil, and others), and reflected the conservative, strong monarchist reaction against the popular enacting of constitutions. The emperor of Brazil, Pedro I, who was also the heir to the Portuguese throne (see chapter 9), had granted a constitutional charter to Brazil, in 1824. When his father, the king of Portugal, died (1826), he immediately granted one to Portugal (April 29, 1826), which closely followed the Brazilian text (which, in its turn, was influenced by the French model).

The Constitutional Charter had only 145 articles. Individual rights (no mention was made of duties) had now been placed at the end. In addition to those expressed in 1822, they also included the right to public help (beneficence), the right to free primary education, the right to have colleges and schools, and several others. As in the first Constitution, freedom of religion to the Portuguese was not expressly granted but nobody could be persecuted on religious grounds, provided he respected the state's religion and did not offend public morals. Among individual rights included in the Charter were respect for the hereditary nobility and its privileges, and the public debt, an effort to get the support of the aristocrats and the bourgeois.

Moreover, the Constitution of 1826 introduced a number of antidemocratic innovations. The state powers became four, instead of three: the legislative, the moderating (*Poder Moderador*), the executive, and the judicial. The first one was vested in the *cortes* composed of two Houses, the Chamber of Deputies (indirectly elected by a limited number of males who owned property) and the Chamber of Peers, appointed by the king for life and with the right of transmission to their heirs—archbishops and bishops also included. The moderating power, which the Charter considered to be "the key of all the political organization," belonged to the king, who, as its head, could appoint the peers, summon the *cortes* and dissolve the Chamber of Deputies, appoint and dismiss the government, suspend magistrates, grant amnesties and pardons, and veto the laws made in *cortes*. The executive power was vested in the king and the government, and the judicial one in the judges and jurors. A Council of State, composed of life-appointed counselors, would assist the king as head of the moderating power.

The Charter of 1826 pleased the nobility and the secular clergy, as well as the landowners and the wealthy bourgeois. It also granted extensive powers to the king. For these reasons, it had all warrants of success and long rule. Indeed, after an initial brief period of almost two years (July 31, 1826, to May 3, 1828), it lasted from 1834 to September 1836, and then, again, from February 1842 to the proclamation of the Republic, on October 5, 1910 (see part 3 of this chapter). In all, seventy-two years.

The third Portuguese Constitution lasted less than four years (April 1838 to February 1842). A compromise between the Constitution of 1822 and the Charter, it was influenced by the Spanish constitution of 1837 and also the Belgian constitution of 1831. It attacked the Charter by reasserting that sovereignty rested upon the nation (not on the king); by suppressing the hereditary Chamber of Peers and replacing it by an elective Chamber of Senators (to which could be chosen only wealthy landowners and bourgeois, archbishops and bishops, top magistrates and full professors, Army and Navy officers of high rank, and ambassadors and ministers); and by accepting direct elections for the Chamber of Deputies, albeit with highly restrictive conditions to qualify as a voter. The moderating power was abolished, but the king kept the right to dissolve the Chambers and veto the laws.

The sixty-eight years of continuous validity of the Charter (1842–1910) depended upon the three amendments, which gave way to a more democratic system and adapted the Constitution to the various changes that had taken place in the country.

Among other things, the first amendment (Acto Adicional), in 1852, made elections to the Chamber of Deputies direct and enlarged the voting capacity, while abolishing the death penalty for political crimes. The second amendment (1885) suppressed the hereditary peers and limited their number to 100, while introducing elective and temporary peers; it also somewhat restricted the moderating power. The third amendment (1896) restored to the king certain prerogatives abolished in 1885, and suppressed the elective peers (although not thoroughly re-establishing the hereditary peerage).

Electoral procedures started within the early months of the Liberal Revolution. The "Instructions" on how to vote and on how the first National Assembly should be constituted were the first Portuguese electoral code. They provided an indirect system, by which all the male heads of family chose a number of electors on the parish-basis, who, in their turn, chose another group of electors on the *comarca* or province basis. The latter would then elect the deputies to the *cortes*. Every head of family could qualify for deputy. National representativeness was one deputy for 30,000 inhabitants. With Brazil and the other Overseas possessions, this brought to the first Parliament 181 representatives: 100 from Portugal proper, 9 from the Azores and Madeira, 7 from the African and Asian territories, and 65 from Brazil. A plurality of votes decided the election of each group of candidates, arranged by provinces.

The adoption of the first Constitution somewhat changed this system. Elections became direct—indeed a more democratic way—but restrictions to deputy qualification were first introduced. To become a representative, one now had to have a "sufficient income." Instead of provinces, the electoral code of June 1822 introduced a larger number of represented units, twenty-six for Portugal instead of six. In all, the number of deputies went down to 118, because Brazil ceased to be represented.

The first elections held after the granting of the Constitutional Charter (1826) clearly reflected the conservative tendencies of the "new order." Up to 1852, with the exception of a brief period (1836–42), all elections were indirect, and the voters' and candidates' qualifications were considerably tightened, on an income basis. To be a voter, one had to have at least 100,000 réis of income, to be a deputy at least 400,000 réis. Such restrictions severely reduced the number of voters. They put parliamentary representation in the hands of the landowners, traders, and industrialists, and parliamentary voting in the hands of a middle class both rural and urban. After the September Revolution (1836), a short interlude of six years made elections direct again but hardly changed the voter and deputy qualifications.

The electoral law of 1852 was a long document which embodied the typical principles of bourgeois parliamentarism. It kept the income qualification for voting and for being elected, but it made elections direct again and altered some other minor points such as the definition of plurality for election purposes (one-fourth or more of the ballots, or else a run-off with victory for any plurality). From 1859 to 1878 plurality gave way to majority in the first round.

Important changes in the electoral system took place with the law of 1878. It greatly enlarged the number of voters, by enfranchising all those who could read and write or had a minimum income of 100,000 réis, or were heads of families. Furthermore, voting age went down from twenty-five to twenty-one. Thus, voting capacity ceased to rest upon money alone and depended now upon literacy or family status. The trend toward a more democratic basis was further enhanced in 1895, when a new law lowered the 100,000 réis basis for the illiterates to about a half (i.e., a minimum 500 réis of taxation, when formerly it was estimated at 1,000). This law particularly increased the number of rural voters, who depended upon local bosses and party structures. Run-offs disappeared in 1884.

Electoral laws were numerous to the end of the monarchy—fifteen such laws in ninety years—but their main concern was generally the circle division throughout the country. Most defended an average two-three deputies for each circle, but several introduced the principle of one deputy to one circle. The total number of deputies did not follow too closely the general growth of population, but as a rule popular representation could be kept the same. In 1820 there were 100 representatives for some three million people (i.e., one/30,000); in 1870 there were roughly the same number for nearly four million people (one/40,000). But the latter figure was afterward maintained by gradually increasing the number of deputies. Total voters went up from 350,000 in 1864 to 500,000 in 1911.

The troubled political life of the country, along with the faculty the king had of dissolving Parliament whenever the government thought it convenient, made it rare to have full four-year or three-year legislatures (determined by the Constitution). After 1834 and to the end of the monarchy, there were forty-three elections for Parliament, which gives an average of one year and eight months per legislature. Elections thus became a usual thing in the political life of the country; moreover, parish and municipal ones happened regularly too. Their organization was an important and expensive undertaking both for the Secretariat of Interior and the political parties.

Which were those parties?

The organization of parties in a modern way came somewhat late in the history of constitutional Portugal. Before the 1860's and 1870's there were currents of opinion, ideological groups, political forces or whatever one wishes to call them, but hardly parties in the sense of duly organized bodies. Until 1834 the two opposing forces were the absolutists, defending the traditional monarchy, and the liberals, fighting for the Constitution. In each group there were different trends, particularly in the latter, where the democrats (sometimes called Vintistas, because they claimed to follow the true doctrine of the Revolution of 1820) opposed the conservatives (who aimed at a compromise between the national traditions and the liberal principles) and the "bourgeois," who leaned toward a middle ground between the two. These three forces within the liberal ideology composed Parliament roughly until the 1840's, although with changed labels and sporadic coalitions. The Democrats, with a part of the bourgeois, triumphed in September 1836 and became known as "Septembrists" (Setembristas). The conservatives, with another part of the center, remained faithful to the Constitutional Charter and were thus called Chartists (Cartistas). A new Center, more related to the Right than to the Left, realigned forces by 1838 under the name of Order Party (Partido Ordeiro).

In the 1840's the Right conquered power and imposed a dictatorship under Secretary Costa Cabral. Opposing this Cabralismo all the other forces rallied together in a "Progressive" coalition, which rose in arms in 1846–47 (being then known as Patuleia) and then, again, in 1851 under the banner of "regenerating" the country. Calling themselves Progressive Regenerators, they preferred the second to the first label and became definitely titled as Regeneradores. It was from this group that the first regular party emerged, always sticking to the same banner and name, and persisting as the strongest and most able party to the beginning of the century.

Cabralism died out without succession. Opposition to the "re-generating" regime, however, soon arose, bringing about a new group known as the Historic Progressives (because they claimed to be the true Progressives), later shortened into "Historics" (Históricos). They encompassed sort of "left-wing" opponents to the ruling party. Re-generators and Historics divided between themselves Parliament seats and governmental tasks for more than fifteen years. Then, a third party, more Left oriented, strove for power in the late 1860's and early 1870's: the Reformists. But the three-party system did not last. In 1876 Historics and Reformists got together and formed the Progressive Party, a true party, with a program and a well-defined structure.

Regenerators and Historics first, Regenerators and Progressists later, a two-party system which tried to follow the English way, rotated in power rather peacefully for almost fifty years, with a few interludes of crisis. Yet this "Rotativism" was soon threatened by the rise of new political forces and the decline of the monarchical regime itself.

In uncompromising opposition the Republican and the Socialist parties emerged, both in the 1870's, the first one with a tremendous appeal to the popular masses, particularly in the towns. But within the monarchical groups, too, new parties were born, fighting for "new life," new principles, and less political corruption. This was the period of dissensions, of rebellion against the party leaders, of asser-tion of younger people who tried to instill new blood into the veins of a dying body. In the 1880's, dissidents from the Regenerators formed the so-called "Dynastical Left" (Esquerda Dinástica), which did not endure but for a while earned the support of many. Between 1900 and 1910, the two big parties came apart, some six or seven major factions resulting from their breakdown. Besides the two main branches, which claimed "true inheritance" and kept the traditional name of the party, the most prominent new groups were the "Re-generating-Liberal" Party (founded 1901, in power 1906–08) and the "Progressive Dissidents" (founded in 1905). The Catholics, too, emerged as a new political force under the name of the Nationalist Party.

The secret and the religious societies provided the framework for much political activity. Their real influence, however, must still be appraised from a historical standpoint, because gross exaggerations have been stated and written on their impact upon government policies and revolutionary acts. Freemasonry was the most relevant among those societies, its action increasing in the early 1900's and becoming almost thoroughly republican-oriented. Yet to be a Mason was also much of a fad, a virile connotation so to say, and Masonry membership should not necessarily account for revolutionary potentiality. More popular and active was the Carbonary (Carbonária), arising at the beginning of the twentieth century after the Italian model of the mid-1800's. Among the religious associations with semi-secret clauses and the purposes of defending God, the Catholic faith, the Institutions, and the like, against subversion, the Society of Jesus Third Order and its by-products should be emphasized.

It was often hard to discern the precise differences among the several parties. The idea of defining ideologies and currents of action in a written program and of carrying on that program to the end was still far from the party conception. The Regenerating Party, for instance, had no written program up to January 1910, a few months before its end. The Regenerators defended the Charter and its amendments (all enacted by them), and emphasized order under a strong government which might permit free individual initiatives. They also stood for intensive public works supported by the state with public loans, particularly in the field of communications. The Progressive Party defended a constitutional revision and dissented from the Regenerators in other minor points related to finance, economy, and political organization. Yet, by the late nineteenth century, its real differences from the other party were reduced to nothing. The Regenerating-Liberals stood for a strengthening of the king's authority and for a much closer intervention of the state in the country's economic and social life. To a certain extent they represented in Portugal state socialism, in the German manner.

Theoretically, the great parties of the monarchy were organized upon the basis of local, freely elected centers. As a matter of fact, such centers existed only in the towns. Elsewhere, and even in many towns, the party basis was the local boss, who controlled everything and everyone. In this way, and as the Spanish author Luis Araquistain has put it, "power did not emanate from the people to the parties and from the latter to the Crown, but from the Crown to the parties and from the latter to the local organizations of bosses. The people voted as they were ordered by whoever paid most for votes." In this way, also, the constitutional regime had much of the character of an absolute monarchy "which entrusted the parties with power; and the parties, by cynically manipulating the political machinery, proceeded to impose that power on a people for the most part ignorant and indifferent." As public opinion was inconsequential and existed only in a few towns, the parties were simply groups of clients depending upon a boss or a leader and eagerly coveting public jobs. Elections were "made" by the government, which always won them by means of a network of local authorities. Consequently, instead of the king choosing the prime minister based on popular voting, it was the king who had to dissolve the House of Deputies, in order that the government might have a majority in the next House, which it "made." Premierships changed from one to the other party, whenever the ruling party, or an agreement between the two, or even the king thought it convenient. Reasons varied greatly from case to case: often a simple fatigue of governing brought about the change; at other times, it was the fear of some responsibility, a parliamentary debate in either House of Parliament, a press campaign cleverly oriented, personal matters affecting any cabinet member, or the like.

Governmental instability was not a feature of the constitutional monarchy in Portugal. But there were times when governments did not last, as for instance in 1820–22 (a five-month average for each), 1826–28 (a four-month average), 1834–37 (a four-month average) and 1908–10 (a six-month average). But those periods corresponded, for the first three, to the troubled assertion of the constitutional monarchy, and for the last one, to its final disaggregation. Averages between 1837 and 1908 were much higher, a year and a half to the "Regeneration" (1851) and more than two years afterward. There were long-lasting governments, of five and a half years (Fontes Pereira de Melo, 1871–77); five years (Saldanha, 1851–56); four years and nine months (Loulé, 1860–65); four years and four months (Hintze Ribeiro, 1900–04); four years and three months (Fontes Pereira de Melo, 1881–86). Such averages and "long" terms in office were certainly much below the long periods of rule in the old days of the absolute monarchy. But times had changed, and nowhere did Liberalism represent too much stability, which it understood as stagnation and corruption. In a European context, the Portuguese governments were as stable as any others.

The Portuguese constitutional monarchy like most constitutional monarchies of the world was, and has often been regarded as, a corrupt regime, characterized by fake elections and general bribery in public administration. Parliaments were defined as organs of systematic obstruction to government, as machines of vain oratory, and as arenas of disorder. Indeed, all those things did happen, but it would be a gross exaggeration to reduce constitutionalism to some examples of poor functioning. Elections, for instance, had little meaning in the countryside but undoubtedly represented public opinion in the towns, particularly in Lisbon and Porto. Thus, if majorities were "made" by the government for most of the country, they were not "made" for the big centers, in those places where the commercial and industrial bourgeoisie were concentrated. In Lisbon the governments often lost an election, and this had a far larger impact on politics than the huge majorities obtained elsewhere in the country. Irregularities of all kinds were usual in every election, but in the capital or in Porto things were smoother and few ever dared to try these practices. Freedom of press, which had practically no limits (at least from a political standpoint), helped to build up a civic consciousness in the large centers which it would be wrong to neglect.

In bribery and political corruption, we have no proof that the constitutional regime went farther than any other before or afterward. As usual, corruption became the scapegoat for every sign of Portugal's weakness or backwardness in a European context. The loss of Brazil, the inability to develop the Overseas territories, several humiliations abroad, lack of funds, illiteracy, all seemed to most contemporaries (and to historians who followed them) a result of incompetence, irresponsibility, and political corruption. Actually, what common sense suggests is that daily control of public affairs by the press and Parliament—regardless of their imperfection and faults—made corruption and poor administration more difficult than in the old times of despotism. This suggestion, however, awaits a historian.

MAIN EVENTS

The triumph of Liberalism in Portugal was preceded by an unsuccessful conspiracy, the goals of which seemed to be more political than ideological. The Portuguese felt abandoned by their monarch; they complained about the heavy sums of money shipped yearly to Brazil in the form of rents and taxation along with the commercial decline and the unbalanced budget. In addition the Portuguese resented the British influence in the army and in the regency. In 1817 several persons were arrested on the charge of plotting against Marshal Beresford's life, the government, and the existing institutions. A short trial brought death at the stake to a dozen people, including the alleged leader of the conspiracy, Lieutenant-General Gomes Freire de Andrade. This execution had a deep impact on the rise of a liberal consciousness among the army and the bureaucrats. Far from preventing any future rebellions, it only fostered them: the opponents of the existing regime fully realized the tyranny of its supporters and the impossibility of any change by other than violent means.

It should be emphasized that to a certain extent the regency understood how grave the situation was, and suggested several ways of coping with it. Yet it mainly stressed the economic and financial problems and simply proposed cuts in the expenditures and petty reforms in administration. Far from Portugal, neither the king nor his government were fully aware of the political and economic tensions, while the regency always tended to ignore facts or dilute them in order to please the rulers.

Early in 1820 Liberalism triumphed in Spain. Contacts between the Spaniards and the revolutionary Portuguese intensified. Beresford decided to go to Brazil in order to get more extensive powers both for improving the army and suppressing the liberal danger.

Taking advantage of his absence, the military revolted in Porto (August 24, 1820) and in a few days claimed full sovereignty in the North. A Provisional Junta was formed, presided over by Brigadier-General António da Silveira. Its main goals were to take over the regency and to summon the *cortes* with the aim of adopting a constitution. In Lisbon, the regency tried to resist and denounced the revolutionaries as enemies of the country. However, it could not prevent a second uprising (September 15), this time in Lisbon, which ousted the rulers and set up a provisional government under the presidency of Freire de Andrade (a cleric and a relative of the martyr of 1817). At the same time the northern revolutionaries started a march south. On September 28, North and South fused into a new Provisional Junta, in which Freire de Andrade held the presidency and António da Silveira the vice-presidency. The great names of the revolution, however, were Fernandes Tomás, Ferreira Borges, and Silva Carvalho, all jurists and bureaucrats who together took over the secretariates of interior (Reino) and finance (Fazenda).

The new government did practically nothing but promote elections for the *cortes*. They took place in December, and a majority of bourgeois landowners, traders, and bureaucrats was elected. One of the first measures of the *cortes* was to request King John VI to return to Portugal. They also elected (January 1821) a new government and a new regency (under the presidency of the Count of Sampaio) to rule the country in John's absence, thus putting an end to the Provisional Junta.

John VI arrived in Lisbon in July 1821 after having sworn to uphold the future constitution. Many Liberals viewed him suspiciously and saw in him the natural leader of a conservative and anticonstitutional current of opinion. Yet John VI did not betray his oath right away and quite willingly accepted whatever the *cortes* and the government imposed on him. It is true that he appointed predominantly conservative ministers but on the whole and for two years he behaved well as the first constitutional monarch. The leaders of the absolutist movement were rather to be found in Queen Carlota Joaquina, along with her son, Prince Miguel.

The "Liberals" were far from united. Most jurists and bureaucrats stood for the revolutionary principles based upon the American and French ideologies, wanted the *cortes* elected by all the people regardless of social class, defended the need for a constitution, and required thorough reforms in administration leading to a truly new order. Among them several wings could still be distinguished. By contrast, most of the military, who had led the revolution, aimed at

Houses of Bragança and Bragança–Saxe-Coburg

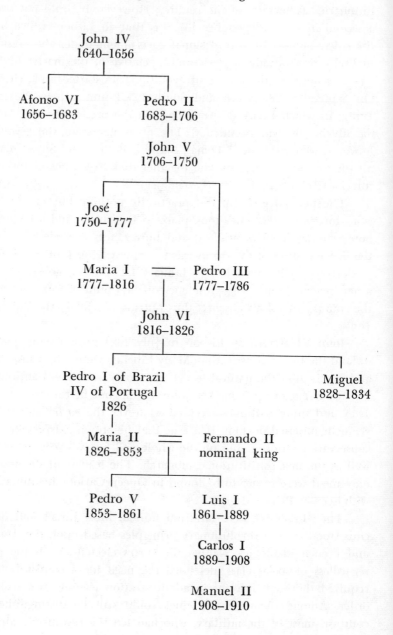

John IV
1640–1656

Afonso VI
1656–1683

Pedro II
1683–1706

John V
1706–1750

José I
1750–1777

Maria I   Pedro III
1777–1816   1777–1786

John VI
1816–1826

Pedro I of Brazil
IV of Portugal
1826

Miguel
1828–1834

Maria II   Fernando II
1826–1853   nominal king

Pedro V   Luis I
1853–1861   1861–1889

Carlos I
1889–1908

Manuel II
1908–1910

Teófilo Braga	1910–1911
Manuel de Arriaga	1911–1915
Teófilo Braga	1915
Bernardino Machado	1915–1917
Sidónio Pais	1917–1918
Canto e Castro	1918–1919
António José de Almeida	1919–1923
Teixeira Gomes	1923–1925
Bernardino Machado	1925–1926
Mendes Cabeçadas	1926
Gomes da Costa	1926
Óscar Carmona	1926–1951
Oliveira Salazar	1951
Craveiro Lopes	1951–1958
Américo Tomás	1958–

much more moderate goals, namely the return of the king, the end of the British influence in the army, and the summoning of the traditional *cortes* with the three-order representation (clergy, nobility, and people). What everybody wanted was to put a full stop to Brazil's total autonomy, and go back to Portugal's former situation of motherland versus colony.

The liberal jurists and bureaucrats took the lead for a while. They controlled the *cortes* and wrote a highly advanced constitution, started the revolutionary work of changing institutions and abolishing privileges, decreed freedom of press, and dissolved the Inquisition. Most government ministers were also bureaucrats. Several top military tried some coups d'état or even armed rebellion, but they failed.

The independence of Brazil (September 1822) inflicted a mortal blow to the liberal *cortes* and made the Liberals highly unpopular. People now realized that one of the main goals of the Revolution, i.e., bringing Brazil back to the condition of a colony, had failed, and they blamed the *cortes* for it. Also, many of the innovations met with the resistance of the great majority of the people, who did not understand

them, not to mention the clergy and the nobility. Soon the ruling
Liberal Party felt isolated and without support. Queen Carlota
Joaquina refused to swear to uphold the constitution, which gave her
wide popularity. In Spain, the French army had just intervened to
restore absolutism (April 1823).

Under these circumstances it was relatively easy for the anti-
Liberal party to rise up in arms at the small town of Vila Franca and
proclaim the restoration of absolutism (May 1823). Yet John VI altogether rejected a return to the old regime. He promised instead a
new and better constitution to the country, while dissolving the *cortes*
to please the victors. In this, he was very wisely trying to prevent future rebellions from the oppressed side.

Although Prince Miguel posed as the head of the anticonstitutional movement known as Vilafrancada, he was no more than a tool
in the hands of a vast group of people, in which some of the revolutionaries of 1820 played a major role. However, as in 1820, the counterrevolution could now be defined as a rebellion against something,
although rather vague in what it actually wanted. This became clear
as time passed and the counterrevolutionaries broke up into an extremist right wing lead by Miguel and his mother and a moderate
center wing symbolized by the king and his government. The former
started plotting again and revolted once more in April 1824 (Abrilada). John VI sought protection aboard an English man-of-war and
from there, backed by England, he forced Miguel into submission. The
prince left the country, and the Center Party regained power. Up to
the king's death (March 1826), a moderate absolutism ruled Portugal,
leaning more toward the Right than toward the Left. No new constitution ever appeared; on the contrary, John VI announced the intention of summoning the *cortes* in the old manner. Numerous liberals fled the country and went to England and France.

John's death posed a difficult problem. His eldest son, Pedro,
was the emperor of Brazil. And although nobody had ever questioned
his rights to the throne of Portugal, it seemed obvious that neither
Brazilians nor British would accept a reunion of the two crowns, even
under separate, autonomous conditions. Thus Pedro, acclaimed in
Portugal as Pedro IV as soon as his father died, promptly abdicated
(a week after John's death was known in Brazil) on behalf of his

daughter Maria da Glória—then a child of seven—provided that she marry her uncle Miguel, who would immediately take over the regency of the kingdom. At the same time, Pedro granted Portugal a highly conservative constitution, which had been hastily drafted. He also declared an amnesty. In this way, Pedro IV tried to carry on his father's policy of compromise, to the extent of calling back Miguel, the head of the extremist faction, and of entrusting to him full government powers for at least eleven years.

In Portugal, despite the fact that many people resented Pedro's abrupt decision without previously swearing the traditional oath of fealty to the nation, and disliked the granting of any constitution, this solution was generally accepted. A regency under Princess Isabel Maria had the new queen (called Maria II) and the new constitution sworn to throughout the country, and organized elections to the new *cortes*. In Vienna (where Miguel was living), the prince and future regent accepted his brother's conditions, swore to uphold the constitution and was bethrothed to Maria. Late in 1827 he left Austria and arrived in Portugal, via Paris and London, in February 1828.

By that time the early atmosphere of conciliation had altogether vanished. The Liberals, with a constitution and a parliament again, proclaimed victory and demonstrated in the streets. Most exiles returned home. The absolutists realized that the maintenance of things as they were meant defeat and a return to the hateful constitutional days. They started invoking all kinds of arguments to prove that Pedro had no rights to the throne—because he had proclaimed Brazil's independence and had therefore betrayed Portugal—and consequently could not transmit them to anyone. Miguel, they argued, was the lawful heir and king. Military uprisings and guerrilla warfare occurred here and there, and an actual, albeit brief, civil war ravaged a part of the country with the support of Spain in 1826–27.

The government was weak and did little to contain such violent methods. It obviously showed more sympathy toward the absolutists than toward the liberals. To protect itself and the status quo, it even required Britain to send a troop garrison to Lisbon, which stayed there for some time.

For the second time Miguel swore his faithfulness to both Pedro and Maria, as well as to the constitution. Pressures on him, however, came from every social class, and particularly from his closest advisers, to pass over his oaths and be proclaimed absolute king. The Austrian and Spanish governments were also favorable to the restoration of absolutism. In March 1828, he dissolved the *cortes* and in May he summoned new ones according to the old style. They proclaimed him king (July 1828), which he promptly accepted. The foreign countries had their representatives removed from Portugal until 1829, when most of them—but not the three major powers, England, France, and Austria—formally acknowledged Miguel's kingship.

The liberal opposition responded with a military uprising in Porto and elsewhere, which failed. Other conspiracies also led nowhere. As a consequence, violent persecutions against the liberals featured Miguel's six-year rule. Thousands left the country, thousands were arrested and kept in jail in the worst possible conditions, dozens were executed or murdered. Repression hit every aspect of Portuguese life and surpassed Pombal's despotism fifty years before. Yet the majority of the population applauded such measures, because they regarded the liberals as pure atheists, enemies of the country and guilty of the worst crimes.

Miguel's repressive system at home seemed to herald a bitter civil struggle. The king was unable to surround himself with able and competent ministers, with the result that both his internal and his external policies were awkward and led to disaster. After 1831 he gradually succeeded in alienating all the foreign support he could expect to obtain, even that of reactionary and neighboring Spain (by backing Carlos' claims against his brother, King Fernando VII). The economic and financial situation, far from improving with the definite return to absolutism, became worse.

Meanwhile Emperor-King Pedro dispatched young Maria to Europe. Her presence in England gave the thousands of exiles new hope, while money arriving from Brazil (which that country owed Portugal according to the peace treaty of 1825) helped prepare an expedition which landed in the island of Terceira (Azores) early in 1829. This island had revolted against Miguel and gallantly upheld the liberal cause for more than two years. There, many exiles and local people set up a provisional regency under the leadership of the Marquis of Palmela. Queen Maria went back to Brazil to await better days.

The absolutists vainly tried to subdue Terceira, but the liberals gradually conquered all the other islands of the Azores. In Brazil, circumstances had forced Emperor Pedro I to abdicate on behalf of his son Pedro II (1831), which gave him full freedom of action to try to gain the Portuguese crown. He left Brazil with his wife and daughter Maria and went to England and France, assuming the direct leadership to the liberal cause. The French government, sympathetic to the liberals after the revolution of 1830, raised no obstacles to his organization of a new military expedition with the purpose of liberating Portugal. Arriving at Terceira (March 1832) Pedro replaced Palmela as regent and left for Portugal with his people in June 1832. The expedition was formed by some 7,500 men, including 800 French and English mercenaries and volunteers. Landing in Portugal took place in July, near Porto. Caught by surprise, the absolutist forces which protected the city retreated, and the liberals entered Porto almost without bloodshed four days later.

The civil war had thus started on the mainland. It would last for two years and bring about considerable devastation. It ruined the country's already shaken economy and made liberals and absolutists both dependent upon foreign creditors. English, French, and others had their share of Portugal's wealth, and imposed their control there more than ever before. Foreign help and direct interference in Portugal's affairs featured the troubled history of constitutionalism to the 1840's. Diplomatic envoys often acted as royal advisers.

In the beginning, the civil war seemed a thoroughly unbalanced duel between a handful of liberal exiles aided by France and England and the overwhelming majority of the country, counting upon a large regular army of more than eighty thousand. Yet the liberals had the advantage of fighting for something new and practically unproved, thus pure and with good propaganda possibilities. They could make promises, herald a reign of prosperity and liberty, compare a dubious and corrupt past and present with a future full of glory. Mousinho da Silveira's theoretical legislation had quite an impact on the minds of the absolutist soldiers and other supporters. Moreover, the liberals included the cream of the Portuguese intelligentsia, the ablest lawyers, bureaucrats, doctors, scientists, and writers, with a significant number of young and daring fighters. Their upper-grade military were few, but they had with them some first-class young officers in the making. From the very beginning, military command supremacy belonged to the liberals, who proudly displayed men like Saldanha, Vila Flor, and Sá Nogueira. Also, the liberals were desperately fighting for a return home, for the right to live in their fatherland, while defeat for the absolutists would not necessarily result in death or exile. Freedom was meant for all, while despotism excluded many.

Yet the absolutists did not give up that easily. After their first disorientation, they rallied together and besieged Porto. The siege lasted one year, but the liberals along with the population of the city gallantly held to the end. In June 1833, they decided to try another landing somewhere, which might relieve the absolutist pressure. A maritime expedition composed of some 2,500 men under the command of Vila Flor (now honored with the title of Duke of Terceira) left Porto and in a surprise operation landed in the South, in the Algarve. Some days later the liberal fleet (under the mercenary English commander Napier) completely defeated the absolutist men-of-war. This fact gave the Duke of Terceira and his men new hope, and helped spread the liberal cause throughout the country. The absolutists were now demoralized and desertions occurred in large numbers. Liberal uprisings and guerrilla warfare resulted here and there, particularly in the South. Terceira marched on, reaching the Tagus in less than a month. The absolutists were badly beaten in front of Lisbon and their government decided to evacuate the capital. A day later Lisbon was occupied with little fighting (July 24, 1833). England and France formally recognized Pedro's government.

The main absolutist forces were still besieging Porto, and Miguel himself was with them. The appalling news from the South forced them to lift the siege and march southward in order to recapture the capital. Yet they were beaten again and again, particularly at the battles of Almoster (February 1834) and Asseiceira (May 1834). Late in that month, Miguel and his partisans were compelled to lay down arms. According to the concessions, signed at the village of Évora-Monte (May 26, 1834), a general amnesty was granted, the military were maintained in the patents they had in 1828, and the civil and church servants were indemnified although not kept in their jobs. Miguel was to live outside the country with a yearly allowance of sixty

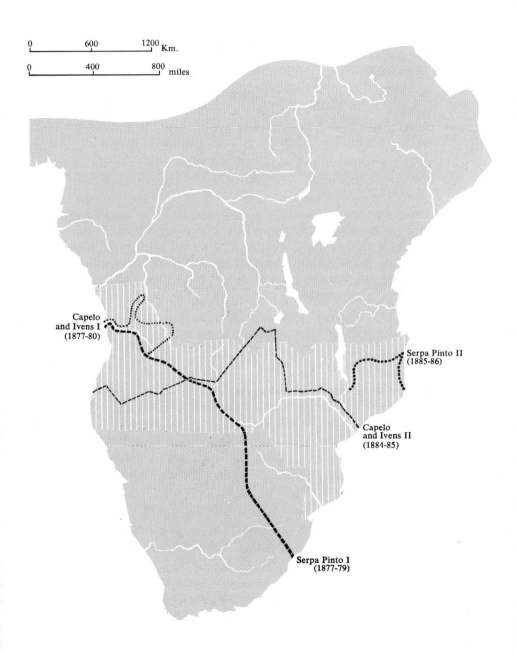

0 600 1200 Km.

0 400 800 miles

Capelo
and Ivens I
(1877-80)

Serpa Pinto II
(1885-86)

Capelo
and Ivens II
(1884-85)

Serpa Pinto I
(1877-79)

contos. He left forever on June 1, but once he arrived in Italy he disavowed his signing of the agreement, therefore losing the right to the allowance.

The end of the civil war did not mean stability at home. The liberals were plagued with internal divisions, and the reintegration of the absolutists in the political family only made things worse. The inevitable persecutions against the defeated side took place, accompanied by confiscations and destruction. The right wing became stronger than ever but the left wing was more aggressive too. The military and all those who had fought for the liberal cause now wanted a reward for their services. The most impetuous and famous army commanders (Saldanha, Terceira, and others) strove for power and considered themselves the natural leaders of the country. Not used to the constitutional practice, most statesmen tended toward a disguised dictatorship which brought them into an almost permanent conflict with the *cortes*. The latter also was riven by the opposition between the upper Chamber of Peers and the lower House of Deputies.

Regent Pedro was the first victim of the new system. He was accused of dictatorial acts and blamed for his lenience regarding Miguel. He quickly became unpopular among the leftists and many of his former partisans. But he died shortly after (September 1834) of tuberculosis. Rather than have a regency, the *cortes* and the government preferred to declare fifteen-year-old Maria II of age. She appointed as premier the conservative Duke of Palmela, who formed a center-right cabinet, supported by the rural landowners, the wealthy traders and bankers, the Church, and most of the old aristocrats.

Until 1836 the conservatives held power. Palmela, Terceira, and Saldanha, along with some moderates, controlled the government and tried to instill some order and inject some prosperity into a country utterly exhausted and still bleeding from its civil war. They had the full support of the foreign powers, who saw in them the warrants of a moderate, English-type constitutionalism, depending on loans from abroad and committed to pay them in time. They also managed to marry the queen to a German prince, Augustus of Leuchtenberg (January 1835) and when he suddenly died, two months later, to another German, Prince Ferdinand of Saxe-Coburg-Gotha (January

1836). The prince was given the title of Commander-in-Chief of the Portuguese Army. When his first son was born (1837), the queen had him proclaimed king-consort with the title of Fernando II.

The troubled situation of the country and the weakness of the several governments which succeeded each other made the conservatives unpopular, particularly in the large cities. The leftist opposition in the Chamber of Deputies, led by Manuel Passos (better known as Passos Manuel), kept the government under constant fire. Parliament was dissolved (June 1836), but in the following elections, the opposition won in several important places, among them Porto. When its representatives arrived in Lisbon, the city garrisons revolted with popular support, and forced the government to resign (September 1836). A new government, with Passos Manuel as the leading figure, assumed power, abolished the Constitutional Charter, and put in force the Constitution of 1822. The elections that followed gave him a majority that drafted a new constitution, more extreme than the Charter but far less than that of 1822.

"Septembrism," or the policies resulting from the September rebellion, quickly evolved toward a Center-Left compromise, where the moderate Viscount of Sá da Bandeira (i.e., the war hero Sá Nogueira) prevailed over the more leftist-oriented Passos Manuel. The 1836 rebellion had pretty much been a reaction of the urban industrial bourgeoisie, allied to middle-class traders (and both acclaimed by the lower classes), against the predominance of the rural landowners and upper business people. But it became clear that the new victors did not possess enough strength to carry on a radical program of their own. Moreover, although their interests were generally urban, they contradicted each other by opposing rich industrialists to petty traders and even to proletarians. Passos Manuel's kind of dictatorial government (actually the nominal premiership did not belong to him) brought about important and revolutionary measures but did not endure: eight months later he had to give up power to more moderate elements.

"Septembrism" lasted until 1842, but it tended to be less and less radical. Moreover, it had to fight constant attempts to restore the Charter: in November 1836, the queen and her advisers tried a coup d'état which failed; from July to September 1837, the Chartists revolted under the two prestigious marshals Saldanha and Terceira; other less important plots were discovered as well. On the other hand, the extreme leftists also rebelled in Lisbon against what they called the "betrayal" of the September revolution. As a consequence, the government tended to emphasize order and to lapse into authoritarianism. From 1839 on, the Secretary of Justice, Costa Cabral (a former radical), practically controlled things, being regarded by the Crown and the Right as the best warrant of order and prosperity.

The final step was taken in February 1842, when Costa Cabral himself restored the Charter at Porto in a bloodless coup d'état. He became the Secretary of the Interior in a new government, presided over by the Duke of Terceira but definitely controlled by himself. Power had returned again to the Right, but this time under an able and authoritarian leader, who knew how to rule and make himself obeyed.

"Cabralism" (from Cabral) emphasized order and economic development. As such, it set up in the country a regime of repression and violence, often comparable to Miguel's rule. But unlike Miguel, Costa Cabral did not want to go back to the past and to its obsolete structures; he rather fostered the development of Portugal in a progressive way, particularly in the fields of public works and administration. Many of his reforms endured, even when his name had become anathema for most people.

Costa Cabral's unashamed despotism, in contrast to his theoretical respect for the constitution and its liberties, together with his inability or unwillingness to carry violence to its limits and get rid of all opposition, brought about the most terrible and enduring civil war between liberals. Curiously enough, one of the main pretexts for a general rebellion was a highly progressive act that forbade burials in the churches and confined them to the cemeteries. Taxation increase also had its impact on the rebellion. A military uprising, early in 1844, had failed. Two years later, however, the common people in Minho rose in arms, with the actual participation of women. One of these, nicknamed Maria da Fonte, became a legendary figure and gave her name to the whole movement.

The Maria da Fonte revolution was a very complex affair. It put together several contradictory forces, encompassing old absolutists and partisans of Miguel, leftist radicals, moderates, and even right-wing Chartists annoyed with Costa Cabral's ruthlessness and shameless corruption. It included generals, aristocrats, clerics, bourgeois, proletarians. And it featured many interesting aspects of popular revolutionary organization in the form of local juntas which controlled local affairs and obeyed no central government.

The first phase of the Maria da Fonte movement lasted only a month (April–May 1846) and came to an end with the ousting of Costa Cabral from the government. He and his brother left the country while the Duke of Palmela headed a coalition cabinet formed by moderate Chartists and moderate Septembrists. This cabinet, however, pleased no one; on the contrary both Cabralists and leftists were against it, as well as the absolutists who aimed at the queen herself. A troubled situation lasted for some time, causing anxiety to the foreign powers and particularly Spain, where the fear of radical rebellions in union with the Portuguese was felt. To make things worse, Maria II and her advisers played politics too, forcing Palmela to resign (October 1846) and appointing Saldanha in his place to head a stronger government. This was the sign for the civil war: the Porto junta, which, like most others, had not been dissolved, rose in arms again carrying along all the North, part of Beira, Alentejo, and the Algarve. The guerrillas reappeared here and there. Many revolutionaries now planned the deposition of Maria II and her replacement by Prince Pedro, the heir to the throne, or even the proclamation of a Republic.

The war lasted for eight months and its results were generally favorable to the rebels. Their final victory, however, would bring about Maria's abdication and a government controlled by radicals. Neither England nor Spain could accept that. And concerning this, the two countries were eagerly supported by the Lisbon government itself. Saldanha asked for foreign intervention. A Spanish army entered Portugal, while the English fleet blockaded Porto. At Gramido, the rebels were forced to sign a treaty (June 1847) according to the terms of which they lay down arms with all honors.

The imposed peace of Gramido brought Costa Cabral and his partisans back. Saldanha still held power for a while in alliance with them, but palace intrigues and accusations of corruption led to his downfall in June 1849. Costa Cabral (made Count of Tomar) reassumed total power, this time as Prime Minister. Cabralism had returned, although in a more moderate, less violent form. Saldanha, personally offended with the government, the queen, and her advisers, became the main leader of the opposition. His enormous prestige and political naiveté made him welcomed by both the Left and the Center, despite his former associations with the extreme Right, including Cabral himself.

In April 1851 Saldanha revolted once again, and was supported by a military uprising in Porto. He called his movement the "regeneration of Portugal," his partisans becoming known henceforth as "Regenerators" (*Regeneradores*). Cabral's government fell, and Queen Maria II was forced to entrust Saldanha with the task of forming a new cabinet.

The rebellion had been in the making for a long time and rallied some of the best people in Portugal, including the great writer Alexander Herculano, who played a major role in its preparation and definition of goals. Saldanha's government gathered together some able and skilled personalities such as Rodrigo da Fonseca (Interior), Fontes Pereira de Melo (Finance and, later, Public Works, too), the poet and writer Almeida Garrett (Foreign Affairs), and several others. Politically, it began as a large and remarkable coalition of moderates, rightists, and leftists that deserved the acclaim of most people and was able to hold power for five years, albeit with several changes in its composition.

The country was tired of so much political turmoil, and desired peace. The bourgeoisie, particularly, required a strong yet flexible government, which could insure tranquillity and economic expansion. Saldanha's prestige accounted for the first; Fontes' plans for developing Portugal assured the second. Moreover, politically the liberal regime and the constitutional monarchy had reached maturity, which actually meant a maximum of freedom for a few, a docile and noninterfering monarch, a state of equilibrium among the several social classes and groups, and a clever manipulation of the political machine. The period of idealism was over. Economic and administrative problems replaced political doctrines as a program of government. The 1852 amendment to the constitution, along with the new electoral law, put an end to the division between Chartists and Septembrists and made the Charter acceptable to almost everyone. The industrial, financial, and trade expansion of Portugal attuned the interests of industrialists, financiers, traders, and rural landowners at the several levels, gathering together upper, middle, and petty bourgeoisie for a common goal. Between aristocrats and bourgeois the difference tended to fade away. From 1851 until the rise of the Republican Party in the 1880's and the 1890's one could say there was in Portugal no real "opposition" to the institutions, the ways of government, the economic and social policies or structures. From time to time there were some attempts to foster such opposition but always in vain. This firm hold on power by a united bourgeoisie would last for half a century and prevent any notions of rebellion from the lower classes. Summing up, one might say that 1851 saw the final adjustment of Portugal to the new conditions which had arisen with the loss of Brazil and the breakdown of the old regime.

Queen Maria II died in 1853, in childbirth. Although she was always respected as a mother and a person, her behavior as a constitutional queen often deserved bitter criticism. Obviously she liked to interfere in politics and leaned toward favorites in her choice of ministers. She listened too much to foreign advisers, including her husband, a German, and the envoys of countries like England and Belgium. She was probably primarily responsible for several political crises which shook Portugal from 1836 to 1851. King Fernando II, who in his youth liked to play politics too, became wiser with age and gained the esteem and respect of his subjects. Very talented and educated and with a disposition toward music and the arts, he had a major role in fostering the development of the arts in his new country and was responsible for the excellent education given to all his children. The heir to the throne, Pedro, was not of age, a regency being assumed by his nominal father King Fernando II. As king, Pedro V began ruling in 1855, but he died very young, of typhus, in 1861. He was remarkably intelligent and mature for his duties, and his death was deeply felt throughout the country. His brother Luis succeeded him on the throne. Not so much inclined toward public affairs as his older brother and his mother, Luis I passed into history as the model constitutional king. He preferred literature to politics and published several good translations of Shakespeare's plays in Portuguese. His marriage to Maria Pia, the daughter of Victor Emmanuel II of Italy, tightened the ties with that country and helped his popularity among the leftist anticlericals.

Portugal's internal policy during the reign of Pedro V and Luis I (1853–89) was one of relative quiet in the general framework of economic expansion and prosperity for the ruling classes. Regeneradores and Históricos (later called Progressistas) followed each other in power, both with a similar number of ruling years (the Regeneradores ruling in 1851–56; 1859-60; 1871–77; 1878–79; 1881–86; the Históricos, the Reformistas, and the Progressistas ruling in 1856–59; 1860–65; 1868–70; 1870–71; 1877–78; 1879–81 and 1886–90; and a coalition of the two parties, named Fusão, ruling in 1865–68), but the Regeneradores can be credited with greater achievements. Here and there, some minor crises shook the political order, but they were of no great significance. On January 1, 1868, for instance, there was some rioting in Lisbon in protest against new taxation. In 1870 old and proud Marshal Saldanha, because of a personal offense again, led an uprising against the government, ruled for some months with a group of talented people around him, and then stepped down. And in 1871 the famous lectures at the Lisbon *casino* formed the very beginnings of a true opposition to the institutions and the bourgeois order.

Portugal's external policy apparently was equally calm. Actually, however, the country had little autonomy, depending rather upon the general European order as decided by the Congress of Vienna (1815). England, France, Austria, and, to a certain extent, Spain controlled Portugal as they controlled most of the other small European countries. England acted as the main "protector" for economic reasons, and prevented a possible Spanish take-over. Yet, when some other important power interfered, England did little to enforce that protection. This happened, for instance, in 1831 when a French fleet paraded before Lisbon and threatened to bomb the city if some French demands were not answered. It happened, again, in 1857–58, when France violated Portugal's rights and imposed on her the payment of a heavy indemnity, because of the confiscation by the Portuguese authorities in Mozambique of a French slave ship (see chapter 11). Both English and French settled down in Portuguese or Portuguese-claimed territories in Africa (see chapter 11) with little respect for Portugal's rights there. Other countries' arbitration, when accepted by the great powers,

generally gave credibility to Portugal's claims. And many other instances could be called upon to show this dependency. On the other
hand, the Portuguese themselves asked for foreign protection and intervention in their home affairs: this happened in 1823, 1824, 1828–34
(both liberals and absolutists), 1836, and 1847. If such an interference
was generally required by the conservative side, which was afraid of
being displaced by radical movements, the leftists themselves were not
entirely free from guilt. Whenever Spain, France, and England showed
some sympathy for their principles, they would also ask for their support.

After 1848, the international order in Europe greatly changed.
Foreign intervention in European countries became somewhat rarer,
and the tendency was to let each nation solve her internal problems
alone. For Portugal, the main problem which arose regarding foreign
relations was that of Iberianism—the union between Portugal and
Spain. This had been, of course, a centuries-old aspiration of both
countries, but the Portuguese had given it up after 1640. Spain became the dangerous partner, and particularly during the nineteenth
century her claims to an Iberian Union often endangered Portugal's
independence. There were undoubtedly partisans of such a union in
Portugal, but their number was small and their practical influence
minimal. The unification of Italy (1859–61) and the trend toward the
unification of Germany (effective in 1871) had an unquestionable impact on both Spain and Portugal. Spanish and Portuguese literature—
including the press—debated the problem, either attacking or defending the union, and suggesting practical solutions. In 1868–70, the
Spanish revolution and the two-year search for a king put the whole
problem in a new light. Both Fernando II and Luis I of Portugal
were thought of and invited as throne candidates, with the forethought
that the two crowns might be united in the future. Both refused because of such a goal. Saldanha posed as a convinced partisan of Iberianism, and his seizure of power in 1870 probably had some Spanish
influence behind it. The question was open again in 1873–75, until
the Spanish throne solidified once more under Alfonso XII. For many
Portuguese intellectuals, including a great number of Republicans, the
dream of an Iberian Union had a strong appeal, as a remedy for the
backwardness of both countries and the dawn of a new era for the

united "Spaniards." They defended, of course, a sort of federation with Spain (or even a confederation of several states dismembered from Spain), which might preserve Portugal's cultural and political identity.

The stability of the 1870's and 1880's was followed by a deep political, economic, and financial crisis. The contradictions of the constitutional monarchy began to be evident to everyone. Its ideology no longer had any appeal to the younger generations. Instead, socialism and republicanism pointed a new way. The Spanish and French revolutions in the 1870's played a major role in the rise of a Portuguese political consciousness opposed to the cynical rotation of the parties and the enrichment of the bourgeoisie. The number of emigrants who left the country year after year suggested that the social problems of the lower classes were worsening instead of improving with the general economic expansion. Anticlericalism also played a major role in the shaping of an opposition.

Republican and socialist groups appeared in the 1870's. A decade later they had crystallized into two parties of some significance, particularly the Republican one. They were becoming more aggressive, more daring in their claims, more threatening in their work of subversion. The first Republican representative was elected to the *cortes* in 1878. King Luis I died in 1889, and the new monarch, Carlos I, intelligent but haughty and married to a very pious French princess, Amélie of Orléans, did not enjoy his father's popularity.

The crisis was provoked by the ultimatum that Great Britain sent to Portugal in January 1890, according to which the Portuguese had to give up their claims to a vast African territory connecting Angola with Mozambique, in what is now Zambia and Rhodesia (see chapter 11). This ultimatum caused a national wave of indignation against England and a widespread movement against the monarchy and the king himself, who was accused of neglecting the Overseas territories and of jeopardizing the nation's interests. There were some riots, and in January 1891 the first republican uprising took place in Porto. It failed, but for the first time it showed the existence of a real menace to the established institutions.

The events of 1890–91 took place in the context of an international economic and financial crisis. The Progressista government, headed by José Luciano de Castro, considered responsible for the ultimatum, fell. The king called the Regeneradores under António de Serpa Pimentel, who were unable to keep power and resigned some months later on account of the treaty to be signed with England. A national cabinet was then formed under a prestigious but aged figure, General João Crisóstomo (October 1890). It was followed by another coalition government under the economist José Dias Ferreira (January 1892), who included historian Oliveira Martins as Finance Minister. Dias Ferreira's cabinet was able to solve the financial crisis and smooth the situation again. As a consequence, the old party system came back to power. Regeneradores under Hintze Ribeiro and Progressistas under José Luciano succeeded each other up to 1906 (the Regeneradores ruling in 1893–97, 1900–4, and 1906; the Progressistas in 1897–1900 and 1904–6).

The political situation, however, was not entirely the same as before the ultimatum. New trends pointed either toward a stronger assertion of the royal power or toward a much more liberal conception of constitutionalism. Both could be ascertained in either party. In 1893, Hintze Ribeiro attempted a compromise with the liberal wing, which failed, the liberal ministers (Bernardino Machado and Augusto Fuschini) resigning some months later. It was the other wing that prevailed, with its main representative in João Franco, the Secretary of Interior. Hintze and Franco even tried a dictatorship in 1895. Party unity could not be enforced because of such trends, which were exacerbated by personal rivalries. In 1901, Franco seceded from the Regeneradores and formed (1902) a new party, the Regenerador-Liberal party, which stood for a new kind of monarchy, somewhat despotic but with social concerns (following closely the Bismarck pattern). On the other side, a small group of dissidents led by José Maria de Alpoim left the Progressistas (1905), clamoring for a more liberal regime, very close to a Republic. Yet the rising force, which more and more threatened and worried the constitutional monarchy, was the Republican Party, particularly after 1903 when Bernardino Machado, the former minister, became a Republican and threw all his influence and ability into reorganizing and strengthening the party.

Meanwhile, if the international position of Portugal had improved in regard to the Spanish menaces to her independence, the security of her Overseas territories was far from guaranteed. Germans and British kept an eye on Angola and Mozambique, and would not give up an opportunity to repeat the ultimatum of 1890. In 1898, both countries signed a treaty envisioning the partition of Angola, Mozambique, and Timor in case of Portuguese financial difficulties. The United States had some views on the Azores. In 1904 Germany planned to take all the Portuguese colonies. Well aware of this fact, the Portuguese governments did their best to appease the big powers' greediness and to a certain extent they succeeded. The secret Treaty of Windsor (1899), between Portugal and England, contradicted that of 1898. King Carlos himself acted as a good ambassador, with his frequent visits to the most important European countries and his playing the host to the rulers of England, Germany, France, and Spain. With his royal colleagues, King Carlos was as popular as he was unpopular with his fellow countrymen. Yet the main obstacle to a partition of the Portuguese colonies was the rivalry among the great powers themselves and the concern for maintaining the European equilibrium.

By 1906 the *cortes* had become an assembly for chicanery and personal debates. Obstruction to any government and filibustering were common practices. The two large parties did little to avoid the accusations of corruption, inefficiency, and uselessness laid upon them. The Republicans made the best use possible of internal monarchical dissensions to attack the regime. Behind them, a majority of urban middle- and lower-class people began successfully to sap the fundaments of the institutions. The king forced Hintze Ribeiro to resign and entrusted João Franco with the task of forming a new cabinet. The new premier first got the support of the Progressistas but soon lost it and decided to try the dictatorial way. The *cortes* were dissolved (1907) and no new elections set. The consequences were disastrous for the regime: Franco had against him the overwhelming majority of the organized forces in the country and could rely mostly on the royal support. It has been made public that the royal family owed the government (i.e., the nation) important sums of money in the form of successive loans, which brought about a campaign against the monarchy. Violence and repression featured Franco's second year in government. The students struck in Coimbra. In January 1908, an abortive rebellion rallied together Republicans and a good many monarchists too. Some of the main Republican leaders were arrested. On February 1, King Carlos and the heir to the throne, Prince Luis Filipe, were assassinated in Lisbon, while the second-born prince, Manuel, was slightly wounded.

Acclaimed as Manuel II, the new monarch, a youth of eighteen, dismissed Franco and called upon a coalition government headed by Admiral Ferreira do Amaral. The prevailing attitude was one of appeasement, in contrast to the fierceness of the fallen dictatorship. The Republicans were given more freedom than ever, and their influence among the people increased. In the municipal elections of 1908 they won in Lisbon. Porto had already a coalition of Republicans and liberal Monarchists in its municipal government since 1906. It became obvious to most people that the monarchy was coming to an end. This also derived from the weakness shown by all the monarchical groups and from governmental instability. From 1908 to 1910 there were six different cabinets, each one accounting for a new split within the two large parties. Behind the scenes, the old Progressista leader, José Luciano, controlled most of the political situation, his party backing all but the last of the six governments. In the general elections of August 1910, the Republicans triumphed in Lisbon and several other places. In a country like Portugal, where the weight of the capital is paramount in the nation's life, this meant the end for the constitutional monarchy. Indeed, on October 4, 1910, a military and popular revolution in Lisbon easily disbanded the last defenders of the throne, the Republic being proclaimed on the following day. King Manuel and his family left the country, never to return.

CHAPTER ELEVEN

AFRICA

TRAVELS AND COLONIZATION

In the nineteenth century central and southern Africa began to be influenced by the growth of European settlement and expansion. Hunters, traders, missionaries, and concession-seekers began penetrating the mighty continent everywhere. The great explorations of David Livingstone (1852 to 1873) and H. M. Stanley (1874 to 1877) were only the best known of a long series in which the French, the British, the Germans, the Boers, the Belgians, and the Portuguese figured prominently as well.

Although not well known, the part played by the Portuguese was also a major one. From the late eighteenth century (see chapter 9) to the 1900's, one expedition after another left the coastal areas of Angola and Mozambique with varied purposes and dissimilar achievements. These explorations made known to the West vast territories between latitude 7° and 27° S., and were instrumental in promoting European settlement not only in Portuguese but also in British areas —in present-day Zambia and Rhodesia.

The first important expedition which the Portuguese carried on after 1820 took place in 1831–32. Major José Maria Correia Monteiro, with Captain António Pedroso Gamito as second in command, and a large force of 420 traders and porters left Tete (in Mozambique) in 1831, heading northwest and following the track which explorer Lacerda e Almeida had made known thirty years before. They went as far as Cazembe, near Lake Mweru (the border between present Zambia and Congo), for economic as well as geographic purposes. Robbed of most merchandise and gunpowder, they decided to return to Tete, where they arrived in 1832. Gamito wrote a report on the expedition.

In 1843, the governor of Angola entrusted Joaquim Rodrigues Graça with the mission of getting to the springs of the river Sena and the region known as Bié and establishing effective Portuguese sovereignty there. His was a long trip, up the Cuanza River and then, northeastward, down the Kasai to Mussumba between that river and the Lulua (in what is now Congo). He went back to Luanda, following the same route, in 1846.

From 1847 onward, to the 1850's, explorer Bernardino José Brochado went from Moçâmedes, in south Angola, to the Cunene River, in which area he traveled extensively, reporting very interesting findings on ethnography and geography. The precise knowledge of the Cunene, in its course, was a result of Brochado's trip.

In the 1840's and 1850's, the Portuguese settler and peddler Silva Porto (1817–90) undertook some of the most important expeditions in present-day Angola and Zambia. Settling down in central Angola, where no other Europeans were then living, he gained a tremendous prestige and influence among the local African rulers, which enabled him to implement a geographic and economic policy. He and his "envoys" got to Barotseland (where he met Livingstone), and regular contacts were established with that area. Besides other trips he also accompanied two Arab merchants (who had crossed Africa coming from Zanzibar) on their way back home almost to the Kafue River, in central Zambia (1853). There he stopped, but his African clients went on to the Indian Ocean (1854) and then back home by sea. Silva Porto's merits as an explorer and a defender of the Portuguese sovereignty in central Angola were rewarded with the office of Captain-Major of Bié. He later committed suicide when some local Bié tribes revolted against the Portuguese flag.

Still in the 1850's the Austrian naturalist Friedrich Welwitsch traveled widely in Angola under a commission of the Lisbon government. Caetano Ferreira departed from southeast Angola and traveled south, up the Cuando River, the springs of which he first saw in 1854. A year later, explorers Montanha and Teixeira left Inhambane, on the eastern coast of Africa, and headed west well into Transvaal (now Kruger National Park). Thus ended a first period of Portuguese geographical expansion.

After a twenty-year interval began a new period, marked by the most significant and the most daring of all the Portuguese expeditions. They were now better prepared and managed, by people with more expertise in all fields. The newly created Lisbon Geographical Society (1875) was instrumental in fostering, patronizing, and subsidizing the exploration movement.

Navy Commanders Hermenegildo Capelo (1841–1917) and Roberto Ivens (1850–98) left in 1877 for their first exploration. Departing from Benguela, they proceeded to Luanda, went up the Cuanza for awhile, then headed north to the Congo, looking for porters, then south again, in a sinuous line which took them to Silva Porto's headquarters, in Bié. They discovered the courses of the rivers Cubango, Luando, and Tohicapa, returning to Luanda in 1880. Their report, a fine piece of geographical knowledge, was widely publicized (*De Benguella ás Terras de Iacca,* Lisbon, 1888). A former companion of theirs, Captain Serpa Pinto (1846–1900), undertook the crossing of Africa, from west to east. From Silva Porto's headquarters (1877), Serpa Pinto went south, following the 1853 expedition tract to central Zambia. He continued further south via the Zambezi River, and then, accompanied by the French missionary Coillard, he proceeded all the way south to Pretoria (Transvaal) and Durban (1879), becoming the first Portuguese and one of the first Europeans to cross Africa. He wrote a famous account of his expedition, "How I Crossed Africa" (*Como eu atravessei a Africa,* 2 vols., Lisbon, 1880).

Within Mozambique, Navy Lieutenant António Maria Cardoso went from Inhambane to Sofala and back, following a wide detour west (1883). Again in Angola, Army officer Henrique de Carvalho traveled from Malange to the Kasai River (1884–86).

Capelo, Ivens, and Serpa Pinto undertook still a second voyage. The first two departed from Moçâmedes (South Angola) in 1884 and went all the way to Quelimane (Mozambique), where they arrived a year later, going as far north as Katanga, in Congo, and following the Zambezi down to its mouth. The report of their daring and successful trip was published in Lisbon in 1886, under the title *De Angola á*

Contra-Costa ("From Angola to the Other Coast"). Accompanied by Augusto Cardoso, Serpa Pinto also traveled in Mozambique in 1885–86, going from the town of Mozambique, on the coast, north to Ibo, and then west to Lake Nyassa.

These were simply the most renowned of all the expeditions, yet there were scores of others, undertaken by peddlers, officers, and scientists, within the present boundaries of Angola and Mozambique, which definitely helped make available better geographical knowledge of both colonies and formed the basis for the Portuguese political expansion in Africa. Indeed, the major motivation for the travels was the assertion of the Portuguese authority over historically claimed territories. Geographical and commercial motivations were also present. The elaborate maps of the late nineteenth and early twentieth centuries were their result, as well as the fostering of interest in trade projects among both blacks and whites. The Anglo-Portuguese treaty of 1890, defining the borderline between English and Portuguese Africa, pointed to the need for thorough and precise knowledge of at least the border region. Setting up the framework for modern Angola and Mozambique, it also stimulated the Portuguese to carry on an entire exploration of their territories, which they did throughout the last decade of the nineteenth and the first ten years of the twentieth centuries. Numerous map committees, geographical missions, and military operations completed the basic tasks started by the explorers of the mid-nineteenth century.

By 1830 or 1840 the Portuguese effective occupation of Angola was limited to a narrow strip of coastal territory, 50 to 80 miles wide, with no definite boundaries inland. In the north, occupation widened a little by encompassing part of the Congo River banks up to present-day Matadi, 171 km. (105 miles) inland where its navigability stops at the Livingstone Falls. In the south, southeast of what is now Benguela, Portuguese sovereignty reached Caconda, some 240 km. (150 miles) from the coast. The coastline itself was only thoroughly known as far as Benguela, before the reconnoitering expeditions of the 1830's and the 1840's, which mapped Angola's coast to the Bay of Tigres, 17° S.

In Mozambique, the Portuguese controlled even less territory than in Angola. From Cape Delgado to Lourenço Marques, occupation of the coastline was not even continuous: running north to south it stopped at Angoche, where the local ruler resisted the Portuguese; then it took over at Quelimane and proceeded to Delagoa Bay. From Cape Delgado to north of Angoche, the strip of land in the hands of the whites did not go beyond 40 km., or 25 miles; from Lourenço Marques to Sofala, it widened a little, mostly at the river valleys; yet only the Zambezi River corresponded to a deep penetration inland, for the Portuguese were well settled down to Tete and beyond, nearly 500 km. (320 miles) from the coast.

In Guinea, Portuguese authority had a mere coastal character and was limited to some fortresses and villages such as Bissau, Bolama (since 1828), Cacheu, Ziguinchor, Geba, Farim, and a few more, not necessarily connected by other than coastwise navigation. The situation in distant Timor was similar.

The reasons for this restricted occupation of the African continent were several. With the exception of Angola, in the late sixteenth and early seventeenth centuries, the Portuguese Crown had really never envisioned a substantial conquest of territory and was simply concerned about protecting the coastal settlements with a minimum hinterland, in the good tradition of the Asian "Empire." Secondly, Africa played a minor economic role for the Portuguese, compared with Brazil and the East, only slaves being of relevance. Thirdly, the African peoples generally offered fierce resistance to the European advance. And last but not least, the climate and the geographical features of the Continent posed insuperable hardships for white colonization. As a matter of fact, it is safe to say that the major stimulus to the Portuguese conquest of Angola, Mozambique, and Guinea was the foreign competition and the growing Portuguese fear of being "robbed" of what they regarded as parts of Portugal. This "uneconomic imperialism," to use Professor R. J. Hammond's words, must be emphasized to understand Portugal's position in Africa in the nineteenth century and attitude toward her colonies down to the present. Only in the twentieth century (in a few cases since the 1890's) did economic advantages clearly justify the Portuguese occupation of continental Africa. Until then, conquest, settlement, and reconnoitering were mostly planned and carried on by the government with political goals, but with very little interest from, and little capital invested by, private sources. Mobilization of a vast public opinion that supported the policy of imperialism—as it certainly did, to the extent of forcing the government to take better care of the colonies—had no other basis than national pride. To conquer Angola, Mozambique, and Guinea, to tell the world of the prowess of soldiers, sailors, and explorers over there, was for the Portuguese—as it still is, though less so—a way of balancing the frustrations felt at home and of lining up with the seven colonizing countries of the world: England, France, Germany, Italy, Belgium, Holland, and Spain (the latter replaced by the United States after 1898).

The several attempts to officially promote colonization in Africa did not meet with great success. Emigrants preferred Brazil or the United States, where well-organized societies needed them and provided them promptly with jobs and high salaries, to Angola or Mozambique, where no one welcomed them and where profits seemed difficult to obtain. Statesmen like Sá da Bandeira tried to organize migration to Africa with poor results. In 1838 land was distributed in Mozambique to orphans and other former pupils of the Casa Pia of Lisbon, but with little success. In 1852 a special fund to promote emigration t the Overseas possessions had meagre results. In 1884 a more promising undertaking was carried on—the colonization of the Moçâmedes tableland by settlers from Madeira. Several companies and regulations to promote settlement failed too. As a matter of fact, deported outcasts and some soldiers were virtually the only ones the government could get to stay in Africa permanently. Because of this the society of Luanda or Lourenço Marques was not very appealing and lacked that minimum of respectability every emigrant wished for himself or for his family.

By the early nineteenth century there were throughout the Portuguese "Empire" less than 10,000 Europeans, and this figure did not change much up to the middle of the century. Cape Verde, Angola, and India absorbed the largest number, a great many of whom were banished outcasts and garrison men. The number of actual settlers was minimal, for most of the white Portuguese returned home after a time. Even the garrisons included a large majority of Africans and Asians under the command of white Portuguese officers. Half-breeds did exist but in small numbers, and they did not necessarily feel at home in the Overseas provinces. Many attempted to go to Portugal and settle down there, some successfully.

After the middle of the century, things started changing but not much. Although the white population of both Angola and Mozambique increased eight or nine times between 1850 and 1910, Angola housed only some 12,000 Europeans when the Republic was proclaimed, and Mozambique half of that number. Miscegenation occurred slowly, not only because of the relatively large number of white females, but also because of the high death rate among children. An analysis of the peacetime garrisons, which the Portuguese kept throughout the eight colonies at the end of the monarchy, showed a little more than 10,000 men controlling the empire, of which less than a third were whites: 5,000 in Angola, 2,800 in Mozambique, 1,000 in India, 500 in Macao, and the remainder distributed almost evenly in the other four colonies. The "Empire" was no demographic burden for Portugal nor did it solve her problems of migration. Manning those huge areas and keeping them peaceful proved a much easier task than keeping order in Lisbon (8,000 soldiers in Lisbon could not prevent the Republic from being proclaimed on October 5, 1910).

"Towns" were little more than small villages, with some few exceptions: Macao (78,000), Pangim (Goa), Luanda, and Lourenço Marques—none of the three exceeding 20,000 in 1910, all races included. This, however, happened to be true of most European cities south of the Sahara, and Luanda could still pose as a large metropolis on the West coast from Morocco to Cape Town.

Although the African peoples of Angola, Mozambique, and Guinea were many, subdivided into several language groups and tribes with different characteristics and traditions, they had some similar traits. Most of them spoke clearly related languages known collectively as Bantu, a sort of African "Latin" mother tongue. Their main activity was grain farming, leading to a rapid exhaustion of soils. As they had limited means of restoring fertility, there was often a shifting kind of cultivation. Many tribes combined grain farming with cattle raising. Culturally, most of the African peoples in contact with the Portuguese had reached a sort of prehistoric metal-age level. They used iron tools (hoes, for instance) but were not familiar with writing. Their religion, though combining fetishism with an often elaborate pantheon of gods, did not shun the existence of a Supreme Being. Their political organization generally lacked a traditional kingship, most of them forming independent or tributary chiefdoms under the control of paramount chiefs (*sobas*). In historical terms, they strikingly resembled the Germanic peoples in contact with the Roman Empire. This, however, varied from area to area. In certain parts of Guinea and of north-central Mozambique (mainly along the coast), centuries of Moslem influence had definitely raised the civilizational level of the Africans and changed many of their ways of life. They were Muslims in religion, many spoke languages (such as Swahili) or dialects with a strong Arabic content, and they were organized in petty Arab-like shiekates or even sultanates.

In Angola, by far the largest tribal group was that of the Ovimbundo (also called Ovampo), occupying a central position in the Benguela highlands. North of the Ovimbundos lived the Ambundos and the Congos, the latter stretching much beyond the frontiers of present-day Angola, well into the former Belgian Congo. South and east of the Ovimbundos there were several smaller tribal groups, among them the Ambo, covering a part of what is now Southwest Africa. They all spoke different Bantu languages.

In Mozambique the tribal groups and the languages spoken were still more numerous than in Portuguese West Africa. In the north there lived the Yao (not distinct from the people of present Malawi), the Makondas, and the Makwas (or Macuas), common to Mozambique and Tanzania and both often Islamized. Central Mozambique was occupied by the Basenega and the Baangoni, of Zulu origin. In the south, there were the Tsonga groups of the Baronga and Batonga, as well as the Bachopi and several other minor Zulu tribes.

In Portuguese Guinea, about a dozen peoples occupied most of the territory: the interior Islamized groups of the Fulani (Fulas), the Mandingo, and the Biafada or Biafar; and the non-Moslem Balanta, Manjaco, Papel, Fulup or Felupe, Bijagó, and Nalu.

Tribal differentiation, rivalries, and frequent warfare always prevented the African peoples in contact with the Portuguese (or with other European peoples) from uniting themselves against the common foe. Except in very brief periods of sporadic "empires," i.e., confederations of tribes under a prestigious leader (like the Zulu Tutsi or Watutsi Empire in South Mozambique), the Portuguese had relatively little trouble in imposing their sovereignty, whenever they were determined to do it. Usually, they preferred cunning to violence, exploiting tribal and subtribal petty rivalries, dividing the blacks, and often posing as protectors or defenders of one tribe against another. They also proclaimed Portugal's "might" and threatened unconvinced tribes with fierce revenge. Centuries-long contact with African peoples had taught the Portuguese how to be accepted as lords and how to rule with a minimum of force. As a counterpart, they usually required very little from the subdued peoples: a theoretical subjection to the Portuguese flag and authorities, and the payment of a tribute. Only the development of white settlement throughout the twentieth century changed this situation.

Whenever peaceful means were insufficient or proved useless, the so-called campaigns of submission took place. Again, the Portuguese were masters in "pacifying" a territory with a minimum of fighting. Few as they were, they often depended upon individual deeds, daring prowess, and the like, which had a deep impact on the minds of Africans. Despite the European superiority in weaponry and military organization, the blacks had many strengths of their own: they knew the ground, they were used to the climate and the insects, and they were overwhelmingly superior in number. From the mid-1800's on, most of the tribes fighting the Portuguese used rifles sold or given by other Europeans—who often wished to foster Portugal's defeat in Africa— or by the Portuguese themselves.

During almost all of the nineteenth century, colonization in Angola, Mozambique, and Guinea interfered little with African ownership of the land. Except in a few areas, such as the Zambezi Valley or along the coast, where Portuguese rule had been a matter of fact for centuries, the Africans were not dispossessed of their property, for the simple reason that settlers were very few and generally uninterested in agriculture. Still, when the Lisbon government and several private companies began systematically organizing and promoting white colonization, open appropriation of the African-owned lands was discouraged for fear of rebellion. It must be remembered that the population density in each of the three colonies was low: not more than 4 inhabitants per square mile in Angola, not more than 8 in Mozambique, about 20 in Guinea. Property demarcations were often vague or nonexistent; shifting agriculture fostered the movement of people, with vast areas belonging to nobody.

Moreover, Europeans preferred to live in towns rather than to scatter themselves about in the countryside. A form of settlement thus developed, similar to that in the South of Portugal, with huge areas of uninhabited land or land sparsely inhabited by Negroes separating relatively dense towns and villages. It was only well into the twentieth century that individual white farming based upon actual settlement could develop as the road network expanded and communications became easier, along with greater security and European familiarity with the environment.

The Portuguese system of colonization—whenever it existed—always aimed at converting the African into a Portuguese. As early as 1820, all natives of the Overseas provinces were considered Portuguese citizens, at least in theory. With such goals in mind, the Portuguese systematically rebuffed whatever might prevent that "Portugalization": teaching was to be in Portuguese and only Portuguese was accepted as the official language; religion and morals were to be Christian and, if possible, Roman Catholic; customs, traditions, and way of life were to relate to the Portuguese fatherland, not to the African past. Consequently, learning and preservation of African languages and cultures could only be envisioned from a strictly scientific standpoint or as a provisional bridge for communication between whites and blacks.

Between the Portuguese and the Africans cultural contacts were almost totally one-sided. The difference in technological advance was too great to make the Europeans permeable to any black influence. It must also be emphasized that the Portuguese always resisted influences from races and civilizations which they considered backward and therefore inferior. Considering the worldwide and centuries-long Portuguese expansion, amazingly few aspects of African, American, and even Asian origin are to be found in the Portuguese culture or way of life, in contrast to their often excessive permeability to European influences. A few words, some new plants, but little else was all that Africa gave Portugal at the time.

The question of slavery hovered over the entire Portuguese colonial administration to the twentieth century. In a disguised way, one could even say that it survived to the 1950's. In this, of course, Portugal was not alone; other colonial powers confronted the same problem.

The great industrial changes of the eighteenth and early nineteenth centuries made possible an anti-slavery movement with good

chances of success. The French Revolution insisted on liberty and
equality for mankind, instilling some freshness into the traditional
but stagnant Christian doctrine of equality of all men before God.
Slavery had already been abolished in most European countries during
the eighteenth century, and fighting it became a sort of fashionable,
enlightened attitude among intellectuals and aristocrats. A public
opinion against slavery in general and the slave trade in particular
developed throughout Europe in the early 1800's. England, where the
industrial revolution had progressed most, could pose as the leading
defender of liberty for the slaves and thus the leading enemy of slavery-
indulging countries. During the nineteenth century, the British vessels
(for they were everywhere in the world) acted as a kind of police body
trying to stop the slave trade in Africa, Asia, and America. This, of
course, had several other implications. Anti-slavery operations were
often a disguise for political attitudes of imperialism. As warrants of
freedom, the British felt a right to interfere anywhere—particularly in
the subequatorial lands—and to meddle with the full sovereignty and
liberty of action of other countries. It was often a pretext to extend
Britain's "protection" to African areas and control their trade to the
detriment of other countries.

Following the Treaty of Vienna (1815), England and Portugal
signed an agreement to curb the slave trade in the Portuguese possessions. Portugal pledged to suppress it north of the equator, which
meant her colonies of Cape Verde and Guinea. Septembrism (see
chapter 10) generalized abolition, when Premier Sá da Bandeira decided to forbid all imports and exports of slaves south of the equator
(1836). Sá da Bandeira also tried to put an end to compulsory labor,
which often competed with and substituted for real slavery. Yet, easy
as such measures seemed in theory, their practical application met
with insuperable obstacles. Slave trade meant prosperity for many
people, in fact the only source of prosperity for colonies like Guinea
and Angola. The Brazilian demand for slaves was a temptation that
few would resist. The acts of the Lisbon government, therefore,
brought about widespread resistance and discontent. For a long time,
enforcement of the anti-slavery policy appeared hopeless. Indeed, it
succeeded only with the final abolition of slavery in Brazil in the
1880's (although the slave trade sharply declined after 1850).

The Treaty of 1842 between Portugal and Great Britain completely

abolished all forms of slave trade in the Overseas possessions of both
countries. Enlightened public opinion in Portugal pressured the government to carry out abolition, by declaring all slaves free. This, however, took a long time and required several intermediate steps. Slaves
belonging to the state were first emancipated (1854), then those in possession of municipalities, charity brotherhoods (*misericórdias*), and
churches (1856). In this same year, another act declared free all the
children of a slave mother. The legislation of 1856 liberated all the
slaves landing in Portugal, the Azores, Madeira, Portuguese India, and
Macao, and abolished slavery altogether in some parts of northern
Angola (Cabinda, Ambriz), in order to stop the British claims there.
An act of 1858 foresaw total abolition with a twenty-year deadline,
but the law of February 25, 1869, reduced it, by declaring an immediate end to slavery in every part of the Portuguese Empire.

The were no more slaves in theory, but some kind of replacement
for labor demands had to be found. The act of 1869, like those from
1854 on, kept the old slaves in the condition of freed-men (*libertos*),
compelled to give services to their former lords until 1878. This deadline was reduced to 1874 in the Cape Verde Islands and to 1876 in all
the other Portuguese Overseas territories. The *libertos* disappeared,
yet the *serviçais* (servants) came into existence according to the new
code of native labor (1875), regulated three years later. Between slaves,
freedmen, and servants differences did exist but in a minor degree.
Clearly, total freedom for many Africans was still far away. Moreover,
the labor code of 1875–78 (with a new version in 1899 and 1902) was
applied to all Africans, following the principle that work civilizes and
that in order to Europeanize the Africans one must start by accustom-
ing them to work. A kind of disguised slavery thus appeared, with
highly different aspects from area to area. As a matter of fact, the great
majority of Africans in Angola, Mozambique, and Guinea continued
to live free, forced only to pay a small tribute, but particularly con-
spicuous was the export of labor to the São Tomé plantations and to
the South African mines.

The economic development of São Tomé in the second half of
the nineteenth century required more and more handwork. When the
condition of *liberto* disappeared, the planters hired free Africans from
Sierra Leone, Dahomey, Liberia, Angola, and even China. Gradually,

however, Angola's position rose, as the *serviçais* meekly replaced the former slaves and freedmen. Between 1885 and 1903, 56,189 *serviçais* entered São Tomé and Principe. At first they were free and, according to their hiring contract, they could go back home after a certain number of years. Later, the São Tomé planters made it more difficult for them to return and virtually imprisoned them within the limits of the islands. This fact worried both the authorities, who wanted to enforce the anti-slavery laws, and the Angolan settlers themselves, who complained of an increasing labor shortage. The situation of the Angola workers attracted the attention of countries like the United States, Great Britain, and Germany, where a campaign against Portugal was launched. The British planters of the West Indies and several other traders and industrialists, worried about the growing competition of São Tomé's cacao and coffee, operated behind the scenes, grossly exaggerating the violence allegedly inflicted upon the African workers. A British chocolate dealer, William Cadbury, was entrusted with investigating the matter. He went to Lisbon, then to São Tomé and Angola, and published a renowned report, attacking the existing forms of labor hiring and equating them with slavery. Cadbury was followed by several others, like J. Buret, all of them stirring public opinion for a while, leading to Parliamentary debates in London, and calling for a boycott of São Tomé's products.

The Portuguese administration tried to correct some of the abuses which it acknowledged: it promoted the hiring of Africans from other parts (namely from Mozambique) under improved and better controlled contracts; it corrected several injustices and published a new labor code (1909); it ordered an inquiry and a raise in salaries. On the Portuguese side several reports were also published—some by foreigners—contradicting Cadbury's conclusions and praising Portugal's labor policy.

The slave trade after its formal abolition continued to be carried on in Portuguese waters by other than Portuguese vessels. French, British, Brazilians, and some others were guilty of violating the trade ban and were often given chase by Portuguese and English cruising ships. An example of national interests and questions of pride prevailing over justice and international law happened in 1857. The French vessel *Charles et Georges,* indulging in slave trade from Mozambique to the French colony of Réunion, was confiscated by the Portuguese authorities and its captain sentenced to prison. Yet the French government of Napoleon III could not tolerate such on out-rage to its flag. By a sort of ultimatum delivered to Portugal, France not only required the restitution of the ship but also the liberation of its captain and the payment of an indemnity. As Britain refused to interfere in a question that could jeopardize her relations with France, Portugal had to yield to the French demands.

The lack of a developed ecclesiastical organization and the shortage of clerics also hampered the Portuguese advance in Africa. To the end of the Monarchical period there were few signs of a mis-sionary revival in the Overseas territories, which in fact simply con-tinued a situation noticeable since the eighteenth century. The deca-dence of the Church was apparent in Africa or Asia, as in Europe.

There were practically no changes in the number or boundaries of the dioceses, which went back to the seventeenth and sixteenth centuries. On the contrary, the bishop of São Tomé and Principe vir-tually ceased to exist in 1816, although the diocese was never formally abolished. The extinction of the religious orders, in 1834, was behind the permanent lack of missionaries, in spite of the fact that the picture was already a dismaying one much before. The religious and political quarrels at home (see chapter 10) had their impact on the Overseas possessions too. In the East, the Portuguese rights of the Padroado were constantly violated by the Holy See through the Propaganda Fide organization, simply because the Portuguese were no longer able to promote an effective Christianization of India or China. In 1836–38, Pope Gregory XVI even dissolved several of the traditionally Portu-guese-maintained sees in the East. The resistance of the local Christian communities, who stuck to their prelates and traditional organization and rebuffed the Propaganda Fide ministers, created a problem dif-ficult of solution, often with chaotic aspects. It was only in 1857–59 that a Concordat signed between the Holy See and the Portuguese gov-ernment somewhat eased the situation. The old dioceses were kept but their boundaries were considerably reduced. The Portuguese Patron-age was maintained in Goa, Cranganore, Cochin, Meliapore, with juris-diction over all British India, Malacca, and Macao. Yet the shortage of priests as well as the poor preparation of many of the existing ones jeopardized the practical application of the Concordat and justified the action of the Propaganda Fide against Portugal. A new Concordat, signed in 1886, further restricted the Portuguese rights in India, although granting the Archbishop of Goa the pompous but meaningless title of Patriarch of the East Indies.

Some measures to foster missionary activity in Africa had meanwhile been taken. A school for preparing priests to be sent to China opened its doors in the 1840's at Bombarral. It simply revived an older college founded in 1791 at Sernache do Bonjardim and closed in 1834. In the 1850's the seminary of Bombarral was enlarged and granted more funds, including the building of the ancient Sernache school. In 1856 the government officially created the Royal College of Missions, aiming not only at China but also at Africa. This date marked the beginning of a new missionary effort in the Portuguese Overseas provinces. Gradually, the Royal College was given larger revenues and its action could expand. Up to 1910 some 317 missionaries had been educated there and sent to Africa and Asia.

ORGANIZATION

The Constitution of 1822 defined the Portuguese nation as "the union of all the Portuguese of both hemispheres" (article 20), encompassing Portugal proper, the Atlantic Islands, Brazil, and the African and Asian possessions, which were clearly and carefully enumerated. No distinction was made between whites and blacks, or between Portuguese from Portugal and Portuguese born in the Overseas territories. The legislators of 1822 were obviously thinking of Brazil or India rather than of Africa. Also, they could argue that most people living in Angola and Mozambique under the Portuguese flag were indeed Portuguese, for they were Europeans and a small number of more or less Europeanized Africans (it must be remembered that only a narrow strip of territory was then controlled by Portugal both in East and West Africa). Yet the principle had been established and was repeated again and again in the future, despite the growing annexation of African peoples who were thoroughly strange to the Portuguese culture. Similar definitions and descriptions were included in the Constitutional Charter of 1826, the Constitution of 1838, and the two Republican constitutions of 1911 and 1933. Unique in the constitutional history of the European colonizing powers was this indissoluble bond between Portugal and her Overseas provinces, for the nation was considered one and indivisible. Such premises, whatever their theoretical aspect, always have a deep impact on a country's policies and political attitudes. As a part of the constitutional law referring to the meaning of nations, they are most difficult to alter. They can be as sacred and unchangeable as religion itself. Incidentally, the Constitution of 1822 had not been revolutionary about the place granted to the Overseas in the shaping of Portugal. Many official acts and countless writings of the "Old Regime" referred to the provinces of America, Asia, and Africa as a part of Portugal. The absence of rigid constitutional texts, however, made it easier to adjust theory to practice and to shift colonial policies according to each case and to general circumstances.

The legislation of 1820-22 went still further. If all the people living under the Portuguese flag were Portuguese citizens, and if all the Overseas territories were simply provinces similar to those in Portugal, then there was no point in keeping a department to administer the Overseas as a whole. Consequently, all the matters relating to the colonies began to be dealt with by each of the departments of Portugal, together with the Portuguese affairs: Interior, Justice, Finance, War, and Foreign Affairs (Act of 1821). The absolutist reaction of 1823 reestablished the Department of the Navy and Overseas, but the final liberal victory, in 1834, again superseded it.

This utopia, which had brought about a considerable disorganization of the public services in Africa and Asia, came to an end in 1835 (Sá da Bandeira). The Secretariate of Navy and Overseas (*Marinha e Ultramar*) was revived, two "sections" being created within it, one for the Navy, the other for the Overseas (1838). In 1843, the Overseas section was divided into four bureaus (*repartições*)—one for Portuguese Asia; another one for Angola; the third one for Mozambique; and the fourth one for Cape Verde, Guinea, and São Tomé. Budgets were to be organized by the treasury bureau of the secretariate. In 1859, this system gave way to a classification by matters instead of by provinces. Four new bureaus replaced the four geographical ones: the first for general administration; the second for external affairs and colonization; a third for central administration; and a fourth for Public Works, Trade, and Industry. The number of these bureaus was later altered: three only from 1868 to 1878, six from 1878 to the Republic, but with no other structural changes. To assist the Secretariate of the Navy and Overseas the constitutional monarchy re-established in 1851 an Overseas Council (Conselho Ultramarino) which it had disbanded in 1833 (see chapter 8). This Council encompassed a body of experts in colonial affairs and had extensive powers. In 1868, its name was changed to Junta Consultiva do Ultramar, and its powers considerably reduced.

In legislation and its practical application to the Overseas, the nineteenth-century tendency could never get away from an excessive centralization. Laws for the African and Asian colonies would result from the decisions taken in *cortes*. The executive, however, had powers to legislate whenever urgency or the simple interruption of parliamentary sessions required it. Local governors were given emergency powers too (Constitution of 1838; First Amendment to the Charter, 1851), but later acts curbed them so much that Lisbon actually had to be consulted in every respect.

The Portuguese administrative, civil, and criminal codes, as well as other European-type legislation, were applied to Africa and Asia with few adjustments to the local usages and traditions. Similarly with the administrative organization. The acts of 1832 created "prefects" (*prefeitos*) for each of the Overseas "provinces," like those of Portugal, to replace the former captains or captains-general. In 1836, however, things were changed (Vieira de Castro): "general" and "particular" governments (*governos gerais; governos particulares*) were established for the Overseas "dominions," the former encompassing (1) Cape Verde and Guinea, (2) Angola, (3) Mozambique, and (4) India (called Estado da Índia, according to tradition), and the latter (1) São Tomé and Principe Islands (with Ajudá) and (2) Macao and Timor. Governors-general and governors, appointed by Lisbon, ruled them, with no interference in judicial affairs. A council (Conselho de Governo) was to assist each governor-general. This system lasted to 1869, when a new reform (Rebelo da Silva) somewhat increased decentralization by granting the governors larger powers and stimulating local initiatives through the newly created general juntas (*juntas gerais*). This reform mentioned "provinces" again, instead of "dominions," and abolished

UPPER LEFT: *Negro chieftains surrendering to the Portuguese in the 1898 campaign, Mozambique.* BELOW: *Main Street, Beira (Mozambique), 1895.* ABOVE: *Portrait of Serpa Pinto.*

the general governments. Later changes separated Guinea from Cape Verde in 1879 (first called "province," then "autonomous district" in 1892, then "province" again after 1895), and Timor from Macao in 1863–66 (as "province") and in 1896 (as "autonomous district"). The governors-general were re-established in 1895 for Angola, Mozambique, and Portuguese India. Rebelo da Silva's decentralization policy led nowhere, because further legislation always prevented the governors from actually ruling with autonomy.

Moreover, the turnover in governors always plagued colonial administration during the constitutional monarchy, continuing in fact a very old tradition. In Angola for instance, there were thirty-seven governors from 1836 to 1910 (besides several interim juntas and councils of government), averaging less than two years each. The reasons for such instability were many: Portugal's unstable governments above all, but also the difficulties in ruling with all kinds of local quarrels and problems; the lack of preparation of many governors; conflicts with Lisbon; health and family motives; the slight appeal most colonial capitals had for a European; and so forth. The results were poor administration, lack of continuity, constant change of methods and manners.

The same concern for converting the African and Asian colonies into overseas Portugals caused the creation of "districts" (*distritos*) with several municipalities (*concelhos*) in each one, in the Portuguese manner, even in areas which had just been conquered and where the number of European settlers was minimal. Electoral representativeness existed from the very beginning of the constitutional regime: to the first Parliament, in 1821, seven representatives were elected by the African and Asian territories, one for Cape Verde and Guinea, one for São Tomé and Principe Islands, one for Angola, one for Mozambique, two for India, and one for Macao and Timor. This number of seven was roughly maintained to the end of the monarchy. Obviously, the electors were overwhelmingly white, not because of racial prejudice, but because only whites by and large fulfilled the qualifications for voting (see chapter 10). As a matter of fact, in most cases representatives were simply "appointed" by Lisbon, and often among people who had few connections with the electoral district, rather than being chosen by the white settlers. Yet some exceptions and real electoral struggle could occasionally be noted.

Colonial finance followed the same centralizing principles. Lisbon had the first and final word in allotting funds and collecting revenues. Yet the wish—which some formulated—that the colonies should pay for their own expenditures and even contribute to some of the motherland's was almost never a reality. Local expenses always proved so huge —particularly when a greater concern with colonial administration and colonial development featured the Portuguese administrations— that, despite the growth in local revenues, there was usually a deficit, which the motherland had to pay. Military expenses, on the rise throughout the whole century, increased the deficit tendency.

Although the reform of 1836 had provided for local budgets for each colony, it was only after 1852 that colonial finance was organized on a regular basis. Finance juntas (juntas de fazenda) were restored in every Overseas province (1837), for the purpose of collecting revenues and paying expenses. In 1888 a new system came into force, which substituted finance bureaus (repartições de fazenda) for the juntas, under the control of finance inspectors. The bureaus were a part of the Secretariate of the Navy, and the whole new policy emphasized centralization in Lisbon. By 1898 centralization was further enforced when the finance courts (tribunais de contas), recently created in each colony to counterbalance excessive centralization, were discontinued. A General Inspection for the Overseas Finance Services, established in 1900, completed the Lisbon-oriented finance policy.

Analysis of the colonial budgets since the late 1830's leads to interesting and highly revealing conclusions. Up to the 1870's, Portuguese India showed the largest revenues, and often a balanced budget. This was mainly a consequence of taxation of well-organized communities where trade played a major role. In India the Portuguese spent little on military affairs and had few internal or external enemies. The budget for 1874–75 first reveals the predominance of Angola in the total revenues, but in 1885–86 India still took the lead. It was only in the 1890's and 1900's that Angola and then Mozambique definitely overtook India. Angola's revenues doubled in the 1870's (263 contos in 1867–68, 281 in 1870–71, 542 in 1874–75, 591 in 1882–83), then doubled again in the 1890's (594 contos in 1885–86, 1,374 in 1896–97), and again in the first decade of the twentieth century (1,677 contos in 1903–4, 2,528 in 1909–10). Mozambique's growth was still more astonishing. Until the 1880's, Mozambique definitely remained behind Angola, although her revenues had increased more than seven times since 1839 (70 contos in 1839, 100 in 1863, 248 in 1874–75, 462 in 1885–86). Afterward, however, and up to 1910, revenues more than decupled, doubling those of Angola when the Republic was proclaimed: 3,592 contos in 1896–97, 3,327 in 1903–4, 5,291 in 1909–10. This was mainly a result of the successful establishment of the "chartered companies," with their regular yearly payments to the treasury. Altogether, the revenues of the Portuguese colonies had increased from a total of 752 contos in 1852–53 to more than 11,000 in 1909–10. In proportion to the revenues of the motherland, the financial position of the Overseas had risen from some 7 per cent to almost 16 per cent, more than double.

As to expenditures, the rule was that they increased faster than revenues. Balanced budgets were only possible for a short time, in the 1870's, when a policy of economy prevailed, but even so neither Angola nor Mozambique ever experienced any surpluses. It was the colonies like India, Macao, São Tomé, or Cape Verde that in the end permitted a total surplus for purposes of political propaganda. Then, in the early 1900's, Mozambique was able to start paying for itself and for the usually huge Angolan deficits. Among the smaller territories, the interesting fact was that while India had increasing problems in balancing her budget from the early 1880's onward, Cape Verde, São Tomé, and Macao were in a satisfactory financial situation. Guinea and Timor were constantly in debt, as well as Angola. The 1909–10 colonial budget showed a deficit of 2,000 contos. Both in revenues and expenditures, Mozambique was in first place, followed by Angola, Portuguese India, São Tomé, Macao, Cape Verde, Guinea, and Timor. Mozambique, India, São Tomé, and Cape Verde could pay for themselves.

Up to the 1850's and even afterward, most of the Portuguese colonial economy rested upon slavery. Guinea supplied Cape Verde, Angola supplied São Tomé, and all of them supplied Brazil; Mozambique exported labor to Transvaal; even Macao derived huge profits from slave shipments to America and Australia. With few exceptions, the estimates of other exports showed poor agricultural or industrial development. This explains why the gradual decline of the slave trade, to its final extinction, jeopardized the development of most

Portuguese colonies and posed the difficult question of restructuring their economies.

Fontism (see chapter 10), and to a certain extent Cabralism before it, attempted in the Overseas dominions, albeit in a much more moderate way, what was being tried at home, i.e., the development of substructures as a means of promoting trade and agriculture. This policy was carried on almost without interruption up to the Revolution of 1910 and then continued by the Republican administrations. In the late 1860's and the early 1870's, however, a concern for economy slowed down state investments in the colonies. In any event, the growth of state expenditures Overseas always depended upon the economic and financial situation in Portugal proper.

Poor communications clearly hampered the economic development of the Portuguese Overseas provinces for a long time. Until the 1860's regular communications between Portugal and her colonies hardly existed. Only with Cape Verde (island of São Vicente) was there a permanent navigation line after 1851, served by the British ships going to Brazil. In the 1850's, the Portuguese government had signed a contract with a French company for the establishment of regular steamship lines between Lisbon and Angola, but with no further consequences. A short-lived Portuguese line (Companhia União Mercantil) did function between Lisbon and Luanda between 1858 and 1864, but failed. From 1864 on the Portuguese government subsidized a British navigation society to carry on ship connections between Lisbon and the West African colonies, which succeeded. The first regular communications with Mozambique and Portuguese India began eleven years later under the same circumstances, a British line being subsidized to take its ships from Lisbon to Mozambique and to Goa, via the Suez Canal. Later on, this same company called at Mozambique ports on its regular run from British India to Durban. In the 1890's, the government subsidized English and German societies to connect Lisbon and Mozambique, via Angola and Cape Town. Macao also began to be served by French and British lines connecting Europe with India and China. As to Timor, no direct connection existed with Lisbon before 1910. Passengers and cargo had to first reach Makassar (in Celebes) before a Dutch line took them to Dili, Timor's capital.

Successful Portuguese navigation companies began only in the

1880's. The Empresa Nacional de Navegação, founded in 1880, started a regular nonsubsidized service between Lisbon and Angola, via Cape Verde and São Tomé and Principe Islands. The same company, this time aided by a government subsidy, established regular connections among the Cape Verde Islands and between them and Portuguese Guinea. Between Lisbon and Mozambique, a regular Portuguese line proved more difficult. It was only after 1903 that the Empresa Nacional extended its navigation lines to Mozambique but depended upon a government subsidy. Two years later, a contract between this same company and the government provided several coastwise lines in all the Portuguese African provinces.

The development of maritime communications went along with better equipment of harbors and other facilities, the building of light-houses, the organization of the customs and the connection of the coast with the interior by means of roads and railways. The most relevant ports were those of Mindelo in São Vicente (Cape Verde), São Tomé, Luanda, Benguela and Lobito in Angola, Lourenço Marques (which gradually superseded Mozambique, up north), Mormugão (Portuguese India), and Macao. Mindelo (also called Porto Grande) was far ahead of all others, with total shipping of more than five million tons in 1908. It was one of the largest coal depots in West Africa called by the navigation lines between Europe and South America. Lourenço Marques came next, with more than two million tons (1910). Sao Tomé reached almost two million tons by the same time. The other harbors had much less, below one million tons.

Connections by submarine cable began in the 1870's, with a cable linking Lisbon to Goa, via Bombay. Contracts between the Portuguese government and British companies gradually connected Lisbon with all of Portugal's Overseas territories (except Timor) during the 1880's. Inside each of the colonies, too, telegraph communications improved much more rapidly than other means of communication.

Railroad building, involving huge capital, many laborors, skilled leadership, and military protection, took a long time to develop and never achieved a satisfactory level. The first rail tract attempted to connect Lourenço Marques with Transvaal, giving northern South Africa easy access to the sea. Begun in 1870, it took twenty-four years to reach Pretoria, although its Portuguese part had started functioning by 1887. It rapidly became one of the most significant railroads in all of Africa. The next railway was built in Goa, relating the port of Mormugão to British India (1881–87), but it could never overcome the competition of other Indian railways. In 1887 a new track began to be built in Mozambique—with the purpose of connecting Beira with present-day Rhodesia—as well as a first one in Angola, from Luanda inland. By the mid-1890's, the Beira railroad had reached the border (some 200 miles), while the Luanda one went as far as Ambaca, 220 miles east. Up to 1910, the Mozambique railway network advanced no further, but in Angola imposing enlargements were in the making. The Ambaca road was getting near Malange (310 miles east of Luanda), a new track from Lobito to Benguela and then east aimed at connecting Angola with the border (200 miles already built between 1902 and 1910), while a third one started at Moçâmedes, heading east too (80 miles constructed between 1905 and 1910). Most of these railroads were built by British firms and with British capital.

The development of internal communications, other than railroads or telegraph, proved a much harder task. Neither Angola nor Mozambique had any road network worth mentioning at the end of the Monarchical period. Whenever possible, rivers made up for the lack of highways. In most cases roads stopped at a short distance from the main towns, and only paths (if any) served as means of communication.

From an agricultural standpoint the great wonder was for a long time São Tomé and Príncipe. This tiny colony, less than 500 square miles in size, economically decadent to the mid-1860's, rapidly improved its status among the other colonies, its public revenues more than trebling from 1863 to 1867, then doubling to 1882, doubling again to 1896 and again in 1903, and nearly doubling again at the proclamation of the Republic. São Tomé's exports had risen from an estimated 18 contos (1842) to more than 8,000 contos (1910) with a positive balance of trade. By the early twentieth century, São Tomé was regarded as a model colony and was proudly displayed to the world as a proof of the Portuguese colonial capacities. This economic "miracle" was attributable to the well-managed coffee and cacao plantations (roças), served by cheap labor and relatively good trade facilities. Coffee (introduced from Brazil in 1800) had taken the lead to the 1890's, and replaced sugar cane as the colony's main product. Afterward, cacao (introduced in 1822) almost completely replaced coffee, reaching 95 per cent of São Tomé's total exports in 1910 and converting the islands into the world's greatest cacao producer. A sort of equatorial botanical garden, the two islands also nurtured many other exotic products like Peruvian bark, vanilla, rubber, cinnamon, clove, cola, tea, cotton, ginger, tobacco, and indigo, most of them introduced throughout the nineteenth century. The plantations and the islands' trade belonged mostly to Portuguese absentee landlords (both individuals and firms), but foreign capital was also well represented.

Agriculture was not equally successful in every other Portuguese colony. In Angola, for instance, despite all the efforts carried on to the beginning of the century, rubber, by far the most profitable export, reached only about one-third to one-half the value of São Tomé's cacao. Mozambique's agriculture, on the rise since the 1890's (oil seeds, rubber, sugar), could not compete with São Tomé's either. Often, the agricultural techniques were extremely primitive, lack of capital and resistance to new techniques preventing any improvements.

The long-standing Mozambique *prazos* (see chapters 7 and 9), thoroughly decadent during most of the nineteenth century, were revived in the 1890's and became productive to the state as well as to the colony itself. Regulations enacted in 1890 and 1896 curbed the exploitation of African labor by the *prazo*-holders and promoted a better use of the land.

Also in Mozambique, the need for a rapid development after 1890 brought about the establishment of chartered companies, some of which acted like states within the state. The example of the neighboring British East Africa Company and British South Africa Company (1888–89) was decisive for the Portuguese ones. In 1888, predominantly British and French capital (£1,000,000 pounds sterling) gave birth to the Mozambique Company (Companhia de Moçambique) chartered three years later. The Mozambique Company was granted extensive powers in central Mozambique, between the rivers Zambezi and Save (62,000 square miles), including administration and police authority. It had a monopoly in commerce, mining, construction, postal services, and the rights to transfer land and collect taxes. It promoted agriculture (rice, cotton, rubber, sugar cane, coffee), trade (5,500 contos in

1899, 8,000 contos in 1907), industry (textiles), and mining activities (salt, diamonds, gold), and was instrumental in developing central Mozambique for more than fifty years. The population of its "capital-city," Beira, rose from about 700 people (1891) to more than 3,400 (1910). The company also built roads and a railroad from Beira to Manica, and considerably improved its harbors. Several smaller companies depended upon it.

The Nyasa Company (Companhia do Niassa) appeared in 1894, with a similar capitalization, British and French in equal shares. It got a royal charter giving it sovereignty over a vast area in northern Mozambique, between the Rovuma and Lúrio rivers (100,000 square miles). With headquarters at Ibo, the Nyasa Company tried to develop its concessions, particularly in mining (iron, coal) but could never compete with its rival farther south. The land was far less developed by any previous European occupation or influence. Native rebellions required army and police activity before any economic progress could be achieved. As a result, the company's total trade did not exceed 1,200 contos in 1905, and declined to 1908, incurring a deficit in its accounts.

Much less privileged was the Zambezia Company (Companhia da Zambézia), founded in 1892 and devoted to the agricultural exploitation of the Lower Zambezi Valley (Quelimane and Tete areas, 60,000 sq. miles). Less wealthy (£600,000) and less independent (the Portuguese government owned one-tenth of the shares and received about 30/100 of the revenues), but also with a much lighter burden, the Companhia da Zambézia had a decisive impact on the development of the area where it ruled, building a railroad from Quelimane to Shire, opening canals and roads, erecting sanatoriums, and fostering mining activities.

Besides these three chartered companies (a fourth one, the Companhia de Inhambane, authorized in 1891, was never constituted), several other societies rose in Mozambique in the 1890's and early 1900's for agricultural (mainly sugar) and mining activities. Some failed but some prospered, and all together contributed to the quick upsurge of the colony's economy. In fact, Mozambique's exports surpassed those of Angola by far on the eve of the Republican movement, while her public revenues displayed the same amazing growth.

Another reason for Mozambique's rapid development after 1890 was the colony's increasing connection with Transvaal and Rhodesia, most of whose international trade made use of either Lourenço Marques or Beira. The international railroads definitely enhanced the position of the two Portuguese cities. In Lourenço Marques, commercial transactions rose from 1,020 contos in 1888 to 27,000 in 1908, of which 90 per cent concerned transit merchandise. By 1910, 57 per cent of the Transvaal external trade used Lourenço Marques, against 32 per cent for Durban and 2 per cent for Cape Town. Several agreements were signed between Mozambique and Transvaal (especially in 1875), then British South Africa (1901, 1904, 1909), for trade and railroad facilities, as well as for the export of African labor. Before the Boer War, an average of 25,000 Mozambique workers were employed annually in the Transvaal mines. By 1903, this figure reached 80,000–90,000.

Nothing of the sort existed in Angola. No developed hinterland made use of its ports and railroads. The colony had to depend on itself exclusively and an upsurge was hampered by a longer tradition of protectionism and old-fashioned economic policy. Shortage of labor (due to export of workers to São Tomé) was coupled with scarcity of capital. Foreign investments came less easily. A chartered company (Companhia de Moçâmedes), founded in 1894 with a predominantly French investment of £570,000, tried to follow in Angola the example of the Mozambique societies but with poor results to 1910. Deficits were registered year after year, and the company related its future success to the completion of the international Benguela railroad.

The economies of the smaller colonies also lagged. Portuguese India could not progress much, owing to the formidable competition of its only neighbor, British India, and it submitted to a situation of almost total dependency. Cape Verde and Guinea stagnated, while the development of Timor to 1910 was too small to be noticed. Only Macao revived after 1845, when the government declared it a free port. Its trade continued to grow (opium, silk, cotton, firecrackers, rice, sugar, tea, wood, tobacco), being larger than that of Angola and rivaling that of São Tomé. Being mostly Chinese and internationally oriented, however, Macao did not mean much either for the state or the Portuguese bourgeoisie.

In the economic and financial development of the Portuguese Overseas territories, the foundation of the Overseas Bank (Banco Nacional Ultramarino) in 1864 had a certain impact. Branches were established in Luanda, Cape Verde, and São Tomé to 1868, and then in Mozambique in 1877. The privileges granted by the government to the bank were several times enlarged, including the monopoly of banknote issues.

The cultural development of all the Portuguese Overseas provinces was slow throughout the nineteenth and early twentieth centuries. Lack of funds hampered all efforts at promoting education, both at the central and the local levels. But often the shortage of money was coupled with a lack of interest in developing the colonies from a cultural standpoint. After all, the number of white settlers was minimal and the concern for the black Africans was nil. And how could it have been otherwise, if the cultural advancement of Portugal itself progressed so slowly and so timidly?

Reforms of education in 1836, 1848, and 1868 tried to do something for the colonies. The act of 1836 even established schools of medicine in each administrative district of the Overseas provinces. Not one ever came into existence. The colonies needed primary schools first before any higher education.

Although statesman Sá da Bandeira—who ruled the Overseas as Navy Secretary in 1835-36, 1837, 1856–59, 1865, and 1870—commended the establishment of primary schools for all the sons of the African chiefs (*sobas*) and normal schools for the teaching of future African instructors, primary education gained only very slowly in the several provinces. The reform of 1848 provided the fundaments for public primary studies, which in the 1850's were introduced in most colonies.

Secondary education also started in the 1850's; in Goa the first *liceu* (high-school) was opened. In the other colonies, however, no *liceus* existed until the 1890's (Macao) and the 1900's. Technical schools appeared in the 1870's in Goa, Angola, and Mozambique, but much later (1900's) in places like Cape Verde and São Tomé. Some more specialized schools had been created in Goa (School of Pilots, 1871) and Macao (School of Pilots, 1862; Nautical School, 1881). In Goa, three normal schools were opened in the 1850's.

As to the university studies, only science and medicine could flourish, and only in Portuguese India. The old Pombaline School of Navy and School of Artillery were combined into a Military Academy, which was reorganized and renamed the Mathematical and Military School in 1841. The first School of Medicine and Surgery (1801) was re-formed twenty years later and then (1842–44) converted into a School of Medicine similar to those of Lisbon and Porto. Attempts to establish Schools of Medicine in Angola, Cape Verde, and Mozambique failed.

As a consequence, scores of young whites, along with some blacks and East Indians, came to Portugal to enroll in primary, high, and upper schools of education at the expense of the government. Many were indeed the sons of influential African and Goans, as Sá da Bandeira had advocated. It has been estimated that between 1834 and 1853 more than one hundred young students from the Overseas enrolled in Portuguese schools. Forty-eight came from Goa.

A printing press developed only very slowly in each of the Portuguese territories (with the exception of India and Macao) throughout the nineteenth century. The first local newspapers appeared, but with little continuity and poor editing. In every colony, the most important paper always was the administration gazette, called "Official Bulletin" (*Boletim Oficial*), which often included general news and even literary subjects. Curiously enough, a timid yet early Black (or Mulatto) African press began in this period: in 1882 a bilingual weekly (*O futuro de Angola*), printed in Portuguese and Quimbundu, made its appearance in Luanda. Local diocesan bulletins and other publications often had a wider readership and a longer endurance than privately owned newspapers and magazines. Up to the early twentieth century Portuguese India, Macao, and Cape Verde clearly led the way in press and literary activity.

In Lisbon, and elsewhere in Portugal, scientific interest in Africa developed considerably in the mid- and late-nineteenth century. In 1851 the government entrusted the Austrian botanist Dr. Friedrich Welwitsch with the mission of studying the flora of Angola, which he did in seven years of fruitful research (1852–59). His counterpart for the fauna of Angola was the Portuguese scientist José de Anchieta, who started his missions to Africa in 1864. The foundation of the Lisbon

Geographical Society (1875) had a decisive impact on the studies of tropical geography, ethnography, anthropology, history, botany, zoology, geology, and other related sciences. The Society fostered by every means an effective knowledge of Portuguese Africa. It helped prepare expeditions. It organized museums and a rich library. It published books, pamphlets, and articles on every aspect of African (and also Asian) science and life. Particularly under the leadership of men like Luciano Cordeiro (1844–1900), the Lisbon Geographical Society reached a remarkable level in the world's scientific associations.

By the late nineteenth and early twentieth centuries, several government-sponsored services were also established to carry on research and knowledge in the Overseas territories. They were particularly active in geology, meteorology, veterinary science, and hydrography. Scientific missions were dispatched to Africa, like those devoted to research and combat of sleeping sickness, where the Portuguese (under Dr. Aires Kopke's leadership) had a world priority. In 1902, an Institute for Tropical Medicine, including a school and a hospital, was opened in Lisbon, quickly ranking among the best in Europe. A school for colonial affairs also appeared in the nation's capital by the early twentieth century.

POLITICAL EVENTS

The political history of Portuguese Africa and Asia throughout the nineteenth and early twentieth centuries was marked by intense diplomatic activity to keep and enlarge the existing territories and no less intense warfare to occupy them permanently.

Up to 1885, no general European policy had been shaped for Africa. Each country with colonial ambitions—England, France, Germany—tried to subdue as much territory as it could, either in "vacant" lands or at the expense of the others. Historical rights, true or false, were often invoked to justify an act of conquest or its counter-defense. Among all the European countries, Portugal in particular followed a historically based policy, simply because Portugal was the weakest of the colonial powers in every respect: military force, manpower, and economic resources.

North of the equator, both the French and the British threatened the Portuguese claims and actual occupation of the coast of Guinea. The island of Bolama was a particular target. The English had landed there once, in the late eighteenth century, returning again in the 1830's. The Portuguese, who had established a small garrison there as early as 1828, resisted and refused to yield. There were several acts of violence from both sides, and in 1860 Britain decided to make Bolama a part of the Sierra Leone Crown Colony. The Portuguese continued to protest, until Great Britain accepted international arbitrage. The American President Ulysses Grant, chosen as arbiter, acknowledged Portugal's rights (1870), and Britain complied.

The French had gradually settled in the Guinea area, and by the late 1820's and the 1830's founded several trade ports along the Casamansa River, which the Portuguese had long considered their territory. An agreement could only be reached in 1886, according to which Portugal gave up her rights in the Casamansa basin (including part of Ziguinchor) in exchange for the French renunciation of the Cacine area.

In the Gulf of Guinea the Portuguese let the French and English advance with little opposition. The Portuguese had only São João Baptista de Ajudá, a useless fortress, and they made no efforts to claim any surrounding territory. In their turn, the French respected Ajudá's Portuguese flag and accepted its inclusion as a tiny enclave in their colony of Dahomey.

Along the coast of Angola, British and French pretensions also threatened the Portuguese interests and led to some loss of effective suzerainty, although Portugal succeeded in keeping most of her claimed territories. The British disputed the Portuguese sovereignty over Ambriz (a good harbor in North Angola) and especially over the mouth of the Congo, including Cabinda on its northern bank. The French had similar pretensions in the Congo area. More precisely, Portuguese rights were questioned between parallels 8° and 5°12' S. Ambriz was an important center for the slave trade, as well as for other commercial undertakings. When the "Septembrist" cabinets decided to occupy Ambriz permanently, after 1839, the British government protested. British ships active in the North Angolan area, under cover of preventing slave traffic, several times attempted to gain the local

Africans to their cause and make them revolt against the Portuguese. In 1855, however, an effective and permanent garrison hoisted the blue-and-white flag and established a firm Portuguese occupation, which the British gradually accepted. On the Congo River, however, the Portuguese were not so lucky, and if they managed to keep Cabinda (where their occupation could not be questioned), north of its mouth, they lost the right to the connection between Cabinda and Angola. Cabinda thus became an enclave in French and Congolese (later Belgian) areas, as it still is.

On the east coast, England and Germany posed the main threats. For a long time England tried very hard to oust the Portuguese from the Lourenço Marques area (Delagoa Bay), realizing the tremendous importance of that harbor for the economic development of interior Africa at the same latitude. The history of European settlement in Lourenço Marques is full of episodes. In the eighteenth century, the Dutch and the Austrians alternated with the Portuguese in sending trading vessels and small garrisons. International debates on Delagoa Bay ownership began in the 1820's: the Portuguese had built a new fortress there and were unwilling to yield to the British, who had replaced both Dutch and Austrians. Again, "diplomatic" activity with the local African chieftains played its role, in an attempt to change allegiances. To make things worse, the local Africans (Zulu Watutsi, called Vátuas by the Portuguese) fiercely opposed any permanent European occupation: they attacked the few Portuguese settlers again and again, beating them badly, killing many, destroying property, and forcing them to leave. Such occurrences made the Portuguese occupation of Delagoa Bay a precarious one and strengthened the British claims to the area. It was only in the 1870's that international arbitrage solved the question: in 1875 the French President, MacMahon, formally acknowledged Portugal's full ownership of Lourenço Marques and the surrounding areas.

In the extreme north of Mozambique the border settlement did not go unquestioned. The Germans had occupied present-day Tanzania (Tanganyika) and decided to hoist their flag on both banks of the Rovuma River. In 1894 they simply landed on its southern bank and replaced with Germans the few Portuguese authorities. Despite the protests of the Lisbon government, they extended their occupation to a sort of triangular area (generally called Kionga) which only World War I would restore to Portugal.

Yet the really big problem for Portugal, and the one where her efforts failed completely, concerned the interior of tropical Africa, connecting Angola and Mozambique.

In the 1870's Great Britain drafted a general plan of colonial expansion which, if carried on undisputed, would give her a foremost position in the world's affairs and destroy the European equilibrium. Germany (under Bismarck) and, to a lesser extent, France (much weakened after the Franco-Prussian war) attempted to check that boundless expansion and to replace it by an international agreement which might establish a new equilibrium in Africa too. For that purpose, an international conference had met in Brussels in 1876.

Officially called a Geographical Conference and summoned by King Leopold II of Belgium, it led to the foundation of an African International Association. This was theoretically a scientific and philanthropic association, organized to promote the exploration and civilization of Central Africa. Practically it implied political goals as well. King Leopold posed as a sort of arbiter of the big powers in conflicts stemming from their greed and competition, with Belgium as a sort of unthreatening competitor of England, Germany, and France. Portugal was not invited, and this corresponded to a deliberate policy of ignoring her pretensions as those of a small and backward country. The Conference of 1876 coincided with Stanley's great expedition to Central Africa. Two years later he became officially engaged by the International Congo Association (*Association Internationale du Congo*), sponsored by King Leopold, which all the European powers (including Portugal) recognized as an independent power with sovereign status in 1884–85.

By that time, the Belgian and French advance in the Congo areas favored a provisional bringing together of English and Portuguese. Under the circumstances, Great Britain acknowledged Portugal's sovereignty to both banks of the Congo River (Treaty of London, 1884), rather than having them fall into more unfriendly hands. Yet Germany, France, and Belgium promptly reacted, which prevented the treaty from being ratified. For the solving of this and other African problems, Bismarck summoned an international conference in Berlin

(1884–85), inviting Portugal to take part in it. On February 26, 1885, the conference drafted a "General Act," which defined "a new colonial public law." According to that General Act, occupation would require the existence of an authority strong enough to enforce any acquired rights as well as freedom of trade and passage. Therefore, effective occupation replaced historical rights. In this way the Berlin Conference invalidated the Treaty of 1884, and forced the Portuguese to display a quick and impossible effort in order to send troops and civil officials to all the areas which they claimed as theirs.

Yet the Portuguese did not give up that easily. From 1885 to 1890 they organized several expeditions and tried to promote the effective occupation of the territories between the two coasts. It was, of course, too late, and the government had neither the funds nor people nor persistence to carry on such a big enterprise. Instead, it became lost in theoretical dreams of establishing a large empire, which, by its very shape, conflicted with the British imperial plans. Cecil Rhodes, active in South Africa at the time, had coined the famous expression "British dominion from the Cape to Cairo," and was the inevitable bitter enemy of Portuguese plans. In 1887, the Portuguese foreign minister, Henrique Barros Gomes, presented to the House of Deputies a map of "Portuguese Meridional Africa" (dated 1886) in which Angola and Mozambique were connected. As the possessions were colored pink, this map became known as the "Pink Map" (*Mapa cor de rosa*).

The "Pink Map" opposed all the British plans, specifically those of Rhodes. Besides the traditional Angola, it designated as Portuguese all the territories south of parallel 11° S. (with a few exceptions) until parallel 18.5°. From meridian 26° (east of Greenwich) east, the Portuguese-claimed lands continued southeast to the Gaza district, in present Mozambique. In current language it gave Portugal almost all of Zambia, Malawi, and Rhodesia.

Meanwhile Portugal had signed (1886) with France and Germany two treaties that regulated the borders in Guinea and South Angola. According to the first one, Portugal lost several territories in the Casamansa River basin, partly compensated by France's recognition of the northern Cabinda border. According to the second one, the southern frontier of Angola was fixed on the Cunene River and the northern

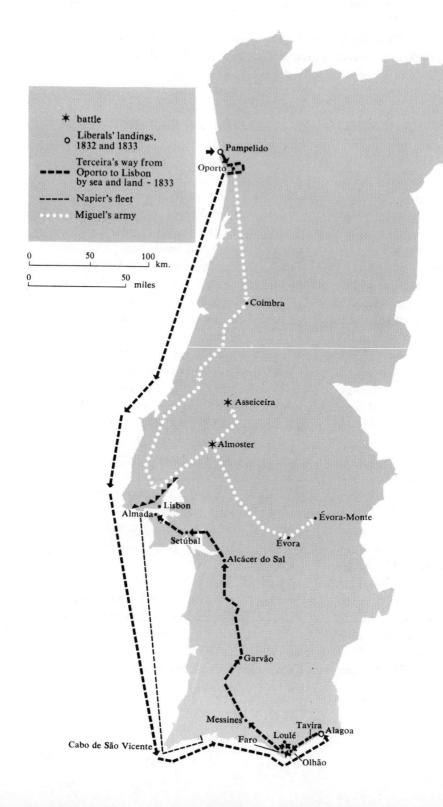

battle ✱

Liberals' landings, 1832 and 1833 ○

Terceira's way from Oporto to Lisbon by sea and land - 1833

Napier's fleet

Miguel's army

0   50   100
km.

0   50
miles

Pampelido
Oporto

Coimbra

✱ Asseiceira

✱ Almoster

Lisbon
Almada

Setúbal

Évora-Monte

Alcácer do Sal

Évora

Garvão

Messines   Tavira
Faro   Loulé   Alagoa
Cabo de São Vicente   Olhão

frontier of Mozambique followed the course of the Rovuma River. Both borders sacrificed Portugal's interests and claims—namely, the western coast to Cape Frio—to Bismarck's aleatory support of Portuguese inland pretensions.

Throughout 1888 and 1889 the Portuguese made it clear that they intended to start the occupation of their claimed territories. Several expeditions were planned, and Major Serpa Pinto was entrusted with studying the area for a future railroad connecting Lake Nyasa and the eastern coast. Some skirmishes arose between the Portuguese and the Makololo tribes, who claimed allegiance to the British flag. This and other incidents roused in England a vigorous and aggressive press campaign against Portugal. As a matter of fact the British government had always rejected the Pink Map theory and warned the Portuguese cabinet about possible unpleasant consequences of its enforcement. Then too, Barros Gomes' pro-German foreign policy overestimated Germany's willingness to help Portugal against England, and he chose to follow a highly imprudent course. Relations between the two countries deteriorated quite rapidly, and on January 11, 1890, Lord Salisbury's government sent an ultimatum to Portugal requiring the immediate withdrawal of all Portuguese forces active in the Shire area (Nyasaland) and the lands of both Makololos and Mashonas (present-day Rhodesia). The alternative was a break in diplomatic relations, with use of force most probable.

Facing a threat of war, the Portuguese complied with the British demands, and withdrew. For months afterward they tried to have Great Britain accept some kind of international conference or arbitrage to decide the matter, but in vain. As neither Germany nor France showed any wish to decisively interfere, Portugal had to yield to all British requirements. Public opinion at home made things worse, by denouncing England and displaying all forms of resentment and anger. In Great Britain, too, feelings against the Portuguese were high. In Mozambique small incidents between English and Portuguese still embittered the situation.

A first treaty, signed by the governments of both countries in August 1890 (Hintze Ribeiro as Foreign Minister), was rejected by the Portuguese Parliament and by people in general. The government fell and the new Foreign Minister, Barbosa du Bocage, managed to negotiate a six-month *modus vivendi,* which confirmed the British occupation of Portuguese-claimed lands. Only in June 1891 was the final treaty ratified. Slightly worse for the Portuguese interests than the rejected one (which still granted Portugal a strip of land connecting the two provinces), it nonetheless gave Portugal some territories where the Portuguese had never set foot. In May another treaty, this time with the "Congo Free State," acknowledged as Portuguese a new and vast area in Angola, east of the Cuango River (present-day Lunda). Paradoxically, by replacing a well-defined country of nearly 800,000 square miles with a vague, unoccupied, and only historically claimed territory, the treaties of 1891 granted Portugal an empire almost as large as Brazil had ever been under effective Portuguese occupation. And, moreover, they granted it at a time when the number of white settlers and white soldiers did not reach 20,000. In Brazil, at the eve of independence, about 900,000 were whites with more than one million half-breed Europeanized settlers.

Some minor border areas were still disputed for a while. In south Angola, for instance, Barotseland was divided between Great Britain and Portugal by Italian arbitrage, in 1903. Much later, in the 1920's, other border adjustments came into force with the Belgian and the South African governments. The same happened in Guinea, where minor frontier changes took place in the 1890's and early 1900's. But, essentially, the map of Portuguese Africa had been drawn by 1891.

In the Far East, Portugal's problems could be solved more easily. In India, Britain recognized the borders of Goa, Damão, and Diu as defined in the eighteenth century (see chapter 9), never questioning the Portuguese presence there. In Macao, the Portuguese decided to profit from China's weakness during the nineteenth century to achieve full sovereignty over that small possession. A treaty with China, however, signed in 1862, was not ratified by the Chinese. Twenty-five years later, a new treaty met with the same resistance, which happened again and again in 1908 and in the 1920's. To the present, the Chinese have always refused to accept Portuguese full ownership of Macao, although for all practical purposes Portuguese sovereignty was complete from the mid-nineteenth century to the Communist takeover of China.

In Timor, financial difficulties led the local governor to sign a

treaty with Holland in 1851 which sold the Portuguese rights to Solor
and the island of Flores, located close-by. Although discovered by the
Lisbon government, its practical clauses embodied a formal treaty
between the two countries, definitely signed in 1859 and ratified a
year later. This treaty defined the border between the Dutch and the
Portuguese sides of Timor, acknowledging as Portuguese the enclave
of Ocussi. Aside from some minor alterations introduced in 1902,
Timor's territory has remained the same up to the present.

Border definition did not stop the greediness of the big powers
concerning the Portuguese colonies. As shown before (see chapter 10),
the Anglo-German convention of 1898 foresaw an economic partition
of Angola, Mozambique, and Timor between the two countries in
case of a Portuguese foreign loan based upon the revenues of the
customs. A secret protocol to that convention mentioned the possibility
of a political partition, "in the event Portugal might give up her rights
of sovereignty over Mozambique, Angola and Timor, or by any other
way lose those territories." Germany would keep Mozambique to
the Zambezi River, the southern half of Angola, and Timor, and England the remaining parts of Angola and Mozambique.

However, the outbreak of the Boer War (1899) brought Great
Britain and Portugal close together again. England needed Portuguese
collaboration and the facilities Mozambique ports offered. By a secret
treaty signed at Windsor in October of that year, Great Britain
pledged to recognize and guarantee the territorial integrity of Portugal and her colonies, while Portugal undertook not to declare her
neutrality and to allow the British troops to pass through Mozambique
on their way to Transvaal. When the War came to an end in 1902,
Portuguese Africa and Great Britain depended on each other more
than ever. As long as Portugal accepted the all-pervasive British economic influence, Britain would guarantee the Angolan and Mozambican borders. Moreover, German imperialism was threatening the
British interests increasingly, and obviously Britain would not welcome German growth in Africa at the expense of the Portuguese. Yet
a new Anglo-German treaty about Portugal's colonies was signed in
1913, more as a provisional appeasing policy from the side of England
than as a real menace to Portugal. Nonetheless, the Portuguese possessions were far from safe on the eve of World War I, the Germans

openly uttering their imperialist designs over Angola, Mozambique, and other colonies. Portuguese diplomatic activity was of course never idle, and credit must be given to men like the Marquis of Soveral, foreign envoy to England during Carlos' and Manuel's reigns, or to his successor Manuel Teixeira Gomes after 1911. However, it was the outbreak of World War I and Portugal's intervention on the side of the Allies that definitely saved the African empire for the Portuguese.

The internal history of Angola, Mozambique, and Guinea up to the beginning of the twentieth century was one of constant warfare, marked by the successful, though difficult, Portuguese undertaking of subduing the African tribes. Financial problems at home always prevented a well-planned and well-executed policy of military subjugation. Expeditionary forces often arrived when it was too late, and their preparation and proper equipment were generally questionable. Thus, final victory depended on individual bravery and boldness, rather than on well-organized military action.

Nineteenth-century campaigns in Portuguese Guinea started in the 1840's, sometimes with eventual French help. More systematic operations began only in the 1880's, and from then on, to World War I, almost every year witnessed one or more campaigns against the fierce Papel, Balanta, Fula, Biafada, and Manjaco tribes. Some were sheer disasters, others quite successful, and the Portuguese authority gradually increased. The final conqueror of Portuguese Guinea was Major Teixeira Pinto (1876–1917), who died on the Mozambique front during World War I. Teixeira Pinto, whose score was already high as a soldier in Angola when he was sent to Guinea, directed four campaigns (1913 to 1915), where he cleverly combined field action with sea coverage and native collaboration.

In Angola a state of peace and obedience to the Portuguese flag was achieved for longer periods and with relatively less effort. After some scattered campaigns in the 1850's and 1870's, a major military campaign started in the mid-1880's under the intelligent command of Artur de Paiva (1858–1900). His main expeditions reached Caconda (1883), the Cubango River (1888), Bié (1890), the Cunene area (1892), and Humbe (1897), and were instrumental in achieving Portuguese sovereignty over most of Angola. As a major hero, Alves Roçadas (1865–1926) replaced him, campaigning in the Cuamato region (1904 to 1907). Pacification of the Angolan tribes was necessary again at the beginning of World War I, when the Germans fostered rebellion against the Portuguese. Alves Roçadas and then Pereira de Eça (1852–1917) enforced Portugal's sovereignty once more in 1914 and 1915.

Of the three, however, Mozambique proved, if not the most difficult to subdue, at least the one where military operations had a larger scope and where colonial heroes displayed their greatest deeds. In the south, the Portuguese faced a better-organized African state than anywhere else. The so-called Vátua empire controlled quite a large territory extending over the present south and central Mozambique and Rhodesia. The Vátua supreme and able leader, "emperor" Gungunhana, posed a permanent threat to the Portuguese sovereignty. The Vátuas were helped by the British and the South African settlers with weapons, money, and advice, as a possible means of weakening Portugal's authority and replacing it by the British one.

The Vátuas were not the only danger. To the north, the Islamized African peoples offered fierce resistance too, rebelling when the Portuguese tried to settle and frequently attacking the coastal villages and towns. The conquest of the Angoche sultanate, for instance, cost the Portuguese many lives, and was achieved only by the 1860's, to be lost again and reconquered in 1910. In Massangano, successive expeditions in 1867–69 met with constant disaster. There were destructive African rebellions and raids all over Mozambique up to the 1880's.

Vátua attacks on Lourenço Marques caused much fear in the 1890's. Former Minister of the Navy and Overseas, António Enes, was appointed Royal Commissioner for Mozambique, with extensive powers (1895). An able colonialist and statesman and aided by some first-class advisers, he prepared with great care a systematic campaign against the Vátuas. Under Major Caldas Xavier a first victory was attained at Marracuene. The Lisbon government sent reinforcements under the supreme command of Colonel Eduardo Galhardo (1845–1908). His troops, directed either by himself or by his seconds-in-command Freire de Andrade, Paiva Couceiro, and others, fought gallantly and achieved several much-celebrated victories (Magul; Coolela). A new military district was created at Gaza, and entrusted to Mousinho de Albuquerque (1855–1902). In a daring feat, Mousinho reached the Vátua capital, Chaimite, and arrested Gungunhana (1895), who was brought to Portugal where he died. Some months later, Mousinho de Albuquerque replaced António Enes as governor-general of

Mozambique and continued the military operations. His successors in government and command carried on Mozambique's subjugation in the late 1890's and early 1900's, to the eve of World War I.

In India some petty wars and rebellions also disturbed the Portuguese rule. There, however, rebellions assumed a much more political character, often reflecting the turmoil in Portugal. In the 1850's a new revolt opposed Hindus to Europeans, and only with difficulty could it be mastered. Early in 1870 there was a military rebellion against the newly created "India army," which, among other things, would bring about an increase in taxation. The uprising lingered on for several years and evolved into a sort of petty guerrilla warfare which lasted for awhile. Then, in 1895, a new anti-European movement exploded. The native Mahratta soldiers revolted and kept the colony in turmoil for months. Violent repression followed and only the tactful administration of Governor Joaquim José Machado (1897–1900) could reestablish order. All these rebellions had complex motivations and progressed for a variety of petty reasons. Racial tension came together with fiscal oppression, personal quarrels, and private economic questions.

In Macao, the only military trouble worth mentioning happened during Governor Ferreira do Amaral's administration (1846–49). The governor followed a violent policy which aimed at imposing full Portuguese control of the colony, both from the political and the economic standpoints. His authoritarian and repressive measures led to open rioting and finally to the killing of the governor himself who was assaulted and beheaded. Ferreira do Amaral's death meant the beginning of a general attack by the Chinese on Macao, which only the heroism of Lieutenant Mesquita—capturing with thirty-six men and one artillery field gun a fort manned by several hundred Chinese—could prevent.

In Timor there were several threats of native rebellion but the Portuguese military system was able to master them with few casualties. Governor Celestino da Silva, who ruled Timor for fourteen years (1894–1908), achieved full conquest of the Portuguese part of the island and maintained order with his skilled and progressive administration.

CHAPTER TWELVE

THE FIRST REPUBLIC

THE MAIN PROBLEMS TO BE SOLVED

About six million people were living in Portugal at the time the first Republic was established. The census of 1911 registered 5,960,056; that of 1920 almost the same, 6,032,991. In between, emigration to Brazil and to other American countries had deprived Portugal of nearly half a million inhabitants (not to mention the clandestine emigrants), the highest figure in all Portuguese history up to the 1960's. Moreover, epidemics and World War I took 80,000 lives. Once the war was over and restrictions on free immigration had been imposed by many countries of the New World, the growth rate went up again, with the census of 1930 registering 6,825,883 inhabitants.

This population, predominantly rural, was irregularly distributed from North to South. The agrarian laws of the late nineteenth century (see chapter 10) had improved settlement in regions like Alentejo, but the overwhelming majority of migrants still came from the North and the Northwest and also from Madeira and the Azores, where the density of population exceeded the means for decent survival. Altogether, three-fourths of the Portuguese population lived in the countryside; only one-fourth lived in the towns. And despite the general urban movement, more than half of that 25 per cent lived in two cities: Lisbon (435,000 in 1911, 486,000 in 1920, 594,390 in 1930) and Porto (194,000 in 1911, 203,000 in 1920, 232,000 in 1930). The rise of Lisbon in the 1920's was highly disproportionate to the general growth of

Portugal: 22 per cent against 13 per cent. As the preponderance of the capital did not diminish, the result was a tendency to reduce Portugal to Lisbon and to centralize there every lever of economic, social, political, and cultural life.

Porto's importance mainly derived from its industrial concentration, which was much greater than Lisbon's. The relative affluence and economic power of this northern city were disproportionate to its actual size. The small town of Coimbra was the only exception to the all-pervasive predominance of Lisbon and Porto. Coimbra continued to be a prestigious university city although this monopoly was lost in 1911. It had a greater cultural significance than Porto, although its demographic or economic rise appeared minimal.

The problems of emigration and of Lisbon's excessive growth could not be solved. It is true that, whereas the continuous flow of people to America created labor scarcity and angered social reformers, it also had a favorable side. Year after year emigrants sent back large sums of money, which helped make up the deficit in the balance of trade. Moreover, it acted as a relief valve, preventing widespread discontent, particularly in the rural areas. In those days, there was little hope of diverting emigration from America to Portuguese Africa, because conditions there were altogether unfavorable to a continuous settlement of people interested in rapidly improving their economic status. As to Lisbon's growth, it has continued unabated to the present, fostering an unhealthy centralization of services and economic functions.

Portugal's economic structure was based mainly on the land. Wine, cork, and fruit were the chief products and the chief exports, and the area devoted to the production of each expanded somewhat in the first quarter of the century. Grain, however, continued to be scarce. Therefore, the problem of wheat supply—particularly in Lisbon—absorbed much effort and concerned many governments in the period 1910–26. Both full protectionism and frank liberalism were tried for a while. Protectionism followed the trend which had started with the 1889–99 legislation (see chapter 10). It developed national production but made bread increasingly expensive because wheat prices had to be kept high in order to favor the landowner's interests. Imports from abroad were only permitted when no Portuguese grain was available. Yet the slight improvement in domestic grain production could not cope with the increase in population, countrywide and in Lisbon. More and more wheat had to be imported from foreign countries, and protective legislation was gradually relaxed. The outbreak of World War I disrupted the whole system of trade and revealed the impossibility of continuing the same grain policy. A more liberal import policy had to be adopted in order to provide cheap bread to the people. This, however, made the balance of trade increasingly in deficit. Domestic legislation reflected this situation, contradictory acts appearing from 1914 onward. Wheat imports rose from a yearly average of 70,000 tons, to 184,000 (1916), 200,000 (1921), 160,000 (1923), 150,000 (1925). In better years, these figures decreased, but rarely to less than 80,000 tons, i.e., consistently above the pre-1911 level.

The "bread question," as it was called at the time, was therefore a permanent one. In fact everybody wrote or talked about it. It was linked with many political and social crises, especially in 1917–23. The postwar governments tried to resolve the problem by importing grain directly from abroad and selling it to the mills at a price below its real cost. In this way bread could be provided quite cheaply for a while —the so-called "political bread."

Most of the economic problems—that of bread like so many others —were the result of poor organization of both landownership and commerce, together with a lack of industrialization in Portugal. Virtually no changes had been achieved in the division of property since the "agrarian reform" of the liberal period, except in the trend toward the parceling of units in the North, a result of the 1863–67 acts. It was these holdings, already too small, that hastened emigration. In the South, a small group of large landowners—absentees as a rule—held the best lands, caring little or nothing at all about yield ratio or increase in production through reclamation or technical improvement.

The problem of agrarian reform was of course posed with increasing urgency in a period so rich in discussion as the first Republic. A number of economists and essayists, partly dating from the monarchical era, recommended reforms in credit and taxation, along with wide-reaching irrigation projects. Among the workers, a socialist policy of property confiscation and redistribution also gained followers. After World War I, the impact of the Russian Revolution and of the social

laws enacted all over the world brought about a more precise notion
of what should be done in Portugal. The Secretary of Agriculture in
1924–25, Ezequiel de Campos, drafted a proposal for rural reorganization, including the parceling of private property, which he submitted
to the Parliament. It got nowhere, because the left-wing government
fell and its conservative successors quickly forgot Ezequiel de Campos'
revolutionary measures. Some months later, a convention of Rural
Workers' Unions met at Santarém and approved a program of complete land socialization. But the final triumph of the conservative
forces in May 1926 prevented any practical results from all this debate.

Industry continued to lag much behind agriculture or commerce.
It undoubtedly expanded during the sixteen years of the first Republic,
but no essential changes were achieved. The country had little iron,
little coal, and few other basic raw materials; these had to be imported
in increasing quantities. World War I stimulated industrial activity,
in Portugal as elsewhere in the world, particularly the production of
canned fish (sardines), the exports of which almost doubled from 1910
to 1926. Chemical industries also developed, including soap, cement,
and phosphate, the production of which, for example, increased tenfold from 1911 to 1916. In Barreiro, facing Lisbon on the southern
bank of the Tagus, industrialist Alfredo da Silva started building up a
remarkable industrial complex which in a few years became the
largest in Portugal. In Maceira (district of Leiria), another industrial
unit of vast proportions based upon cement rose in the 1920's due to
industrialist Sommer's efforts. Yet the main Portuguese industry was
still textiles, employing about a third of the workers and located
mostly in the North. Industrial concentration also developed, for example in the milling industry which supplied Lisbon with bread and
other doughs.

Most such industries aimed only at home consumption, including,
of course, the colonies. In exports only the sardine industry was significant—actually occupying second place in the export figures for
1926. Except for some cotton, cork, and timber goods, there were
practically no manufactured items in the Portuguese outgoing merchandise either in 1900 or in 1930. Iron and steel, industrial and
agricultural machinery, coal, cotton and woolen textiles, mineral oils,
railway rolling stock, automobiles, and paper ranked among the first

twenty articles of Portugal's imports in 1923–25. Yet some signs of greater industrial expansion in the near future were shown by the growing imports of raw cotton (4,736 gold contos on the average for 1903–14, 6,962 in 1926), coal (4,377 to 6,691), machinery (6,613 to 13,522), and other fundamental industry materials. Also, the number of industrial societies and their capital showed an increase. Those whose livelihood depended on industrial activity of some sort (including craft workers) reached 25 per cent by 1930.

External trade thus had to depend heavily on the products of agriculture to assure a viable economy. The kind and the relative place of the main exports hardly changed up to 1930: wine first, three times the value of any other item before World War I and more than double that of the second-ranking item in 1926; then cork (declining in favor of sardines); sardines (rising to second place after the war); cheap textiles (mainly sent to the colonies); and fruit. The main imports, ranked by value, were wheat, textile fabrics (surpassed by machinery after World War I), machinery, raw cotton, coal, codfish (on the rise after World War I), sugar, steel and iron. The commercial balance showed a permanent deficit, which was partly compensated for by the money sent home by immigrants. According to the official statistics, imports generally were twice the value of exports. In any case, the balance of trade deficit appeared huge, particularly in the years 1919–21.

England was Portugal's main client, absorbing 70 per cent of her exports. In imports, however, the situation was more nearly balanced, England's share declining from 26 per cent (1913) to 23 per cent (1924). English ships entering the Lisbon and Porto harbors also carried a heavy share of Portugal's external trade: in 1924–25, more than one-fourth of the total tonnage was British, four to one over the Portuguese.

British, French, German, and Belgian investments in Portugal also controlled a large part of the industrial, trade, banking, and transport activities, as they had been doing for a long time (see chapter 10).

The communication and transport system was not always adequate to the country's needs, accounting for some of her economic difficulties. True, the railway network had increased since the early 1900's: 2,974 km. in 1912 and 3,282 km. in 1924, one-fourth of which were state-owned. Yet, judging by the standards of those days, railroads had not kept pace with progress. Only 300 km. were double-tracked, no electric lines existed, and the rolling stock was not in first-class condition, despite the government's efforts to acquire better materials. Roads had very much declined since Fontes' days, mainly because of the development of railways and the stress on trains rather than on carriages. The economic crisis of the 1890's further prevented the carrying on of Emídio Navarro's plans. When automobiles and—later on—trucks were first introduced in Portugal, roads were in poor condition, and they became worse up to the 1920's. The state of the roads, indeed, merited the bitterest protests, and pressure was put on the governments to do something toward their repair. An important plan, submitted to the Parliament in 1922, led nowhere. After 1924 more credits began to be voted, but very little had actually been achieved by 1926. Despite this, however, the road network increased from 11,000 km. in 1910 to 13,000 km. ten years later, mainly a result of municipal activity.

Motor cars and trucks were imported in increasing volume from Europe and the United States, particularly after World War I. There were some 6,500 automobiles in 1924 and double that number in 1927. Long-distance hauling by trucks could not develop properly because of the poor road system, but interurban bus transportation increased. In northern Portugal about eighty bus lines were in operation by 1926 out of such towns as Porto, Braga, Viana, Aveiro, and Coimbra. In southern Portugal about fifty lines were in operation, mainly for short distances. Inside Lisbon and Porto, however, the only passenger transportation continued to be the streetcar. A subway was planned for Lisbon, but never materialized. The telephone and telegraph networks also expanded greatly in the 1920's: the number of places served by phone lines in 1927 was four times that of 1924.

Even worse was the situation of the seaports. Portugal's main harbors—Lisbon, Porto, Leixões—lacked up-to-date accommodation for trading and for communications with the other European countries. This prevented a greater volume of traffic with America from being handled at Portuguese ports. The local "autonomous Juntas" (Juntas Autónomas), established after 1910 for the purpose of undertaking public works of several kinds, generally failed for lack of funds, which the state was also in no condition to provide. Yet some minor improvements, particularly in the Leixões port, could still be achieved. Coastal shipping partly compensated for the deficiency in internal means of communication.

The Portuguese merchant marine showed some signs of prosperity, particularly after 1916, when the taking over of seventy-one German and Austrian ships sheltered in Portuguese harbors suddenly increased the tonnage from 73,000 to 307,000. Of those ships, however, twenty were ceded to England while thirty others were lost because of the war. With the remaining twenty, the government created the state-owned merchant marine (Transportes Marítimos do Estado), which operated for a few years. The experiment, however, was premature. Poor organization and private pressure led to an almost complete failure. The ships were finally sold to capitalist societies in 1926.

These societies, including six large ones, continuously improved their services and the tonnage of their ships. All of the Portuguese Empire, to remote Timor, could be reached through them. Two acts of 1921 favored the Portuguese over foreign maritime vessels by establishing flag discrimination, rewards for shipbuilding, reduced taxation, and other advantages. In 1925, with similar measures, another government decree protected and stimulated Portuguese navigation between the Azores and Madeira Islands and the ports of northern Europe. By 1926 Portuguese ships from Lisbon reached a number of ports in Belgium, Holland, Germany, and France. In this way, new prospects for the country's merchant marine opened up, and the situation of 1920 (when 87.8 per cent of the total imports and 89.4 per cent of the exports were carried in foreign ships) gradually improved.

Financial equilibrium was a primary problem in the country's political life. Surplus in the public accounts had been impossible to achieve since the early nineteenth century (see chapter 10), and one of the Republican party's main goals in its attack on the Monarchy was balancing the budget. After 1910 public finance gradually improved, and the coveted aim was at last a reality under Afonso Costa's severe and able management of the state's moneys. Parliament voted the "brake-law" (lei-travão), according to which no deputy or government minister might propose any law that brought about a decrease in the public revenues or an increase in the public expenditure once the budget was approved. The final accounts for the fiscal years 1912–13 and 1913–14 showed surpluses, respectively, of £117,000 and £1,257,000, a result of reducing expenditure considerably. Afonso Costa also attempted some fiscal reforms aiming at a rise in the public revenues, but in this he failed.

His immediate successors in government were not able to carry on his work. The outbreak of the war posed the whole problem again. Even before actually joining the Allies, Portugal had to send troops to Africa, which weighed heavily on the budget. Afonso Costa's return to the secretariate of finance (1915–17) did not result in new balanced budgets. War had been declared (March 1916), and total disaster for the public accounts was in the making. The years 1917–18 and 1918–19 were those of heaviest expenditure, although revenues substantially increased because of war taxation. The budgets of 1920–21 to 1922–23 saw a constant decrease in the public revenues, owing to the debasement of the currency. Receipts in 1922–23 reached only one-third of what they had been in 1919–20 and little more than a half of the prewar figures. A severe compression of expenditures brought the figures to less than they had been under Afonso Costa's strict control of finance.

From the standpoint of a balanced budget, the situation improved in 1923–24 to 1925–26. Premier António Maria da Silva had a taxation reform voted in Parliament (1922) which, first tentatively, then definitely after 1924–25, put up the state's revenues to a level comparable to that in the prewar period (£12,063,000). Debasement stopped altogether in 1924. Expenditure, too, after a year of severe contraction, in 1923–24 (£8,305,000), rose to more acceptable standards in 1924–25 and 1925–26. In this year the deficit was minor.

Regular public debt, on the other hand, hardly increased. In pounds sterling, the Republican governments were able to reduce the debt from £137,668,000 (1910) to £114,685,000 (1916). The war raised it again to £140,455,000 (1919); but the debasement of the currency, now acting as a deterrent, had lowered it to £68,344,000 (1924). In the following two years it rose again a little.

War debts, of course, followed another trend. They reached £22,-000,000 in 1925, all of it to England. The usual attempts by every allied country to make Germany pay led nowhere. It was only in the

1930's that the problem could be solved, but in an entirely different way (see chapter 13).

Regarding currency, the Republic started by making thorough reforms in an attempt to put the Portuguese unit on the same footing with other countries of Europe and avoid the disadvantages of too small a unit (the real). Thus, the escudo was introduced (1911), with the value of 1,000 old réis, subdivided into one hundred centavos. The act of 1911 established gold coins of 10, 5, 2, and 1 escudo (which were never minted); silver coins of 1 escudo; 50, 20, and 10 centavos; and bronze coins of 4, 2, 1 and ½ centavo (the latter one never minted either).

Problems with the new currency started shortly afterward. The official value of 1 gold pound = 4.5 escudos could never be maintained (parity with the 1,000 réis had already dropped before the Republic) and debasements had reached 17 per cent when World War I began. The escudo went down to 6.34 to the pound (1915), 6.88 (1916), 7.37 (1917), 7.85 (1918), 7.54 (1919). Coins were short in the market, particularly in the smaller denominations, which led to many locally issued slips of paper and stubs. The lack of available metals brought about new coins with cheaper alloys, including iron. Silver coinage ceased altogether after 1916, with paper money becoming all-pervasive for many years.

The governments paid their rising budget deficits with bank notes, the circulation of which grew immensely, particularly in the 1920's. The amount of the Bank of Portugal notes in circulation early in 1926 was about £18,500,000, equivalent to the total sterling value of the currency of Portugal in 1914. In nominal values, fiduciary currency went up from 78,071 contos in 1910 to almost ten times that value in 1921, and to 1,820,899 contos in 1925. Yet, regarding the debasement of the escudo, the bank notes in circulation had actually risen from £17,349,000 (1910) to only £53,130,000 (1920), and then dropped to £25,236,000 (1921), £15,467,000 (1923) and £16,114,000 (1925), i.e., less than the prewar level. Thus the fall in the value of the currency was notably greater than the increase in the nominal value of the notes in circulation, in spite of the fact that prices had increased. This brought about a general decline in the internal and external purchasing power of the Portuguese people.

From 1919 to 1924 the value of the escudo dropped almost twenty times, its par to the pound going down from 7.54 (1919), to 11.54 (1920), 29.23 (1921), 45.78 (1922), 91.70 (1923) and 127.40 (1924). Several government acts put in circulation bronze and nickel coins which formerly had been in silver: 1 escudo, 50, 20 and 10 centavos, besides a new 5 centavos one. The smaller denominations disappeared altogether.

In 1924, Premier Álvaro de Castro was able to stop the ruin of the escudo. All over Europe a return to more normal times and stability permitted the gradual end of currency debasements. By a number of strict control measures and by the sale of vast amounts of silver which were kept in the National Bank, the government could fix the value of the escudo, which even improved in 1925 and 1926 (127.40 to the gold pound in 1924, 113.03 in 1925, 94.74 in 1926). The legislation of 1924 also reformed coinage by increasing alloy again and reducing the real value of the coins. Attempts were also made to get rid of paper bills for the smaller denominations.

One of the reasons for the inflationary tendency should also be looked for in the continuous transfer of capital abroad. After 1910, members of aristocratic or upper bourgeois families migrated or chose foreign banks (especially English) as a safe place for their deposits. This flight increased after the war. The amount of pounds sterling accumulated by Portuguese citizens abroad was estimated at about eight million, i.e., more than six times the total monetary circulation (mid-1920's). Besides, some one or two million pounds were in Spain for the smuggling of cattle, wheat, and salt. The large quantity of gold hoarded by the people—particularly in the countryside—should also be considered. Indeed, the Republic was never able to get support from the rich. It also did little to prevent the export of capital. It is not surprising, therefore, that the gold reserves of the National Bank constantly declined. Around 1925 they were among the lowest in Europe, but the worst period had already passed.

The world economic crises of course had their impact on Portugal too; however, the local crises often affected the country more than the general ones. Thus, the crisis of 1913-14 (that ended with the beginning of the war) was felt moderately in Portugal. Nonetheless, at least two banks closed their doors, while a rise in unemployment led to social disturbances, which were behind Afonso Costa's downfall early in 1914. World War I came along to solve the problems and bring about a general expansion of trade and industry after the first half of 1915. Yet it caused other and much worse economic and social dislocations, owing to the shortage of food, the inflation, the revolutionary activity, the state control of the economy, and so on.

In 1919–20, once the war was over, there was a boom in Portugal as almost everywhere else. The wine, cork, and sardine trade expanded. Excessive expenditures on luxuries were the inevitable result of the wartime scarcity. Imports increased. Eleven new banks opened their doors, a clear sign of capital affluence. When the boom came to an end, a new international crisis, that of 1920–22, soon spread throughout the country. As in Germany and elsewhere, it persisted through 1923, 1924, and even 1925, with a deep impact on Portugal's life. Money debasement and speculation characterized the first years. The discount rate of the National Bank rose from 5.5 per cent to 6 per cent (July 1920), then 6.5, 7, 8, and finally 9 per cent (September 1923), a rate which did not change for almost three years. The interest rate on treasury bonds also rose from $4\frac{3}{4}$ per cent to 5 per cent (July 1920), then successively up to 11 per cent (March 1924). Some fifteen banks went bankrupt. This severe depression, coupled with rising social and political disturbances, meant death for the Democratic Republic in May 1926.

The religious question hovered over Portugal during this whole period. At the beginning of the century, the Catholic Church had reorganized its forces in most countries after a long period of decay and had begun to launch a wide-reaching offensive against atheism and Christian apathy in their varied forms of expression (free-thinking, scientism, tolerance, republicanism, democracy, socialism). The first Vatican Council (1869–70) reasserted the traditional principles of the Church, underlined Papal centralization, and set up the bases for the struggle against "modernity" and its evils. A wave of piety led to the rapid spread of new devotions, new saints, and new religious orders primarily aiming at charity and education. It was this revival of the Catholic Church as a fighting body, not the contrary, that brought about a counteraction of violent anticlericalism, especially in France, Italy, and Portugal.

Despite the confiscation laws of 1820–34, the Portuguese Church persisted as a powerful force. The secular clergy had hardly been affected by the legislation against the orders. It continued to own property both in the towns and in the countryside. It had a part in commercial, industrial, and financial enterprises. Moreover, many religious orders had returned in a disguised way—see chapter 10—and joined forces with the secular clergy in restoring the Church's strength and influence. In the field of culture and education, the Church possessed the seminaries which provided free secondary education throughout the country, mainly to the poor. In 1910 there were in Portugal a dozen seminaries, with a total enrollment of several thousands. For the wealthier classes, the Church owned several schools (some of them excellent), which were highly fashionable among the middle classes and the aristocracy. It also controlled a few centers of research, and several newspapers and magazines. In charity, the Church influence was everywhere present through hospices for children and aged people, hospitals, and food distribution to the poor.

The Church revival of the late 1800's and early 1900's was particularly felt by the upper classes. In Portugal, the Church controlled the majority of the nobles, as well as the court, through the person of dowager-queen Amélia, who was deeply religious and devout.

Among the newly introduced religious orders, the Jesuits were predominant in influence (though exceeded in number of houses by the Franciscans, the Dominicans, and the Dorotheas; the latter, however, were under the Jesuits' control). By 1910 the Jesuits owned, both in Portugal and Overseas, more than twenty houses (eleven in Portugal alone) with 386 members. They had organized, and strictly controlled, a lay association with religious purposes called Apostolado da Oração, which in 1909 had 1,500 centers in Portugal with more than two million members. Operated by them or under their control were a dozen schools—among them the two foremost colleges of Campolide (in Lisbon) and São Fiel (in Beira Baixa)—with a total enrollment of more than 2,500 pupils. They directed a famous scientific and literary review called *Brotéria*. They had even helped organize a political party, the Nationalist Party, where their influence was all-pervasive; this party won some seats in Parliament after 1904.

Against the Church, the Republican Party organized a formidable offensive. By any and all means—including calumnies—it tried to convince the masses, as well as the élites, of the dangers of clericalism in a modern society. Books, newspapers, pamphlets, public speeches, and other methods were used to spread atheism (or at least a nonclerical Christianism), scientism, socialism, and other doctrines, along with well-chosen historical "facts" that denounced fanaticism, Jesuitism, the Inquisition. The Republicans also stressed the alliance between Church and ruling oligarchies, thereby managing to join together anticlericalism and antimonarchical feelings. In the towns, especially in Lisbon and Porto, this propaganda found fertile soil and became an effective combat weapon.

Once proclaimed, the Republic identified itself with the fight against the Church. All religious orders were again expelled (1910); the Jesuits particularly were humiliated and sometimes treated as criminals. In a few months all friars, brothers, nuns, and sisters had left the country or had been forced to disavow their habits. Religious houses, colleges, and charity centers were all closed down, their property passing to the state. This time, however, the anticlerical laws affected the secular Church too. Closely following the French legislation of 1905, an act of April 1911 separated Church and state in Portugal, declared religion altogether free (till then some restrictions affected the non-Catholic faiths), forbade the teaching of Christianity in all schools and teaching in general to the clerics, nationalized Church property (including churches, chapels, and their belongings), and strictly controlled every cult manifestation. All over the country, special committees in charge of the religious services were promoted. The wearing of long habits, which had no tradition in Portugal, was forbidden outside the churches, as well as any processions or other public religious displays which might provoke some disturbance. The state lent the Church for cult purposes all the temples. Bishops' and priests' dwellings were kept for their provisional use. Only five of the existing seminaries were left to the Church. All state expenses for religion were abolished both at the central and the municipal levels, but the law provided permanent allowances to the priests who asked for them. Papal bulls and similar documents could not be made public without the government's approval.

The Separation Law of 1911 had been preceded by some other

acts which clearly showed the anticlerical policy of the new regime. Thus, official religious oaths, including those taken in schools, were abolished; Catholic holidays were suppressed; and civil registry (Registo Civil), i.e., compulsory recording of births, marriages, and deaths by state officers instead of by priests in the churches, was decreed for all.

Along with a law introducing divorce for everyone, these measures caused general discontent within the Church ranks. Already, on Christmas Eve, 1910, the Portuguese bishops met together and issued a collective pastoral letter which was made public late in February 1911. They protested against the suppression of the religious oath, the abolition of church holidays, the expulsion of the orders, the law of divorce, the projected extinction of the School of Theology, the prohibition against teaching religion in the schools. The government promptly forbade the priests to read the pastoral letter in the churches. Many, however, defied the authorities, particularly in the North. The bishop of Porto was found guilty of encouraging disobedience among his subordinates, and was deposed.

Throughout 1911, 1912, and 1913 the religious struggle went on. Most priests gave up their right to state allowances, less than 20 per cent actually accepting them. The government charged the bishops with pressuring the priests to refuse those pensions and also to "strike" in their religious functions. All over the country, Catholics and anticlericals opposed each other, often to the point of violence. The patriarch archbishop of Lisbon, the bishops of Guarda and the Algarve, the new governor of the diocese of Porto, and finally all the remnant bishops were punished with a two-year banishment from their bishoprics. The bishop of Beja had to leave the country and was finally deposed too. Pope Pius X tried to interfere (bull *Jandudum in Lusitania,* 1911, confirmed 1912), but the government forbade the public reading or spreading about of his words. The legation in the Vatican was closed, and diplomatic relations with the Holy See were broken (1913). In October 1913 the International Congress of Free-Thinking solemnly met in Lisbon, with wide publicity.

It is true that the anticlerical laws displeased the majority of the people, particularly in the North. However, this meant little, for the majority were idle, passive, illiterate. Most of the active population,

especially in the towns—and most particularly in Lisbon—welcomed
the antireligious policy as theirs. They had made the Republic and
they were supporting it. They justified the government's anticlericalism and made it popular among the town masses.

Yet the need for a smoother situation that would end the open war
between the Church and the Republic was felt by everyone. Premier
Bernardino Machado talked on behalf of it and acted in that direction
by reinstating the bishop of Porto and granting an amnesty to all the
priests found guilty of defying the government's orders, while the
Separation Law began to be discussed in Parliament (1914). The
Catholics, in turn, organized themselves better and realized the uselessness of a violent struggle as before. By 1912 the framework of a
Catholic party was revived in Coimbra under the name Academic Center for a Christian Democracy (Centro Académico de Democracia
Cristã), a group existing in the old days of the Monarchy but virtually
inactive afterward. Its leaders were young and able students and
scholars, among them the future statesman Oliveira Salazar. Other
Catholic circles formed here and there, while the Catholic press
acquired better management and a more clever combat attitude. The
elections of 1915 brought the first Catholics to the Chambers. Some
religious orders returned to Portugal in a very disguised way, the first
ones being the Dorotheas, in 1916.

The outbreak of World War I and Portugal's intervention after
1916 made easier a revival of the Church influence. Public opinion
forced the government to grant religious assistance to the soldiers.
Bernardino Machado, elected President in 1915, tried to restore diplomatic relations with Rome. The Church also sought new weapons
for achieving its goals: it allied with the most conservative Republican
elements, as well as with the Monarchists, exploiting discontent
aroused by less popular measures and by the economic crises. It
strengthened and developed important contacts with the representatives of high finance, trade, and industry. And it sought new methods
of stimulating faith and reconquering souls. In May 1917 the Church
or some of its local elements possibly prepared—and certainly explored
—the so-called Fátima apparitions, which soon had a great impact on
the masses and caused an upsurge of devotion. In October of the same
year, the last "apparition" took place, exactly at a time when the

anticlerical elements were launching a new wave of persecution and punishment. The Church felt strong enough to defy the government once more. As a consequence, the bishops of Porto, Lisbon, Braga, and Évora were temporarily dismissed again.

The installation of a conservative and proclerical regime (December 1917) brought peace once more to the Portuguese Church. The deposed bishops were reinstalled, the Separation Law was finally revised, and diplomatic relations with the Vatican were re-established (1918). Five Catholic representatives entered Parliament. The return to power of the radicals in 1919 did not change things. The trend pointed now to a compromise between Church and state, just as the epoch pointed to a revival of Christianity and a decline of anticlericalism. President António José de Almeida even placed the cardinal biretta on the apostolic nuncio, in the manner of the old Portuguese kings (1923), while a radical Secretary of Education (Leonardo Coimbra) dared to propose to Parliament the reintroduction of religious teaching in the schools. More orders continued to return to Portugal —including the Jesuits—albeit always in a disguised way. Catholic representatives entered Parliament in every election. Things had obviously changed.

Among the essential points that the Republican Party had inscribed in its program was the relevant role of the family. It defended freedom for women and legal protection for children. It supported some of the most advanced principles being commended in speech and writing, if not in actual legislation, all over Europe and America.

In Portugal, as in most Mediterranean countries, women were in a backward condition; their rate of illiteracy (for those over seven) was 77.4 per cent, according to the 1911 census. Plunged into ignorance, women were an easy prey for fanatic priests, witches, clairvoyants, charlatans, and demagogues—a dangerous force acting behind the scenes in their influence on husbands and children and a permanent vehicle of resistance to progress. This fact was clearly realized by social and educational activists, who, by a slow yet persistent campaign, endeavored to promote the gradual emancipation of the female sex. A small group of clever and well-educated women helped them and strove for the same goal with still more determination and knowledge. The Republican League of the Portuguese Women, founded in

1909, played a remarkable role for that purpose, despite its small membership (less than five hundred in 1910). Its main leaders (Ana de Castro Osório, Adelaide Cabette, Maria Veleda) should not be forgotten in their efforts to create a new Portugal, open to modern ideas and closed to the traditional dictatorship of the male sex. According to its statutes, the League wanted new laws about the woman, the wife, and the child; it wanted equality of rights between husband and wife, economic autonomy for the wife, equal rights before the law, and the establishment of divorce, besides a whole program of education for the female sex. Once the Republic was proclaimed, the League fought for women's suffrage. Some women even wanted military service to be compulsory for both sexes.

The new regime brought about a number of interesting and highly progressive laws. The act of November 3, 1910, allowed divorce for all couples, regardless of the form of their wedding, and considered husband and wife as equal in respect to the causes and the results of divorce. Two acts published on Christmas Day, 1910 (which the Republic had renamed "Day of the Family") made civil marriage compulsory for all, granted equal rights to both sexes in marriage, and protected the legal rights of children (in cases of legitimacy, adoption, and illegitimacy). The first woman university professor—Carolina Michaëlis de Vasconcelos—was appointed in 1911. The electoral law of 1911 neither forbade nor permitted women voters, which enabled one female doctor to demand her enrollment and be accepted as a voter. Yet the new electoral law of 1913 promptly denied the vote to women; this was granted only in 1931 and then in a very limited way.

All over the world, the development of the industrial society was accompanied by social ferment. In Portugal, too, despite the moderate aspects which capitalism showed there, the first quarter of the twentieth century was a period of turmoil. The strike movement was on the rise when the Republic triumphed over its adversaries. The Republicans, who had succeeded in getting popular support by attacking capitalist exploitation and by defending a new order based upon work and justice, were now forced to fulfill some of their promises. Indeed the Provisional Government very soon proclaimed the right to strike (December 1910), albeit after the workers had already embarked on a strike movement without precedent. In the two last months of 1910 and throughout 1911, 247 strikes shook the country. They included workers of all kinds, both blue- and white-collar: railroad employees, telephone operators, masons, streetcar employees, stevedores, cork industry workers, bakers, shoemakers, salesclerks. More than seventy of the strikes affected rural workers. The motives for striking involved salaries (in about half the cases), but also sympathy with other strikers, working hours, etc. A majority succeeded in their objectives; many were solved by compromise; and a few had to accept defeat. Lisbon and her suburbs were of course the favorite areas, but the strike wave touched all of Portugal and even the islands of Madeira and the Azores.

This sudden social agitation caught most people by surprise, particularly the bourgeois elements. If it reflected, above all, the poor condition of most workers and their struggle for a better standard of living and more reasonable working-hours, it also suggested the rising force of the unions and their coordination with the workers' international movement. As time went by, it clearly revealed the divorce between the republican governments—controlled by the bourgeoisie—and the workers' aims.

As early as 1911, much of the sympathy previously accorded the blue-collar workers by the petty bourgeoisie was fading in view of the ever-increasing wave of strikes, which bourgeois public opinion regarded as untimely and favoring the enemies of the Republic. From then on, the gulf between the bourgeoisie and the proletariat continued to broaden, a fact that plunged the workers into a widespread opposition to the regime and led them to strange alliances with Monarchists and right-wing elements. And as the number of workers was relatively small—only some 100,000 real proletarians by 1910—in comparison with the bourgeois active population of Lisbon and Porto, one can easily understand why the workers' demands had little chance of full achievement and why the threat of a social revolution could never reach the level it did in other countries.

Yet the several administrations tried hard to solve or at least to lessen the social problem. In the framework of a noninterventionist, liberal state, the governments could do little, but they did what they could.

Secretary António José de Almeida (Interior) proposed, early in

1911, a law limiting the work week to six days and regulating the hours of work per day but only the former provision was enacted. Practically nothing else was achieved, and there was extreme violence throughout 1912 and 1913. Isolated strikes did lessen (35 in 1912, 19 in 1913); but organized labor action developed and managed to launch the first general strike (January 1912), which led to the declaration of a state of siege in Lisbon, the closing down of the workers' main seat (Casa Sindical), and the arrest of hundreds of people. Workers' conventions and Anarchist organization (paradoxical as it may seem) filled the years 1911 to 1914 with assertions of growing strength, social hatred, anti-government actions, and frequent bomb-throwing. Afonso Costa's government, while trying to appease discontent by enacting a quite progressive law on labor accidents (1913), repressed labor demands and persecuted many workers. The years that followed were relatively quiet, but had some important features. The workers of all Portugal, to start with, united in the National Workers Union (União Operária Nacional, 1914), in close contact with the international organizations. The Azevedo Coutinho Democratic government finally enacted a law (January 1915), which regulated the working hours: 7 for offices and banks, 8 to 10 for factories and workshops, 10 for commercial stores with a 2-hour break for lunch. In 1916 a Secretariate for Labor Affairs (Ministério do Trabalho e Previdência Social) came into existence.

Portugal's intervention in World War I signaled another period of social turmoil, which lasted to the end of the Democratic Republic. Opposition to the war and the rising cost of living set off a new wave of strikes in 1917, with a general strike in Lisbon, open fighting, arrests, and persecutions. Afonso Costa's third cabinet tried to get some support from the workers for his government's war effort. In a speech of July 1917 for instance, he showed his sympathy with the class struggle and his leaning toward Marxist theories. He also condemned the employers' exploitation of the workers and realized their need to strike. Yet there was little that either his government or his followers could do to solve the problem. Salary raises did not keep pace with the ever-rising cost of living and the debasement of currency. In real figures, for instance, civil servants were being paid in 1917 61.6 per cent of prewar wages, a percentage which declined further to 1920–21.

The governments of 1918 to 1920, threatened by the rising social disturbance, adopted several measures on behalf of the workers and lower civil servants, which, on the one hand, seemed too timid to appease discontent and, on the other, helped jeopardize the traditional support of the middle bourgeoisie to the regime. A series of laws in 1919 fixed a maximum of 48 working-hours per week for most blue- and white-collar workers and 42 for banks and offices, established compulsory social insurance for all employers (in case of illness, accident, old age) and established an Institute of Social Insurance. At the same time housing for workers was instituted on government initiative.

Wages, however, continued to be low. Middle civil servants saw their real salaries decline to 35.8 per cent (1918), 22.6 per cent (1920) and 22 per cent (1921) of the prewar level. Lower civil servants were in a somewhat better condition: 54.6 per cent (1918), 50.5 per cent (1919), 65.2 per cent (1920), 76.5 per cent (1921). Industry and trade workers, too, saw their efforts rewarded by improvements of the situation. This was the result of both the powerful organizations they had managed to build up and the permanent striking movement. Indeed, the strong Labor General Confederation (Confederação Geral do Trabalho) had replaced the U.O.N. after 1919, its control of the workers' movement being widely spread. As in Spain the Portuguese C.G.T. was anarchist in doctrine, repudiating political communism and subordination to Moscow. In 1924, by an overwhelming majority (104 syndicates out of 115), it voted its affiliation to the anarchist Workers' International Association.

Social agitation after 1919 appeared also in the form of bomb-throwing, individual clashes and killings, often with a political flavor. Despite the official workers' position of neutrality in the political struggle, considered a "bourgeois" affair, countless white-collar and blue-collar workers took part in the several revolutions that shook the country throughout the whole republican period.

The strike movement showed very few signs of abating. Although the actual figures fluctuated (21 strikes in 1919; 39 in 1920; 10 in 1921; 22 in 1922; 21 in 1923; 25 in 1924; 10 in 1925), strikes continued to be a permanent problem. General strikes were declared in 1919, 1920, and 1921, but only the first one met with some success. It is interesting to note that wage and working-hour objectives declined to only about

52 per cent of the cases (60 per cent in 1910–11), while sympathy strikes rose from 17 per cent to 24 per cent. These figures show that some of the workers' grievances had lessened, but also that their class consciousness had increased. Partly because of this, actual triumph could only be reached in 27 per cent of the strikes, whereas 44 per cent had succeeded in 1910–11. Compromise was the result for most others.

From the employers' side, things had also changed. In the beginning of the Republic, the employers were isolated and felt no need for union. Gradually, the rise of the workers' movement and the weak support employers received from the government (so they believed) led them into several forms of active organization. An Employers' Confederation (Confederação Patronal) appeared after World War I, its first leader being promptly killed by enemies of the organization. In 1925 a group of landowners, bankers, and other capitalists organized the Union of the Economic Interests (União dos Interesses Económicos), to fight what they called the "social subversion" and defend their capitalist interests.

Summing up, one could say that the labor movement succeeded in a good many objectives. A better standard of living had been achieved, despite the economic, social, and political troubles resulting from the strikes. The British consul in Lisbon could write in 1924 with some truth that "there is practically no unemployment and the manual worker was never so well off as he is today." The purchasing power statistics also show that the lower civil servants, although far from being overpaid, were nevertheless in 1926 in a slightly better situation than they were before the war (76.5 per cent in 1921, 137.5 per cent in 1922, 119.1 per cent in 1923, 94.4 per cent in 1924, 109.5 per cent in 1925).

Once the battle for the eight-hour day was won (the act of 1919 was being fulfilled only by 1922), the unions had immediately started another fight, for the six-hour day, which to most people looked thoroughly utopian.

Social problems had now shifted to another direction. It was the middle class and the upper civil servants who showed their dissatisfaction. True, many bankers and many capitalists had profited from the war and from the consequent speculations. True, a certain number of parvenus and carpetbaggers had risen in the social scale, forming a group of "nouveaux riches." The middle tradesman, the middle and upper civil servant—including the army and navy officers—the rural and urban owners, all those who in 1910 had been the pillars of the Republic, were now full of complaints against it. They complained about the fall in their real salaries (for the civil servants, 100 in 1914, 22 in 1921, 36.5 in 1922, 49.4 in 1923, 37.7 in 1924, 43.7 in 1925), about the small margin of profit in their business, about the tax increase, about the rise of labor unions and the labor movement.

The Republican propaganda before 1910 had insisted upon the urgent need to solve the cultural problem. The monarchical governments since 1820—and even before—had undoubtedly considered the question. Reforms of education, creation of schools and other institutions of culture, were of concern to several administrations, often with excellent results (see chapter 10). The rate of illiteracy for those over seven years of age had decreased 5.3 per cent in the last eleven years of the regime (1900–11), a quite remarkable achievement.

Yet results did not seem satisfactory to a great number of people. The Portuguese, always comparing their country with the most progressive and the wealthiest nations of the world, felt their cultural backwardness in relation to France, Belgium, and Switzerland. Indeed, by 1911, Portugal's total rate of illiteracy was 75.1 per cent with an actual 69.7 per cent for those older than seven. Moreover, the monarchical administrations were undoubtedly more concerned with railroads, trade, or banking than with education. Their emphasis rested more on the material than on the spiritual development of the country.

The Republican program was exactly the opposite, and this fact should be stressed in order to correctly appraise and understand the achievements of the Democratic Republic. Studies and discussions of culture, education, school teaching and methods of teaching interested a large public and most of the country's élite. In 1876 a famous poet, João de Deus (1830-96), had published a no less famous primer (*Cartilha Maternal*), where a quite revolutionary method of teaching how to read was introduced. Based upon the division of the word into its elements and reacting against the "learn by rote" tradition, this analytical and intuitive system deserved the approval of most progressive educators—despite its many opponents—and became a sort

of banner for the Republican cultural propagandists. João de Deus'
son, João de Deus Ramos (1878–1953), continued his father's struggle
for a better education for children. He was the founder of child-
centered experimental schools in Portugal, which he called "kindergartens" (jardins-escolas), and where the modern principles based upon
the concept of the total development of the child, the individualizing
of each pupil, and the effort to develop his creative ability and emotional maturity were carried on. The number of such kindergartens,
however, did not increase very much, because of the lack of funds to
build them. As a rule, the Republican governments gave their enthusi-
astic support to the initiative, but no money. Consequently, progress
was slow: the first kindergarten opened its doors in Coimbra in 1911,
the second and the third in 1914; by 1927 only five had been established. The kindergartens provided education for young children (4 to
7), including elementary reading and writing.

The Republican reforms of primary education and the spirit behind them had an unquestionable impact on the quality of the education officially available to everyone. Their effects on mass education,
however, were poor, because of the state's permanent poverty. The
acts of 1911 established free, public education for all children—before
and after reading age—and compulsory attendance at school from
age 7 to 10. Methods and disciplines followed the most up-to-date systems. The stress on decentralization as a general administrative principle had led the government to entrust the control of elementary
education to the municipalities, a principle maintained to 1918 (when
it returned to the central government again). Elementary teaching was
classified as pre-primary (infantil) and primary, the latter still divided
into three levels. Temporary or movable schools were also established,
particularly for the teaching of adults. Salaries paid to the teachers
were increased. The total number of primary official schools jumped
from about 4,500 in 1910 to about 7,000 in 1927, while the number of
teachers increased from some 6,000 to some 8,500. Parishes with no
school were reduced by half: 702 in 1910 (i.e., 17.5 per cent of the total
number of parishes), 345 in 1926 (8.6 per cent). There was one school
for each 19.4 kilometers in 1911 and one for each 13.2 kilometers in
1927. Yet the rate of illiteracy decreased only slightly: 75.1 per cent
in 1911, 70.5 per cent in 1920, 67.8 per cent in 1930. In almost twenty

years, illiteracy had declined 7.3 per cent, certainly more than in any comparable period of the monarchical regime (3.8 per cent from 1878 to 1900, or 4.1 per cent from 1890 to 1911), but less than was expected from the new order. When the Democratic Republic came to an end, in the mid-1920's, more than half of the population was still illiterate, again posing the problem of mass education.

For the preparation of primary schoolteachers, official concern led to the creation of more normal schools, with improved methods and equipment.

Secondary teaching received comparatively less attention. The excellent reform of 1894–95 was kept and enforced with only a few changes. However, one new high school (*liceu*) was built and the number of teachers increased. Two normal schools were established in 1911. Much more important were the reforms in technical education. By an act of 1911 (António José de Almeida) the School of Industry and Commerce gave place to two, raised to university level: the School of Engineering (Instituto Superior Técnico) and the School of Commerce (Instituto Superior do Comércio), both with new plans of studies and up-to-date disciplines, methods, and equipment. The School of Agronomy and Veterinary Science was also divided in two: a School of Agronomy (Instituto Superior de Agronomia) and a School of Veterinary Science (Escola de Medicina Veterinária), both considered upper colleges of education too. The act of 1918 (Alfredo de Magalhães) reformed the lower technical schools and established a second upper school of commerce in Porto. All over the country several new schools for the teaching of agriculture, commerce, and industry opened their doors year after year. In 1923 there were 54 technical schools at the secondary level, a rate of one per 120,000 inhabitants. The number of pupils surpassed 8,000, which meant a school for each 150 students.

University education also received the attention of the Republican governments. As a basic principle, the Republic tried to put an end to Coimbra's centuries-long university monopoly. Toward this end the provisional government brought together the existing schools (see chapter 10)—which were renamed "colleges" (*faculdades*)—and created (1911, António José de Almeida) the University of Lisbon and the University of Porto. The only new schools set up by the new regime (1911) were a School of Law (Faculdade de Direito) in Lisbon—the most important step to enforce the above-mentioned principle—and a School of Arts (Faculdade de Letras) in Coimbra, replacing the School of Theology, which the prevailing anticlericalism had closed. Deep reforms of structure affected all the colleges, both in the number of disciplines and teachers and in the introduction of many up-to-date scientific devices and methods. Furthermore, the republican ideology abolished compulsory classes, the university tribunals, and decentralized upper education by making university presidents and other authorities elective and giving financial autonomy to the schools. Scholarships for needy students were also created. Under Afonso Costa a Secretariate for Education made its appearance (1913) and was kept afterward.

To promote research and postgraduate studies, the government established in 1924 a Junta Orientadora dos Estudos, where leading scientists and scholars met together. And in December of that year, the leftist government headed by José Domingues dos Santos even talked of making education totally free at every level.

Nevertheless, lack of material resources prevented the enforcement of many of these measures, at least at the rapid pace both governments and public opinion wished. If the great merit of the Republic was to provide the legislation and the general framework for a cultural revolution in Portugal, scarcity of funds prevented new schools from being opened rapidly enough and hindered the recruiting of instructors and the adequate equipment of libraries, laboratories, and other research centers.

A small part of this progressive legislation was later disavowed by some more conservative governments, or whenever political circumstances forced the state to interfere. Thus, centralization took the lead again after 1918–19, university presidents becoming government appointees once more. Political reasons, also, were instrumental in the failure of the attempt to deprive Coimbra of its School of Arts and to transfer it to Porto (1919). Compromise led to the maintenance of the Coimbra School and to the confirmation of Porto. Yet, when political events gave Coimbra a prominent role again, the School of Porto was closed down (1927).

Besides the official system of education, the Republican period witnessed a highly interesting cultural ferment, particularly in the fields of free learning and the popular spread of culture. Throughout the country, but especially in the cities, public and free classes of all kinds and at all levels burgeoned, often maintained by and through the initiative of cultural leagues and other associations. Among the most important ones, the so-called free universities (Universidades Livres, founded 1912) and the so-called popular universities (Universidades Populares founded 1913) should be mentioned. Set up in Lisbon and Porto, they provided permanent series of lectures and courses by voluntary specialists to a wide public, where the workers were often represented in large numbers. Many of those lectures were published as small booklets, distributed or sold cheaply to vast audiences. Along with them, several private publishers and associations undertook some interesting publishing programs, trying to spread culture to the masses by turning out international and Portuguese works of scientific, historical, or literary note. A literary association founded in Porto in 1912 (Renascença Portuguesa) had a major role in that field.

This same attitude of mass education as something urgent and vital for the country's survival and progress appeared in many other areas of culture, such as music (concerts for the people, opera shows in Lisbon transferred from a small and highly formal opera house to a 5,000-seat informal coliseum), art (exhibitions and museums all over Portugal), and literature. Archives and libraries were also very much reformed. Public archives were created in each capital of a district, and attempts were made to centralize in them the most valuable items still dispersed by local archives. Many important documents came to the National Archives in Lisbon. A number of libraries opened reading rooms for children. The National Library of Lisbon tried to lead the way in promoting higher culture, particularly from 1919 to 1927, when the writer (and later renowned historian) Jaime Cortesão was appointed its director. Through the initiatives of the Free Universities, open-air libraries were created in public gardens after 1922. An almost completely free press (despite some destructive raids on newspaper offices in revolutionary periods and some sporadic government confiscations), where every modern and "fashionable" subject could be debated, was behind the burgeoning of newspapers and magazines of all kinds. In 1919 there were in Portugal 337 daily and weekly papers, i.e., one per 18,500 persons. Political papers predominated, but there was no shortage of cultural magazines and even some good newspapers. They had a very wide circulation throughout the country despite the high illiteracy. In small towns and villages, the paper was often read aloud by some "intellectual," an amorphous mass of people gathering around to listen and to comment.

The political whirlwind (see chapter 10 and the present chapter), which heightened after 1910, was in a way harmful to the cultural development of the country. It engulfed some of the best authors, artists, and professors, draining their productive powers and enlisting them against each other. Everything was politicized. Literary and artistic movements always had a political side. Yet this stress on politics also had its benefits. It developed free discussion and free argument. It proved a good school for democracy. From the philosophical and the stylistic standpoints, it resulted in clear reasoning and in literary speech and writing. It was the final flourish of oratory (António José de Almeida, Alexandre Braga, Afonso Costa, Bernardino Machado, Cunha Leal). Yet it did not prevent the country from keeping up with the world's scientific, cultural, and artistic progress. Portugal's writers, doctors, lawyers, scientists, and artists were in close contact with their colleagues abroad, who respected and praised them.

In the fields of science and technology, the Portuguese made some contribution to the world's progress in those days. Tropical sciences (medicine, botany, and zoology) continued to be among their main research areas. Angola, Mozambique, and the other Portuguese colonies, along with the metropolitan area, had their flora and fauna carefully studied and inventoried by a small, competent group of scientists, which included some foreigners. In the 1920's Ricardo Jorge's work on epidemics was decisive for understanding pestilential disease and its transmission. Research on cancer was promoted with the creation of a Cancer Institute (1924), where some renowned doctors started working. Neurology, psychiatry, anatomy, and physiology also had their researchers, of world importance. Gomes Teixeira (1851–1933) published his major works on mathematics between 1904 and 1915. In astronomy, Campos Rodrigues (1836–1919) had his research rewarded by the Academy of Paris.

However, the greatest scientific achievements of Portugal during the Republican era took place in aviation. Closely studied and fol-

lowed in Portugal from its very beginnings, aviation got a decisive push
with World War I, the few Portuguese pilots ranking among the best
aviators. After the war, the Portuguese attempted some wide-reaching
air voyages: Gago Coutinho and Sacadura Cabral flew an uncharted
course from Lisbon to Madeira in March 1921, with no ships to guide
them, and then again in March–June 1922 without guidance they flew
across the South Atlantic for the first time in a daring Lisbon–Rio de
Janeiro hop, with stopovers in the Canary Islands, Cape Verde Islands,
São Pedro and São Paulo rocks, Fernando de Noronha Island, Recife,
Baía, Porto Seguro, and Vitória. Sacadura Cabral's death in 1924
prevented another scheduled air hop, this time around the world. But
in the same year aviators Brito Pais and Sarmento de Beires flew from
Lisbon to Macao (China), and in the next six years, several other air
trips connected Portugal with her far-distant colonies. Gago Coutinho
perfected a flying device (the sextant), which played a useful role in
those days.

The literary movement should be studied by an analysis of groups
and currents rather than by focusing on individual authors. The first
third of the twentieth century showed the last reflection of a great
epoch in literature (see chapter 10) and the small beginnings and
experiments of a new literary era. Thus, it did not encompass many
great writers (with one exception) but contained many genres. Essayists
and journalists prevailed over novelists, poets, or playwrights, just as
the short article, the newspaper serial, the lecture, the speech, and the
interview prevailed over the long and deep novel, the sensitive poem,
and the detailed monograph. On the other hand, the pervasive democratic concern of reaching a vast, popular audience instead of a small,
sophisticated public often diverted authors from profound and subtle
themes in pursuit of more superficial and vulgar, albeit educative or
revolutionary, matters.

Good examples of such a tendency were Guerra Junqueiro (1850–
1923) and Gomes Leal (1848–1921) in the field of poetry, two of the
most beloved and cherished authors of their time, yet rather mediocre
when considered objectively. Popular bourgeois drama and fiction
were best represented by Júlio Dantas (1876–1962) and Henrique Lopes
de Mendonça (1856–1931), both of whom wrote for an always at-
tentive and responsive audience. Historical fiction, often presented in

newspaper serials or sold in cheap fascicles, had a tremendous impact on the liberal public of the early twentieth century (Campos Júnior, 1850–1917, Rocha Martins, 1879–1952, Malheiro Dias, 1875–1941).

The most valid Portuguese literature of the time was generally characterized by a nationalist tendency, in a reaction against the cosmopolitan realism of the late 1800's. Such nationalism was expressed in the stress, for example, on historical themes and heroes; the cult for the "typical Portuguese" values, manners, and landscapes (the picturesque, the folklore, the countryside); the emphasis on tradition and religion. In form and style, symbolism set the tone. Authors like Teixeira de Pascoais (1877–1952), Afonso Lopes Vieira (1878–1947), and António Correia de Oliveira (1879–1960) were perhaps among the best representatives of that tendency in poetry. Less "nationalist" were António Feijó (1870–1917) and Eugénio de Castro (1869–1944), also poets. In prose, essayists António Patrício (1878–1930) and Raul Brandão (1867–1930) should be mentioned. Most authors started or developed their careers in a well-known magazine, where they published their works, which gathered together intellectuals with cultural affinities. An outstanding example was the Porto magazine *A Águia* (1910–30) and, in the field of history, the Lisbon *Revista de História* (1912–27), which reacted against positivism and materialism in history.

Narrow nationalism and excessive symbolism were strongly attacked by a much more cosmopolitan and French-influenced thought and style, rationalistically oriented and aiming at the development of a critical consciousness. Its best representatives were in the domain of politics and essay, with João Chagas (1863–1925) perhaps the leading exponent. After 1921 the weekly *Seara Nova* displayed a courageous effort in the same direction and rallied several of the best authors of twentieth-century Portugal: historian Jaime Cortesão (1884–1960), polemicist Raul Proença (1884–1941), philosopher and essayist António Sérgio (1883–1969), among others. Close to them in thought, although oriented more toward the aesthetic and sensualist in his novels and essays, was Manuel Teixeira Gomes (1860–1942), who was elected President of the Republic in 1923.

Modern currents got under way by 1915 but had little impact on the Portuguese society of the time. A series of periodicals (*Orpheu,* 1915; *Centauro,* 1916; *Portugal Futurista,* 1917; *Contemporanea,* 1922–

23; *Athena,* 1924–25) completely failed to effect a cultural revolution which would question the very bases of society. With their attacks on bourgeois morals and on common sense, their young founders and collaborators were considered lunatics by the great majority of the people. Mário de Sá Carneiro (1890–1916), Almada Negreiros (1893–1970), António Boto (1897–1959), and especially Fernando Pessoa (1888–1935) had no recognition at all in their generation, although they were among the most prominent. It is significant that Pessoa, the major Portuguese poet since Camões, was only "discovered" during and after World War II, most of his works being posthumously published (see chapter 13).

In the arts, the persistence of old forms and styles was felt still more than in literature. Naturalism and nationalism prevailed in painting, sculpture, and architecture, with the general approval of the public. The art exhibitions (which increased after 1910) clearly displayed the monotonous, yet ever-growing succession of neo-Romantic painters, indulging in the same themes, wherein the Portuguese farmer and the Portuguese landscape were beautifully and artistically exalted, with little concern for the city and its inhabitants. Historical or pseudo-historical facts were also very popular. Such a trend, despite the general quality of its representatives (Carlos Reis, Falcão Trigoso, António Saúde, Alves Cardoso, Alberto de Sousa, and the older masters previously mentioned), showed no innovations and did not reflect the great changes which were taking place in Portugal and abroad. The same situation prevailed in sculpture (where several "monumental" statues were constructed for the public squares and buildings of the country) and in architecture, where Neo-Gothic buildings were in great esteem, along with typical nineteenth-century public buildings and the so-called "Portuguese house" style, more or less inspired by traditional Portuguese models. The pavillions of Portugal in the several international exhibitions (Panama-Pacific, 1915: Rio de Janeiro, 1922; Seville, 1929) were good examples of traditionalism, albeit with some innovating traits—the systematic use of pictured tiles, for instance—and a fusion of elements resulting in a new aspect as a whole. Still stranger in their final display were the bourgeois dwellings in Lisbon that were yearly awarded the so-called "Valmor" prize.

"Modern" trends in the arts had only a few followers and met with little or no public support. The Salão dos Humoristas (Humorists Salon) of 1912 was the first to exhibit some innovating tendencies. The return to Portugal at the outbreak of World War I of painter Amadeu de Sousa Cardoso (1887–1918), who had studied in Paris, had some impact on the development of cubism and other "modernisms." Sousa Cardoso died quite young but left behind a remarkable and up-to-date collection of works. Painters Santa Rita (1889–1918) and Eduardo Viana (1881–1967) followed a similar trend.

Music flourished in this period compared with the nineteenth century. Composer Viana da Mota studied abroad and was later appointed director of the Lisbon Music Conservatory. He and his disciples produced some interesting concert and chamber music of high quality which placed him foremost in the history of Portuguese music.

National cinema also had an interesting phase of success and development. In the 1920's a few high-quality movies were produced, and a short-lived national school of cinema was even opened.

IDEOLOGIES AND POLITICAL STRUCTURE

Although a Republican ideology in Portugal can be traced back to 1820, it was only by the mid-century that it started to be clearly expressed and responded to. Costa Cabral's dictatorship and the general rebellion against him (see chapter 10) brought about much discontent and questioned the possibilities of a liberal monarchy. The French revolution of 1848 also had its impact on Portugal, where many of the younger generation showed their sympathy for democracy in demonstrations, pamphlets, and short-lived newspapers. From 1851 on, the economic expansion of Portugal, expressed by Fontism, meant compromise after compromise for the ruling groups. Monarchical ideologies had a smaller and smaller place in a country geared to business and practical considerations. Bourgeois prosperity did not favor widespread reactions against a moderate, tolerating, and all-embracing regime. Furthermore, King Pedro V (1853–61) and his successor Luis I (1861–89), at least in the beginning, were truly popular monarchs, arousing no hostility whatsoever. Nonetheless, a man like Henriques Nogueira (1825–58), one of the most active among the generation of 1848, was still able to write a sort of gospel of Portuguese Republicanism, emphasizing the principles of republicanism, municipalism, federalism, and association. He called for a decentralized republic (accepting historian Alexandre Herculano's idea of a renewed municipal organization), socialistic in Fourier's and Louis Blanc's terms, with a strong emphasis on voluntary association, and federalistic within a general federation of the Iberian peoples. This would bring happiness to Portugal and restore her glory and prestige.

It can be said that Portuguese Republicanism after 1858, with only one later addition, simply developed and made precise Henriques Nogueira's master ideas, which, after all, were common to other Republican ideologies throughout Europe.

The second great push to the growth of Republicanism in Portugal came with the generation of 1865–70 (see chapter 10). As they had twenty years before, a small group of young people proclaimed their faith in the Republican ideals and their hatred and contempt for the monarchical regime. But unlike their predecessors, the most active elements of the new generation (although not necessarily its best minds) did not die nor did they subscribe to the "establishment" when they grew older. Conditions in Europe had changed, and the prospect of a future Republican world seemed more hopeful. The Republic had triumphed in France (1870), was proclaimed in Spain (1873–74), and had found a fertile field in Italy. Also, Fontism had lost some of its early, all-pervasive, vigor, and economic crises were, from time to time, jolting the overconfident bourgeoisie.

Men like Teófilo Braga (1843–1924), Elias Garcia (1830–91), Basílio Teles (1856–1923), and Sampaio Bruno (1857–1915) were paramount in spreading the Republican ideals for more than thirty years, defining many of the vaguer points and enriching the contents with philosophical, political, and social elements. Scientism and positivism were preached with passion and accepted by most Republicans as an antidote to religion. Antireligiousness was indeed a newer addition to Republicanism, a reaction against the so-called Ultramontanism or excessive Papal centralization (the First Vatican Council, in 1869–70, had indeed defined the new dogma of Papal infallibility). As a counterpart, however, Portuguese Republicanism gradually lost the earlier socialist element. A social Republic began to be considered a utopia by many Republicans, who realized that actual conditions and possible achievements were very far from social equalitarian aspirations. In a country like Portugal, where industrial workers represented only an insignificant minority, to tie the dream of a Republic to their peculiar class goals would postpone an actual change of regime for several generations. It seemed more realistic, in order to appeal to the bourgeoisie, to give up "socialist" principles and carry on the political "democratic" ones. Yet social ideals were never forgotten, at least from a theoretical standpoint. To a certain extent, one could say that Portuguese Republicanism became "socialist" in principle but bourgeois in practice.

This solution proved to be the right one. The mid-1870's witnessed the creation of the Portuguese Socialist Party, divorced from the Republican orthodoxy, and with it the gradual expansion of the Republican Party. From the 1880's on, the Socialists always made a poor showing in contrast to the vigorous forward sweep of the Republicans.

Federalism was never completely forgotten, but the imperialist dreams of many Spaniards did not help its enforcement. Also, the deep trauma caused by the British ultimatum of 1890 renewed the spirit of nationalism, which carried along all the leading members of the generation of 1890.

From a strictly political standpoint, the Republicans followed the model of Swiss institutions. They defended universal suffrage—which they later abandoned—predominance of the legislative power over the executive, and minimal presidential power. They subscribed to the abolition of the compulsory military draft and of the diplomatic corps (only consuls were to continue). They were against several forms of taxation and fought for the development of cooperatives.

The rapid growth of Republicanism also had its disadvantages and weak points. To become an ideology of the masses, as it certainly did become (to the extent one could speak of "masses" in nineteenth-century Portugal), Republicanism lost in constructivism and consistency while gaining in destructivism and heterogeneity. To be a Republican, by 1890, 1900, or 1910, meant to be against the Monarchy, against the Church and the Jesuits, against political corruption and the monarchical parties, and against the oligarchical groups. But for what? The answers were vague and varied. Decentralization certainly remained a precise goal. As to the rest, and despite many exceptions, the tendency was rather to endow the word "Republic" with a mystical charisma, and to believe that its proclamation alone would liberate the country from all injustice and all evil. It is important to underline this fact in order to understand the disillusionment and contradiction of the Republicans when they finally triumphed, in 1910. Indeed, Republicanism ended as a sort of utopia too, in the sense that it implied a perfect regime "of the people, for the people," based upon complete equality, freedom, and "democratic justice." As a matter of fact, the Republican ideals in their last phase were little different from those of 1820 (i.e., those of the French Revolution), which the constitutional monarchy had tried to interpret and apply in a pragmatic way. The Republic was thereby deprived of a great many practical achievements, which had cemented and institutionalized the liberal monarchy, and almost reduced it to the difficult or impossible task of perfecting formulas already experimented with.

The Ultimatum of 1890 had humiliated the Portuguese and awakened interest in their colonies. The Republicans included in their program a full development of the Overseas provinces, which they carried on with vigor after 1910. Thus, colonialism, along with an exacerbated nationalism, also characterized the Republican ideals, evoking all kinds of romantic dreams for the future. Portugal was compared with Belgium or Holland in the potential for building up an empire. The national anthem adopted in 1910 was a symbol of such hopes and beliefs. "Oh sea heroes, oh noble people . . . raise again the splendor of Portugal; . . . may Europe claim to all the world that Portugal is not dead! . . . Hail the sun which dawns in the bright light of your sky; may it be the echo of an affront, the signal for resurge."

It would be wrong to state that Republicanism stopped with the proclamation of the Republic. If there were few or no changes in basic ideology, an actual policy of government was established and evolved, as reality opened the eyes of the Republicans and showed them the need for more precise goals. Many of the Swiss-based premises simply dissolved. Changes were also related to the history of party organization throughout the sixteen years of the Democratic Republic (1910 to 1926).

The basic structure of the Republican party system after 1910 encompassed a large and well-organized Center-Left party—the Democratic Party, officially sticking to the traditional designation of Portuguese Republican Party (P.R.P.)—and several marginal groups which grew up, declined, and faded away according to circumstances and to the personalities who led them. The P.R.P. held its strength and organization from the unified, thirty-five-year-old Republican Party, with a tradition of collective leadership, which made it highly malleable and capable of overcoming personal rivalries and quarrels. Although certain figures from time to time enjoyed enough prestige, political ability, and strength to impose a definite direction to the party—such as Elias Garcia and Bernardino Machado before 1910, Afonso Costa from 1911 to 1917, and António Maria da Silva in the 1920's—the P.R.P. never had a "boss." It was organized in parish, municipal, and district committees and ruled by a "Directory" elected every three (later two) years by the Party Convention, which also met for general policy supervision and discussion.

All the other parties were exactly the opposite. In 1911, the will to build up a strong conservative group that might check the pervasive influence of the P.R.P. broke before the stubbornness of two would-be bosses—António José de Almeida and Brito Camacho—who could not compromise with each other. Two conservative parties thus arose, the Evolutionist and the Unionist, with vague and little differentiated ideologies. In 1919, as the two "bosses" retired, a conservative party did come into existence, the Liberal Party, but too late to affect the positions acquired by the P.R.P. Moreover, the Liberal Party never overcame the same "boss" principle, but always lacked an able and undisputed boss. The result was poor organization, party indiscipline, and anarchical leadership. By 1923 the Liberal Party disbanded itself and tried to reorganize its forces under a new name and with the entrance of a relatively numerous group of dissidents from the P.R.P. This reshuffling led to the birth of the Nationalist Party, which proved no better and provoked two internal secessions in three years.

Dissident groups from either the P.R.P. or the other parties were still weaker and less organized. From the Evolutionists there sprang up in 1916 a small number who formed, a year later, the Center Party. Together with the so-called Decembrists—the revolutionaries who attained power in December 1917—they gave birth to the National Re-

UPPER LEFT: *Afonso Costa.* BELOW: *The first Normal School, built in Lisbon, 1916.* ABOVE: *A group of Republican revolutionaries, October 5, 1910.*

publican Party, a sort of loose popular front blindly following the President-Dictator Sidónio Pais. When he was shot (December 1918), the National Republican Party split up into several groups. Some joined the Liberals, some others decided to go on alone under the name of Republican Presidentialist Party. In 1925 they too joined the Nationalists. From the Nationalists seceded, early in 1926, the Liberal Union, headed by Cunha Leal.

In 1920 the Partido Reconstituinte, led by Álvaro de Castro, seceded from the P.R.P. The Reconstituintes, together with the former Liberals, gave birth to the Nationalists, three years later. But some months after this new party had come into existence, Álvaro de Castro and his people seceded again and started the Republican Action. Another dissension within the P.R.P. brought the Democratic Left Party into existence in 1925.

Finally, to finish the story of the splits in the once united Republican Party, one has to mention the Reformist Party (active 1911–18) and the Popular Party, which broke with the Evolutionists when the latter decided to fuse with the Unionists, in 1919. The Popular Party got together with the revolutionaries of October 1921 to form the Radical Party.

Summing up, when the Democratic Republic came to an end, there were six party branches, all deriving from the Republican Party: from the Left to the Right, these were the Radical Party, the Democratic Left Party, the P.R.P., the Republican Action, the Nationalist Party, and the Liberal Union.

This division did not exhaust all the Republicans. New groups had risen in opposition to and in no connection with the existing parties, although subscribing to the Republican form of government. These were the Portuguese Maximalist Federation (1919), later called Communist Party (1921), and the Seara Nova group (1921). There was still the old Socialist Party, always alone and always insignificant. The Anarchists also rose as the most important group among the workers.

The Seara Nova group was undoubtedly the most significant of all Republican and non-Republican groupings—with the exception of Integralismo Lusitano and the Socialist-Communist-Anarchist factions—in presenting a coherent ideology aiming at a thorough reform of the Portuguese mentality and politics. It was born as a reaction against the parties—as they were—and always claimed not to be a party but only a "group" willing to "help the parties to perfect themselves and to rule well." As such, Seara Nova posed as a defender of national interests against the exclusivisms of oligarchies, groupings, classes, and parties. Its goals and programs combined a rather vague assertion of the usual Republican slogans with some other more precise ideas: democratic socialism, non-Jacobin radicalism, internationalism, and pacifism. It strove for a national public opinion based upon truth and reason rather than upon pseudo-facts and emotion.

On the Right, political groupings had less of a "boss" orientation and a more ideological definition. In Coimbra, some active scholars under the leadership of Oliveira Salazar and Father Gonçalves Cerejeira revived and restructured the Centro Académico de Democracia Cristã (Academic Center for Christian Democracy, C.A.D.C.) by 1912. This was a student and teacher organization less concerned with the monarchy-republic dualism (although most of its membership leaned toward the monarchy) than with a Catholic-Social society based upon Leo XIII's encyclicals. Basically, the same people founded, in 1917, the Portuguese Catholic Center (Centro Católico Português) with similar goals but a wider-reaching organization. Both groups fought against the Republic as an atheist-oriented, anticlerical and individualistic regime.

Integralismo Lusitano, on the rise since 1914, had a more original and more radical program of future government and social organization, which opposed practically all the Republican ideologies (see chapter 13). A monarchical party, it accepted ex-King Manuel's rights up to 1919, but later (1920) subscribed to the anticonstitutional line.

After the suicide of the old monarchical parties, late in 1910, the orthodox monarchists started reorganizing by 1914 under Bernardino Machado's more tolerant government. Gathering together, they formed the so-called Causa Monárquica (Monarchical Cause), which, with few changes, subscribed to the regime dethroned in 1910. Causa Monárquica had ex-King Manuel's full support and was directed by a "lieutenant" appointed by him. As an "official" royalist party, it enjoyed great prestige and largely oriented or influenced most monarchical initiatives after 1914. Dissension, however, soon plagued its ranks, leading to an open party rebellion in 1923. A group of extreme Rightists, who subscribed to a new form of Monarchy close to the Integralist program, seceded and constituted its own group, the Acção Realista Portuguesa (Portuguese Royalist Action).

The fourth group of monarchists was the Legitimist party. It had virtually no ideology of its own except subscribing to Austrian-born Prince Miguel (whom they called Miguel II), a son of ex-King Miguel (see chapter 10), and rejecting Manuel's line. The Legitimists were very few in Portugal, until the Integralists joined them in 1920. Yet they started playing a role in active politics as early as 1912, siding with the Manuelists in the short-lived second "invasion" of Republican Portugal. They also succeeded in convincing Manuel to meet Miguel at Dover (1912) in an effort to reconcile the two branches. Later on (1922), Manuel declared he would, in the absence of a direct heir, accept the successor appointed in future *cortes*. "Miguel II" later "resigned" on behalf of his younger son, Duarte Nuno.

An interesting attempt to build up a consistent class party took place in 1925, when several large landowners, industrialists, financiers, and other businessmen founded the Union of the Economic Interests (União dos Interesses Económicos), as a defense against radical and socialist threats.

The secret societies were very active, particularly in the period immediately before and after 1910. One must be careful, however, in appraising their actual share of responsibilities and real political influence, because the usual tendency is to ascribe everything to the Freemasonry and the Carbonária and to impute all crimes to them. The truth is that we know very little about either society and that bibliography on the subject is nonexistent. The Carbonária, which may have counted some 40,000 members, declined very quickly after 1910, and practically disappeared, giving way to some sort of clubs or groupings which acted as private police bodies at the service of several parties (particularly the Democratic party) and the institutions themselves. Thus were born the Formiga Branca ("White Ant"), the Defensores da República ("Defenders of the Republic"), the Lacraus ("Scorpions"), the Grupo dos Treze ("Group of the Thirteen"), the Legião Vermelha ("Red Legion"), and others, where a clear line between political and criminal goals was often difficult to draw. The religious half-secret societies should also not be forgotten. The Freemasonry's role seems to have declined too, although believed by the Rightist public opinion generally to stand behind every revolution, assassination, public assault, or even rumor. In 1912 there were probably no more than 2,887 Portuguese Masons, with 148 lodges. Yet it survived the Republican period under the able leadership of Magalhães Lima (to 1928), posing as a sort of wordly club to which every Republican would be proud to be admitted.

The Republican Constitution of 1911 largely followed the Brazilian Constitution of 1891, as well as the Swiss, French, and monarchical-Portuguese constitutional laws. Based upon democratic-liberal premises, it emphasized the rights and warrants of the individual. In this, formulas adopted in the nineteenth century (such as freedom, individual security, and property) were combined with proper Republican principles, such as social equality (defined as the rejection of all privileges depending upon birth, nobility titles, and even honorary orders) and laicism (expressed by equality and freedom for all religions, secularization of public cemeteries, religious neutrality in teaching in public schools, prohibition to all religious orders to establish themselves in Portugal, and compulsory and exclusive civil registry). Paragraph 37 of article 3 granted the right of resistance to any orders which might violate the individual guarantees.

The Constitution of 1911 went back to the three-power doctrine, stressing the legislative power, which in fact became the relevant one for most purposes. Parliament (officially named Congress) encompassed a Chamber of Deputies, composed of representatives aged 25 or over elected every three years, and a Senate, composed of representatives aged 35 or over of the districts and the Overseas provinces, elected every six years (half of the Senate would be elected every three years). Both Chambers were directly elected by the people. The President of the Republic was elected by the Congress every four years and could not be reelected for the following term. He appointed the Prime Minister and the cabinet ministers, who were to attend the Congress meetings and whose maintenance in power became practically (although not constitutionally) dependent upon Congressional majorities.

The Constitution of 1911 was twice revised, in 1916 and in 1919–21. A product of war circumstances, the First Amendment simply re-

stored decorations and authorized the death penalty only for cases of
treason or defeatism on the battlefield. The Second Amendment gave
the President the right to dissolve Congress, created a Parliamentary
Council to advise the President, and provided the bases for colonial
decentralization. In March 1918 and in 1928 (see chapter 13), dictatorial laws altered some articles of the Constitution, namely the manner
of electing the President, which was to be by popular ballot. However,
election by the Congress was again restored in December 1918.

The Republican emphasis on democracy and popular representation enhanced the importance of the electoral body and underlined
the meaning of elections. Yet the concern in preparing a conscious
body of citizens by means of education and in avoiding traditional
bossism prevented a substantial enlargement of the number of electors
and rejected universal suffrage. The electoral law of 1911 enforced
the voting restrictions of the monarchical era by granting the right
to vote only to those aged 21 and over who could read and write or
were heads of family. The taxation basis disappeared altogether. From
the resulting 850,000 electors, only some 60 per cent actually went to
the polls to elect the all-Republican nominees. Two hundred and
thirty-four representatives composed the first provisional Parliament.
Thus, excluding the colonies, representatives roughly corresponded to
one deputy for 27,000 people, a number far above that of the monarchical era (one/40,000). However, when the Constitution was adopted,
representatives dropped to 1/36,000, because the 71 Senators—i.e., three
for each of the 21 administrative districts of Portugal, Azores, and
Madeira, and one for each of the 8 colonies—were chosen among the
234 representatives. In the following elections, representativeness was
kept at 1/36,000 (163 representatives since 1915) and went down to
1/39,000 in 1918 (155 representatives). The electoral codes of 1913
and 1915 restricted voting to literate males only. Electors dropped
to 471,000. The electoral law of 1918 established suffrage for all
males, irrespective of literacy. As a result, the electoral body jumped
to some 900,000. However, the law of 1919 brought back the former
state. In 1925 there were 574,260 electors registered.

The electoral history of the Democratic Republic was far from
peaceful. In sixteen years there were seven general Parliament elections—in 1911, 1915, 1918, 1919, 1921, 1922, and 1925 (besides sup-

plementary ones)—and eight presidential elections—in 1911, 1915 (twice), 1918 (twice), 1919, 1923, and 1925—not to mention elections for the municipalities. Part of them were featured by violent acts here and there, as well as by questionable results in some districts. Yet there has been too much exaggeration in speech and writing about the elections of the Republican period. As a rule, they were more free than any of those held before 1910, and control by opposition groups to the government was much more effective than ever before. Also, complaints against alleged irregularities were duly accepted by the electoral tribunals and careful inquiries were frequently carried on. It seems beyond doubt that some progress toward a legitimate popular representation had been achieved and continued to improve. Therefore, studies of electoral geography in terms of party representation are much more meaningful than for the monarchical period. Again, towns had a greater significance than rural areas in legitimate and conscious balloting.

The Republican governments, however, were never able to mobilize a vast body of electors, as they became less and less interested in the too frequent visits to the polls and were gradually disillusioned with the Republican achievements. In 1911, at the peak of enthusiasm, only 60 per cent of the electors voted. It may be assumed that most of the remaining 40 per cent were monarchists, and that the elections were thus genuinely free. The percentage of abstentions always went up, despite the several campaigns carried on by the parties to convince people to vote: more than 50 per cent in Lisbon, both in 1913 and 1915; 64 per cent also in Lisbon in 1918; and similar or still higher figures afterward. The presidential elections of 1918 had 40 per cent abstentions despite all of Sidónio Pais's charisma. These facts made popular support of the Democratic Republic increasingly questionable and helped explain many of the events after 1926. Nonetheless, abstentions should not be interpreted only as a rejection of the Republican regime, especially when Monarchist and Catholic candidacies were available. They often stood for apathy, depolitization, negligence, and other customary attitudes in democratic countries.

The electoral laws of the Republican period always provided for incomplete ballots giving a proportional representation to minorities. How large this representation should be was a matter of much dispute.

Before 1910, the legislation in force granted the minorities more than 22 per cent of the seats in the Chamber of Deputies (35 out of 155). Such a proportion was roughly maintained by the 1911 and 1913 electoral laws. Increasing complaints from the opposition parties (particularly after the nearly complete Democratic victory in 1913) raised the minority allotment to almost 27 per cent after 1915 (44 in 163). Also debated was the electoral division of the country into districts (generally coinciding with the counties) and the allotment of Parliamentary seats to some key districts such as Lisbon and Porto. The study of its changes, which has not been done, may bring some highly revealing conclusions on the predominance of the capital and the reactions against it.

A general characteristic of the Portuguese political life after 1910 was doubtless the parliamentary, presidential, and governmental instability. In sixteen years there were seven general parliamentary elections, eight presidential elections, and forty-five governments. This situation had certainly begun much before, during the monarchical period, and the Republic was simply the climax. Actually, parliamentary stability improved a little, for in seventy-six years of constitutional monarchy there had been forty-three elections and as many Chambers with a different party composition, i.e., an average of one year and eight months per legislature. With the Republic, however, governmental instability grew worse and presidential instability was introduced. With cabinets having an average duration of four months, the Portuguese Republic was ahead of all Europe in instability, exceeding France (both the Third and Fourth Republics) and Spain (Second Republic).

The reasons for this were manifold. Undoubtedly, the excessive weight of Parliament in the political life of the country accounted for much instability. In 1923, Parliament met eleven months throughout the year. In eleven other years, it convened from seven to ten months a year. In all, the average number of months in which Parliament met each year was seven. This system, if it had some advantages in preventing large-scale corruption and forcing a constant dialogue between rulers and popular representatives, also had tremendous disadvantages. Parliament meddled with every aspect of governmental life, constantly demanding explanations to the cabinet members, filibustering on the side of the minorities, attacking just for the sake of personal and party effects, insulting and posing more as an assembly for chicanery than for the care of national interests. Governments entirely depended upon Parliamentary majorities: they often fell because of petty questions, personal dislikes, or whimsical actions. About twenty cabinets had to resign because of parliamentary distrust.

Loose party discipline also accounted for political instability. Even when the Democratic party had majorities in both Houses, stability did not necessarily result. The inability to build up a strong opposition party which might rotate in power with the Democrats and win substantial gains in the electoral race brought about permanent frustration, hatred, and impatience among the opposition. Unable to gain the electorate and displace the all-pervasive Democratic machine, the opposition parties sought a refuge in illusory arguments such as defective electoral laws, fake elections, political corruption, and the like. The growing feeling (whatever its actual veracity) that Portugal was dictatorially and corruptly governed by the Democratic party and that freedom was at stake as long as the Democrats kept power, led to the conviction that only violent methods could displace them and improve the situation. The Democrats, of course, retaliated with more violence. A general climate of mutual suspicion poisoned the relationships between government and opposition throughout the sixteen years of the First Republic. The results were revolution after revolution, another motive for political instability: eight cabinets and four presidents fell because of uprisings or murders. Practically each year saw a successful, unsuccessful, or abortive plot to overthrow the existing order. Some years there was even more than one.

Obviously, violence could not have developed if a strong authority had prevailed. Indeed, government weakness was another feature of the Republic. Neither the Armed Forces nor the National Guard nor the Police Corps were disciplined enough to obey the government all the way. On the other hand, they had no internal cohesion of their own to force the government to accept their orders. The Republic, unable to reach an equilibrium, seesawed between the civilians (generally in command of administration and government) and the military (reflected not only in actual force but also in ideals and ways of life).

Finally, one should not forget the maneuvers, still little known, of anti-Republicans, Catholics, and foreigners (especially Spaniards), all aimed at subverting and discrediting the regime. There was civil war thrice, always promoted by the monarchists. Clerical and international participation in conspiracies and uprisings still awaits its historian.

THE EVENTS

Once in power, the Republican party set up a provisional government symbolically headed by the aged and respected professor Teófilo Braga; the actual leaders, however, were the secretaries of the Interior (António José de Almeida), Justice (Afonso Costa), Foreign Affairs (Bernardino Machado), and Public Works (Brito Camacho). In less than one year, this government achieved some of the main objectives of the republican program, as well as tranquility inside the country and foreign recognition for the new regime.

Among the alterations which almost immediately took place, some symbolic acts must be emphasized, because they helped dissociate the new generations from the old, monarchical ones: the flag, which changed from white and blue to green and red; the national anthem, which was the *Portuguesa* instead of the *Hino da Carta;* the currency, which adopted the escudo instead of the real; and the ortographical reform, which simplified spelling. Although regarded by many as minor, these changes succeeded in building up a psychological distinction between the old days and the new ones. World War I, in which the Portuguese intervened, definitely imposed the green and red colors as the symbol of the fatherland, preventing later emotional rallies around the white and blue flag.

To the general elections of May 1911, only the Republican party presented candidates, plus a small number of independents. The so-called Constituent National Assembly, where the middle-class bourgeois including army and navy officers and civil servants had a majority, drafted and approved a parliamentary constitution. Rivalries among the cabinet members led to a very quick split of the Republican Party into three branches, Afonso Costa leading the bulkiest and

most radical faction (Democratic Party), António José de Almeida a
hodgepodge of Center, Right, and even some Left-wing elements (Evolutionist Party), and Brito Camacho the smallest, most conservative
group (Unionist Party). Such a division was further enhanced by the
rise of a small, yet aggressive faction of angered Republicans, headed
by Machado Santos (Reformist Party), who thought they should play
a role in politics too.

These dissensions first became evident to everybody in the presidential elections (August 1911), which followed the approval of the
Constitution. The partisans of António José de Almeida and Brito
Camacho, who together had a majority in Parliament, succeeded in
electing their candidate, lawyer Manuel de Arriaga, instead of Afonso
Costa's nominee, former university professor Bernardino Machado.
The new president, who wanted to prevent Afonso Costa's rising control of the country, stuck to the rule of not appointing any ministers
who had taken part in the Provisional government. He also defended
the principle of national nonpartisan governments. Therefore, to
January 1913, coalition cabinets ruled the country, with a plurality
of Evolutionists and Unionists. Such governments were weak, met with
little popular support, and had no possibility of carrying on any definite program of their own. In a short time, Parliament ceased to represent the political reality of the country, for its members reflected
only the situation of May 1911, when the Republican Party was still
united.

In spite of this, the new regime increasingly got the support of
the nation. Several monarchical plots and attempts to foster civil war
and the return of the king failed. The old monarchical parties had disbanded; no organized force opposed the Republicans. A majority of
the Army sided with the Republic, and the Navy almost entirely. The
only real danger to the regime was the Church, and therefore against
the Church an almost continuous fight took place from 1910 on.

By late 1912 it became evident that the Democratic Party had
enough strength to govern alone. It had gained an immense popularity
among the townspeople, while the other parties were losing it. Quite
unwillingly, President Arriaga was forced to entrust Afonso Costa
with the task of organizing a new cabinet (January 1913). With the
support of the Unionists in Parliament, Afonso Costa and his group

legislated intensely, balanced the budget, strengthened the government's authority and raised his popularity among the bourgeoisie. He
lost it, however, within the lower classes by ruthlessly suppressing
street demonstrations, discouraging strikes, and sending to jail numerous workers. He also roused the hatred of the monarchists, the Church,
and the upper classes by repressing their plots and imprisoning their
leaders. Elections held for many vacant seats in Parliament gave the
Democrats an overwhelming victory and a majority in the House of
Deputies.

Petty parliamentary quarrels and Arriaga's undiminished dislike of
Afonso Costa brought about Costa's downfall a year later. The president called upon Bernardino Machado, who organized another cabinet, less Democratic, yet supported by them. Up to January 1915, the
Democratic Party ruled Portugal for all practical purposes.

Meanwhile World War I had started. It became clear to most
responsible people that Portugal's national interest was to join the
allies. There had been much talk of a 1913 secret treaty between England and Germany for the partition of the Portuguese colonies, similar
to that of 1898. If Portugal helped England and France to win the
war, that danger might be considered over. Also, Spain's foreseen neutrality (quite sympathetic to the German cause) would contrast with
Portugal's share of international responsibilities and help reassert
Portugal's prestige and independence in the Europe of the future.

Both Democrats and Evolutionists agreed to that. The Unionists,
however, thought the contrary, and wanted to wait for a clearer picture of the war outcome. Many among them sympathized with the
German cause and the German conception of government. A good
number of monarchists, army officers, and Church people felt the same
way. After all, to side with the allies was to side with atheistic France,
protestant England, and schismatic Russia. And moreover, it was to
side with Afonso Costa, the symbol of all evil.

Bernardino Machado did not entirely commit Portugal to the
allied cause. His government made clear the intention of intervening
in the struggle, but only if and when England required it. Yet a strong
wing within the Democratic Party felt that Portugal should join the
allies without any further waiting, in order to force England to accept her collaboration on the same footing as the other countries. This

point of view was supported by the several German border violations and attacks in Portuguese Africa.

Alarmed with the bitter political struggle and the gradual taking over by the Democrats, President Arriaga staged a coup d'état in January 1915 and entrusted a personal friend of his, aged General Pimenta de Castro, with the difficult task of pacifying the country and presiding over impartial elections. Behind him stood the Evolutionists (because of their opposition to the Democrats), the Unionists (because of the same, plus the war policy), a part of the army, the monarchists, and the Church. Pimenta de Castro gave seven of the nine portfolios to the military and tried to appease discontent. The war policy was practically forgotten, persecutions against the monarchists and the Church stopped altogether (with many dismissed officers and civil servants being reinstated), and discrimination against the Democrats started. In March army troops prevented Parliament from meeting.

It was too early, however, for a Right-wing government in Portugal. The Democrats, along with others who also resented the old general's dictatorship, had behind them the bourgeois support of the major cities. Most people saw in Pimenta de Castro's measures a disguised way of restoring the monarchists to power. In May 1915 a violent rebellion in Lisbon, backed by some army corps, the navy, and popular elements, threw the government out and reinstated the Democrats. President Arriaga resigned, old Teófilo Braga being sworn in as provisional head-of-state. General elections gave the Democrats a majority in both houses of Parliament. In August, regular presidential elections put Bernardino Machado in control of the situation. Nothing now prevented Afonso Costa from getting back the premiership (November 1915).

Early in 1916, increasing problems in sea transportation led Great Britain to ask Portugal to seize a number of German and Austrian merchant ships, which had sought shelter in Portuguese harbors since the beginning of the war. When Portugal did so, Germany (and a little later Austria too) declared war upon her (March 1916). Democrats and Evolutionists got together in a so-called Sacred Union (União Sagrada), shaped in the French way, Afonso Costa stepping down from the premiership on behalf of his old foe, António José de Almeida. The Unionists also backed the new government. For all practical purposes, however, the Democrats kept control of the situation, and Afonso Costa, as Finance Minister, had the final word in most important decisions. Later on, a cabinet reshuffling gave him the premiership again (April 1917).

This war government undertook the difficult task of organizing an expeditionary force to fight in France, besides the several expeditions sent to Angola and Mozambique. The Portuguese army was in poor shape, lacking modern equipment, training, and even discipline. The War Minister, Norton de Matos, achieved what people then called a "miracle" by preparing an army corps in a remarkably short time. The first Portuguese troops arrived in France early in 1917 and, if not the best in the struggle, they did not discredit their flag either.

At home, however, the war effort and the world's situation in general brought about disastrous results. There was a shortage of food and even hunger among the lower urban classes. Many things were rationed. The increasing number of troops who had to leave Portugal to participate in the struggle aroused widespread discontent and reaction against the government. For many, the war was unpopular and the need for Portuguese intervention highly questionable.

Moreover, throughout 1917 and into the summer of 1918, the fear of a German victory haunted many people and made them wish for a Portuguese pullout as soon as possible.

Afonso Costa's conduct of the war and the general administration was good, but his popularity sank from day to day. Social unrest plagued the country, forcing the government to adopt severe measures of repression. On the other hand, the cabinet and its leader seemed to try an approach with the workers and supported many of their demands, producing uneasiness among the bourgeoisie. The Church and the monarchists profited by all this by intriguing and plotting against the regime.

In December 1917, with most of the army fighting in France and Africa and the head of the government abroad, some Lisbon garrisons revolted with popular support, under the leadership of the former envoy to Germany, Major Sidónio Pais. The government surrendered, President Bernardino Machado was forced to leave the country, and Sidónio Pais set up a military dictatorship. He changed the Constitution, introduced a presidential regime in the American style, and had himself elected as President in April 1918. General elections held at the same time, but in which the three main parties refused to participate, gave birth to a House of Deputies and a Senate, where the new government party had the majority but where the Monarchists and the Catholics were strongly represented too.

Sidónio Pais' regime (called the "New Republic"—República Nova) was one of increasing confusion and terror. Though well-intentioned and skilled, enjoying an immense popularity because of his gallant presence, boldness, and demagogical attributes, Sidónio always lacked cadres to help him in complex tasks of administration and warfare. The Unionists (who were fellow party members) backed him at first but soon refused to go along with his dictatorial schemes. The small group headed by Machado Santos supported him too, but it lacked able people itself. Therefore, Sidónio had to rely more and more on the extreme Right (monarchists, Clericals, upper bourgeois groups), whose support pushed him away from the Republican public opinion. He had to change minister after minister, with the result that political instability worsened and administration became chaotic. The consequences of the war were deeply felt, and the problems that fomented the revolution of 1917, far from being solved, increased. The influence of pacifists and Germanophiles, the presence of the military who did not want to fight, all this accounted for a lessening of the war effort. Troops were not relieved, some army corps were called home, the main defenders of Portugal's intervention were calumniated, tried, or arrested. Social unrest went on undiminished. Many workers, who had trusted Sidónio Pais, now realized that his policies were the same, or worse, than those pursued by the Democrats. Repression was the consequence of all this. Thousands were arrested and often tortured or badly beaten, a good many fled the country, censorship increased.

The liberal opposition revived, strengthened by Sidónio Pais' successive failures. There were several plots against the "New Republic" and one effective uprising. In December 1918 the President was assassinated and Portugal was plunged into the worst political crisis of her modern history.

Even before Sidónio's death, the government was losing control of the situation in several parts of the country. Military juntas had risen in the North and the South, with the alleged purpose of defending

Portugal against subversion, but in fact with monarchical goals. The War Minister himself was a confessed Monarchist. After Sidónio's murder, the juntas increased their power, particularly in the North. The cabinet hastily had its dean, Admiral Canto e Castro, elected President by the two Houses of Parliament (according to the 1911 system and revoking Sidónio's act of 1918), and tried to compromise with the Left and the Right at the same time. Its weakness became increasingly obvious to everyone. The monarchists prepared the restoration of the regime deposed in 1910, calling upon ex-King Manuel's approval. Alarmed by such a prospect, the Republicans attempted to get full control of the situation. They revolted in January 1919, but failed. Almost at the same time, the military juntas proclaimed the Monarchy in Porto and in Lisbon, and hoisted the white-and-blue flag again.

It was relatively easy to master the uprising in the South. Most of the capital's garrisons remained faithful to the government. Helped by the Navy and by tens of thousands of voluntary civilians who rushed to save "their" Republic, the rebels had to lay down arms and accept defeat. In the North, however, the situation was not so easy to handle. For a month the monarchists held on, controlling all of Minho, Douro Litoral, Trás-os-Montes and part of the Beiras, with headquarters in Porto. Major Paiva Couceiro, a former hero of the African campaigns, headed a provisional junta of the government. From England, ex-King Manuel II, without formally denying his support to the insurgents (as he did later), waited for the results. They were a semblance of civil war, which ousted the monarchists and reinstated the Republican authorities.

In Lisbon, a coalition cabinet of "old" Republicans and Sidonists had, in the meantime, been organized. It even included a Socialist as Labor Minister. It was followed (March 1919) by another coalition but where the Sidonists no longer participated. This meant that the "New Republic" had come to an end and that the "Old Republic" was back in power. Indeed, the June general elections gave a plurality to the Democrats and installed an all-Democrat government presided over by Coronel Sá Cardoso. For the Presidency, old party leader António José de Almeida, who had given up the direction of his Evolutionists, was chosen (August 1919). Most Evolutionists and Unionists fused into a new party, the Liberal Party, which tried to oppose the all-pervasive Democrat influence in government, administration, and popular trust.

Meanwhile, the Allies were meeting together at the Peace Conference. Portugal's prestige had sunk greatly because of Sidónio's rule and the country's general instability, and therefore Portugal's representatives at the conference (Egas Moniz and later Afonso Costa played a fundamental role in all this) had a hard time securing equal representation with the other belligerents. In the end, they managed to get back Kionga from the Germans (in north Mozambique), to obtain a share in the German war payments, and to get integrity of the colonies guaranteed.

The new "Old Republic" was not the same as before. To start with, international and national circumstances had very much changed because of the war: inflation, currency debasement, economic and social problems, generation conflicts, were shaping a new order. Communism and Fascism were on the rise. Political murders occurred frequently. All over Europe, anarchy and instability marked the years 1919 to 1923.

The old politicians were gone. Afonso Costa retired to Paris and, while accepting commissions from his government such as representative at the Peace Conference and the League of Nations (he even presided over the League of Nations General Assembly convened to approve Germany's entrance in 1926), never returned home. António José de Almeida, prematurely old and ill, had been elected President of the Republic, which put him in the role of an arbiter rather than an active politician. Brito Camacho accepted the office of governor of Mozambique and then faded from the political scene. Others had retired, lost interest in politics, or preferred to act as observers rather than participants. The leading positions in government fell to second-rate personalities, unskilled or unprepared to cope with the rising problems of postwar Europe. The results were incompetence, chaos in administration, widespread discontent. Moreover, high-level military officers coming back from the war, with prestige and popularity, thought they should play politics and be the best warrants of Portugal's entry into a new era. Yet their ability for administration was often poor, their political intelligence questionable, their preparation incomplete. Tired of anarchy and social unrest, people of all classes saw in them the saviors of the country and eagerly supported them against the civilians.

From 1918 on, the number of army and navy cabinet ministers steadily increased. Up to 1926, twelve out of twenty-six cabinets (46 per cent) were presided over by military men (before Sidónio Pais, the figure had been only 15 per cent). In Parliament a similar situation was taking place. It is true that the military in the government acted as individuals, not as representatives of the army or navy. Nonetheless, many people realized that it would not take long for an active participation of the armed forces themselves as a conscious body.

One of the main reasons for political instability was the failure of the Democrats to obtain a majority that allowed them to rule by themselves. They always had to depend upon the other parties, which made and unmade alliances as they pleased. Petty questions brought down cabinets and prevented any continuity in administration. Coalition governments had few bases for enduring, because party interests clashed. Governments lasted three to six months on the average; but there were even one-month and ten-day governments! Instability went along with periodical revolutionary attempts, plots and coups d'état. In 1919, for a better defense of the Republic, the Democrats had armed the National Guard with artillery and granted it extensive powers. As a result, the National Guard practically made and unmade governments for two years.

The year 1921, in Portugal as in many other countries of Europe, was a terrible one. Corruption, political crime, and lack of authority were more rampant than ever. Lt. Col. Liberato Pinto, chief of staff of the National Guard, Prime Minister for three months, was accused of embezzlement by the cabinet succeeding him (a coalition presided over by the former President, Bernardino Machado), and was tried and convicted. This brought about a strong reaction in the ranks of the National Guard, which ousted Bernardino Machado by violent means and accepted an all-Liberal regime under businessman Barros Queirós (May 1921). The general elections which followed gave a plurality to the Liberals, although the Democrats won in Lisbon, as always. Another Liberal Cabinet replaced it, headed by António Granjo, one of the most honest and prestigious statesmen of the time. Yet passions had risen too high for the moderate-conservatives to hold power for long. The trend pointed to the Left, to radical and extremist situations. A radical rebellion brought down the cabinet (October). One night several well-known politicians, including Granjo himself and Machado Santos, were murdered. It seems that the crimes were not directly related to the rebellion but to a mixture of elements where personal issues predominated but where Rightist influences were present (the monarchists, the Church, even Spain behind the scenes). The Radicals could not endure, and early in 1922 new general elections put the Democrats in power once more. The National Guard was extensively disarmed and ceased to present any danger. Only the Army now showed a certain cohesion and prestige.

Political fatigue made the years 1922 and 1923 somewhat calmer, António Maria da Silva being able to head an all-Democratic cabinet for twenty-one months. The general ambience tended to improve, along with the gradual fading away of the war problems. In August 1923 Parliament elected the Democrat nominee, Manuel Teixeira Gomes, a writer and ambassador to London, as President. On the political scene, the Liberal Party, with a reshuffling of its elements, became the Nationalist Party, where the Right-wing trend predominated. In the Democratic ranks, the Left-wing aggressively clamored for reforms and for a clear social policy. It was backed by an influential group of intellectuals, the Seara Nova group previously mentioned. Seara Nova people entered the government in 1923–24, then again in 1924–25, when the Left Democrat José Domingues dos Santos presided over a three-month government. This "Leftist" tendency collided with most of the Army which showed its sympathies toward authoritarian regimes like Mussolini's in Italy and Primo de Rivera's in Spain. Two suppressed Army uprisings during 1925 clearly showed such sympathies.

The general elections of 1925 gave another victory to the Democrats, but not a complete one. António Maria da Silva organized what would be the last government of the First Republic. President Teixeira Gomes, constantly attacked by the Nationalists, resigned, and old Bernardino Machado stepped in for his second term as President.

The general situation of Portugal had undoubtedly improved since 1923. The budget tended to be balanced, public debt went down, the currency became stable again. The concern for public works, reforms, and social welfare was in the minds of most statesmen and expressed itself in some timid acts. It seemed possible for the Republic to adjust with the country and start a new era, comparable to the constitutional monarchy after 1851.

But it was too late for that. Dissatisfaction was general. Everybody complained about the regime, even some of the Democrats themselves. All the other parties conspired against the supremacy of the Democrats and strove for power. Also, the Republic was logically tending toward radicalism in the socialist way. Agrarian reform, increase of taxation of the wealthy, nationalization, development of social welfare, improvement in the living standard of the lower classes, all these subjects were under discussion if not in operation. Such an evolution, however, if it seemed too slow to some people—the intellectuals and workers— seemed, on the contrary, too rapid to others—the rural landowners, the capitalists, part of the middle class, the Church. The upper and the middle ranks of the Army, as well as the upper and middle civil servants, had their purchasing power reduced to a half of what it had been in 1910. The bankers, top traders, and industrialists felt burdened with taxes (or threatened by them) and with the economic crisis, and were frightened by the rise of socialism and anarchism. The clergy wanted to regain its lost influence. Some of the workers were made impatient by their social grievances. Part of the intelligentsia (including many young people) were disenchanted with republicanism and enraptured by the novelty of fascism.

The middle- and lower-class people of Lisbon, who had been the best supporters of the Republic, were tired of the constant revolutions, street agitation, and interruption of normal life which were always taking place, resented anarchism in its daily violent manifestations, longed for a strong government that might restore order and tranquility. And like a huge backdrop were the agrarian, conservative, and feminine elements, the majority of the country, reacting against the progressive minority in the two leading towns—Lisbon above all. It must also be emphasized that, unlike nineteenth-century liberalism, the Democratic Republic was not the beginning of something structurally new but was rather the last phase of something which had started much before, in 1820. The Republic meant the climax of a process, the natural result of the evolution of monarchical liberalism.

To a certain extent, it might be compared to enlightened despotism as the end of an historical period. Thus, it had no future. It must die and be replaced by something totally different. That something was Fascism.

On May 28, 1926, General Gomes da Costa, one of the most prestigious war heroes, rebelled in the North (Braga) and marched on the South. Most of the army joined him or accepted the coup. In Lisbon, the government resigned (May 30), and the President entrusted one of the revolutionary leaders, Navy Commander Cabeçadas, with the task of organizing a new cabinet. On May 31, Bernardino Machado himself resigned. Early in June, Parliament was dissolved. The revolution had won.

CHAPTER THIRTEEN

THE "NEW STATE"

PORTUGUESE FASCISM

A well-defined, Right-oriented ideology arose in Portugal after 1914. This was Integralismo Lusitano (Lusitanian Integralism), a political trend primarily patterned after French Maurrassism (Action Française) but also with highly original views of its own. Integralismo Lusitano combined a body of radical objections to current political doctrines with a system of relatively precise views on how to organize a future new regime. Against liberalism, both political and economic, it was also against most doctrines which originated in or resulted from the French Revolution. Therefore, Integralists violently denounced individualism and popular sovereignty, with their practical political forms of constitutional monarchy or republic. They denied almost completely the nineteenth-century *en bloc* with its "fallacious" belief in progress and liberty. They pointed out the dangers of ill-interpreted scientism, leading to atheism, positivism, and other doctrines which tended to deny God, religion, and absolute virtues. Naturally, they most strongly condemned what they called the corollaries of "demo-liberalism": collectivism, with its forms of socialism, and (since 1917) communism. From Maurras, Integralists also took over a dislike of Semitism, both in its racial and religious aspects, but they never carried on anti-Semitism to the extent that other pre-Fascist and Fascist ideologies did. They regarded Semitism in the same way as the Reformation and the whole Protestant movement, as something that threatened the all-pervasive influence of both the Church and tradition.

Integralismo Lusitano gradually presented a full program of beliefs and policies. It stood for unbreakable tradition and for the cult of the past as the best teacher of the present. Consequently, it defended a pre-constitutional monarchy, based upon religion, authority, and corporatism. It accepted the social organization as defined by the Church, namely by Leo XIII's encyclicals (*Rerum Novarum*, 1891). It emphasized nationalism and the perpetuity of the "nation," against cosmopolitanism and international doctrines. It also stood for decentralization as it had existed in medieval times, with extensive municipal, provincial, and regional autonomies. Integralists were at first willing to accept ex-King Manuel II, provided that he yielded to their doctrines and complied with their program of a "total remodelling of Portuguese society." But when Manuel refused to do so, sticking to his constitutional oath and to the parliamentary institutions, they withdrew their support and chose the Legitimist cause instead. In 1920, they formally acknowledged as their monarch King Miguel's grandson, young Prince Duarte Nuno, who was living in Austria, as well as the legitimacy of his branch. In doing so, they were certainly being consistent with their beliefs, by rejecting the constitutional line on behalf of the absolutist.

As time went by, Integralismo Lusitano found its leaders, its apostles, and even its martyrs. It also defined some important points in its doctrine concerning real problems of the time, such as the agrarian question, the structure of the future "Parliament," the financial problem. António Sardinha (1888–1925) was the main philosopher of Integralism, José Pequito Rebelo its greatest economist, President Sidónio Pais—who was never an Integralist himself, but who welcomed Integralists as his advisers and cabinet ministers—its martyr and sole (partial) executor.

But Integralismo Lusitano meant also a generation gap, a rebellion of young people (most of them belonging to the generation of 1910–14) against the "establishment" of their time. In this sense it was extremely fashionable (like Fascism in general) and appealed to many youngsters, who cared less about ideologies than about fighting something they abhorred because it stood for their parents' convictions.

The romanticism of physical violence, which Integralists preached and sometimes put into action, added to that appeal. For many, Integralism was the doctrine of an elite in opposition to the vulgar "demo-liberal" principles shared by a majority of mediocrities. Indeed, Integralists rarely sprang from the lower class; they were recruited from upper and middle-class aristocrats, landowners, and bourgeois.

Portuguese Fascism had other origins too, although with much less impact than Integralism. There were the pure Catholic groups, such as the CADC (Centro Académico de Democracia Cristã) of which future President Salazar was the general secretary; the Catholic Center (Centro Católico), which was neutral on the monarchist-republican issue and of which Salazar, too, was a leading figure; and even certain Right-wing political groups within the parliamentary Republic (the Nationalists, for instance).

Italian Fascism (since 1922) and General Primo de Rivera's authoritarian regime in Spain (1923–30) also had a strong impact on the building up of Portuguese Fascism. Both President Carmona and Premier Salazar were great admirers of the two dictators and undoubtedly learned some lessons from Mussolini's and Primo de Rivera's experiments and experiences. By 1926 Fascism was becoming increasingly popular in Portugal among the intelligentsia, its solutions being pointed to as "the solution" for the Portuguese case. This worried intellectuals of the Left and Center very much, particularly the Seara Nova people, who launched a "week against Fascism" two months before the revolution of May 28, denouncing the dangers of authoritarian regimes, emphasizing the negative sides of Fascism, and warning the country against Fascist demagogy.

It would be hard to call the army rebellion of 1926 a Fascist movement. Action had been taken against the "corruption" and "degradation" of the parliamentary republic rather than against the parliamentary institutions as such. The demo-liberal Constitution of 1911 was not abrogated or repealed until 1933. Many leading Army officers stood for a democratic republic and for a return to "constitutional normality," which might imply some changes in the constitution and some purges against the "bad" politicians, but nothing else. This actually was the hope of all parties but the Democratic, which had supported or welcomed the movement as a means of breaking the

electoral machine and the all-pervasive influence of the Democrats.
The "program" of the Revolution encompassed a long series of vague
aspirations which everybody in the country wished to realize, from the
Left Democrats to the Right Conservatives: inquiry into the public
services, suspicious civil servants, and the "great fortunes"; economies
and good administration; valorization of the escudo and decrease in
the cost of living; road repair; an end to nationalization and return to
private companies of the nationalized services; reforms of the army
and the navy; increase in the number of schools; reforms in justice;
better administration of the colonies. There was little or no ideology
in all this, a fact which permitted a general rally in support of the
revolution and explained the difficult task of carrying it on.

The military dictatorship of 1926–28 carefully avoided any action that might be interpreted as aiming at a restoration of the monarchy. Not only were the majority of the ruling officers republicans,
but the government felt that it needed the support of the nation,
which certainly was against the king. Quite wisely, the monarchist
elements decided to wait for a better opportunity. In 1932, however,
ex-King Manuel's death inflicted a blow to any monarchical hopes. It
substituted an unknown, foreign young pretender, related to the still-
hated Miguelist faction, for the beloved, respected, and unhappy last
king of Portugal. With Manuel's death, all serious chances of a monarchical restoration died too. Most Monarchists, including Salazar
himself, realized this, and supported the Republic. A good many Integralists, waiting for Duarte Nuno's being of age, were not hostile to
Republican institutions.

By 1928 the first steps in shaping a new order were being undertaken, but rather slowly. In the fall of 1929, Salazar described the
future constitutional reorganization as one based upon a "solid,
prudent and conciliatory nationalism"; emphasized the roles of the
family, the moral and economic corporation, the parish and the
municipality; and uttered the slogan which would become famous:
"Nothing against the Nation, all for the Nation." This emphasis on
nationalism was to recur in Salazar's and his partisans' speeches and
writings as a leitmotiv for the regime. Quite artificially, the new order
seized upon nationalism as something new, something typical of itself
and in contrast to the former antinational or at least a-national policy.

By repeating it again and again, a method probably learned from Italian Fascist practices, Salazar managed to convince a great part of the population, and perhaps himself too, of the truth of such an assertion. In 1931 he defined the goals of the government as the setting up of a "well understood political, economic and social nationalism, controlled by the unquestionable sovereignty of the strong state."

This doctrine of a strong state, another of the regime's slogans, appealed to a bourgeoisie tired of political instability. With his usual exaggeration when appraising the immediate past, Salazar opposed the old "disorder" to the new order. Thus in 1930 he said: "One single word—*disorder*—defined in every field the Portuguese situation," and further, "we all know where we come from—one of the greatest disorganizations which may ever have existed in Portugal, in economy, finance, politics, public administration; . . . the same spectacle of permanent disorder . . . we can say that seriousness and justice had disappeared from Portuguese life: thus, indiscipline was general" (1932). Such a strong state should rise by strengthening the Executive Power, abolishing the parties and class unions, enforcing censorship, and reorganizing the Army, the Navy, and the Police. Yet Salazar always spoke against totalitarian regimes and criticized both the Italian Fascist and the German Nazi systems. He clearly distinguished between authoritarianism and totalitarianism.

The New State—the word was coined by 1930 and never dropped since—should be social and corporate. Its fundamental cell was the family, its basic elements the moral and economic corporations, where the interests of both employers and employees would together aim at a common "national" interest. Following the Integralist doctrine, Salazar rejected the class struggle as inevitable and regarded it as thoroughly opposed to the principles of the New State. Therefore, the National Labor Statute (Estatuto do Trabalho Nacional), enacted in 1933 and very much like the Italian Labor Charter, followed by a complex number of other laws and regulations, defined a corporate organization for the industrial sector and for agricultural employers. The so-called "Primary Elements" encompassed (1) the national syndicates, composed of employees or members of liberal professions; (2) the *grémios,* gathering together individual employers or firms and extended to the farmers too (casas da lavoura, grémios da lavoura);

(3) the *casas do povo,* rural unions of both employers and workers; and (4) the *casas dos pescadores,* associations of fishermen and their employers. The so-called "Intermediate" or "Secondary Elements" encompassed the National Federations or Regional Federations, i.e., associations of identical syndicates or *grémios,* and the unions, or associations of similar syndicates or *grémios* having common interests. Finally, the "Corporations" proper would constitute, according to the law that created them, "the unitary organization of the production forces, completely representing their interests."

It took a long time to achieve a thorough regulation for all these bodies and make them all operative. Besides the general resistance and indifference to them, it soon became clear that real economic benefits deriving from the corporative organization were few (other than employment of some thousands of new civil servants) and that, on the contrary, many of the Primary and Secondary elements only hampered production and trade. The labor organizations quickly became instruments of government policy which dictated the timing and terms of labor contracts. Most of the labor associations were made compulsory, while internal regulations restricted freedom of self-government and closely defined their powers in dealing with the *grémios.* The working agricultural population was only partly encompassed by this scheme (in the 1960's, only one-fifth of the rurals belonged to the *casas do povo*). The initial enthusiasm with which some had welcomed the birth of the corporative system rapidly faded, and it was only in 1956 that the government, more for reasons of consistency than for anything else, decreed the basic rules for the setting up of the corporations. Down to the present, only the economic ones have been established: agriculture (1957), industry (1958), trade (1958), transports and tourism (1957), credit and insurance (1957), fishing and fish-canning 1957), press and graphic arts (1959), and show business (1959).

Besides these three orders of "Elements," the government also instituted the so-called "organs for economic coordination," sort of precorporative bodies aiming at relating the state to the corporations. They were the "regulating committees" (*comissões reguladoras)* to control imports, the "national juntas" (*juntas nacionais*) to develop and control exports, and the "institutes" to supervise and officially guarantee the quality of exports. Several other organs appeared to direct and orient professional and corporative activities.

The real consequences for the country of all this complex system are still to be appraised, and its final destiny remains questionable. But it seems beyond doubt that the corporative state shaped a new Portugal, very much in the socialist way, which will be hard to destroy. Regardless of its faults and poor results in production and standard of living, the corporate system built up an economically organized country, an interventionist state essentially different from the liberal, "laissez-faire" Republican order. Almost forty years of actual performance have made the Portuguese accustomed to, and more and more dependent upon, the state. To contrast this new "order" to the one before 1930 would be as legitimate as to contrast the liberal order to the one before 1820. In this sense, the corporate system brought about a true revolution for Portugal, for it changed the country's basic structures. This fact must be emphasized to understand the continuity of a regime forty years old.

The anti-democratic characteristics of the New State should also be mentioned. In his key speeches of 1930, Salazar clearly put aside the concepts of individual freedom and party organization, although emphasizing the "legitimate individual and collective freedoms." The party—which he regarded as a fiction—must be replaced by the association—which he called a "reality." And in 1934 he went on to say that the 1926 movement "tended to proscribe definitely liberalism, individualism, and partisan or social struggles." Therefore, all political parties and secret societies were finally disbanded when the new constitution was put into effect in 1933, and only a "union of all the Portuguese," typically christened as "National Union" (*União Nacional*), allegedly nonpartisan, was tolerated. It was only after the allied victory of 1945 that a new and vague wording, "organic democracy," came into existence, a term invented by the regime to keep up with the needs of the present.

After 1936, the trend toward a fascistization of the New State intensified. The old Integralist element received the growing influx of the Portuguese Fascist groups, namely the National Syndicalists (very active in 1932–34, which later blended with the National Union), and obviously that of the Fascist experiments all over Europe. The outbreak of the Spanish Civil War led to the birth of the regime's militia, the Legião Portuguesa (Portuguese Legion), a paramilitary organization, which, in its beginnings, had much of a spontaneous movement

UPPER LEFT: *Bridge over the Tagus, opened 1966.* ABOVE:
Centennials Exhibition, 1940. OPPOSITE: *Salazar.*

of volunteers. Its purposes were to participate in the "anti-bolshevik crusade" and to defend "the spiritual patrimony of the Nation" as well as the corporate order. It is said to have reached some 20,000 members in the late 1930's and early 1940's, membership becoming virtually compulsory in certain public employments, but it quickly faded away and ceased to be taken seriously, as generally happens in Portugal after awhile. The Legion still exists, and from time to time it has a sudden and short-lived outbreak of activity.

Another Fascist paramilitary group, very much modeled along the Italian and the German patterns, was the Mocidade Portuguesa (Portuguese Youth), a compulsory organization destined to embrace the entire school and university population, but later restricted (in its compulsory form) to the ages of eleven to fourteen. The Mocidade blended some interesting aspects of scouting with political and religious indoctrination. Also established in 1936 (with a precedent in the Associação Escolar Vanguarda, existing since 1934), it rapidly declined and became a subject of contempt or ironical comment for most adolescents.

Both organizations stuck to the typical Fascist uniforms (green shirts), the Roman salute (with the hand position slightly different from the Italian and German ones), the terminology, the internal structure, certain slogans, and so on. Much of this was discontinued from 1945 on, yet it was still possible to watch the Minister of Education raising his arm in the Roman salute by the late 1950's. Regardless of the criticisms against both Legião and Mocidade, they were able to survive to the present, being given new and more up-to-date tasks (for instance, civil defense for the Legion, student welfare for the youth), in an attempt to revive them and instill new enthusiasm into them. Quoting H. Martins, these two examples "illustrate a characteristic behaviour pattern of the régime: the tenacity with which it holds on to its key symbols and the resilience with which it revives dormant organizations after periods of international discredit."

The other totalitarian institutions of the New State were the repressive mechanisms: censorship, Police Corps, and several more.

Censorship of periodicals was instituted shortly after the revolution of May 1926, and maintained ever since. It was gradually extended to other media, such as theater, cinema, radio, and television.

In every case, no word could (or can) be published, uttered, or broadcast without the censors' prior approval. Of all the repressive mechanisms, censorship can be regarded as the most efficient, the one that certainly has done more to keep things little changed for forty years. It maintained a check not only on political or military matters but also on morals, patterns of behavior, religion, and every news item or address susceptible of influencing the people in a "dangerous" way. Thus, censorship might ban the description of a revolutionary plot at home against the government, as well as the news of some social grievance abroad, or even the tale of a scandalous orgy somewhere. As censors varied greatly both in ferocity and in culture (not to mention intelligence), it happened that their action might reach absurd limits, and sometimes let pass important materials. Also, censorship was rarely centralized, each district or each town having its own body of censors. As a consequence, harshness of censorship varied with geography too. Yet censors were far from free in the use of their "blue pencil." Besides being trained on the "subversive" matters they must ban, they were constantly receiving fresh instructions from their superiors (who ultimately depended upon the Prime Minister). Yet there is no doubt that a part of their activity depended on the censors themselves.

The ultimate consequences of a censorship extended for so long a period were to self-discipline authors, journalists, impresarios, and all those concerned with public media, and to force upon them a self-censorship, in order to avoid having their production constantly harassed and mutilated. This self-censorship has often led to extremes of caution with little real justification. It has also led to the rise of a highly original crypto-writing on the part of authors and to a sharp understanding on the part of readers and listeners. Another obvious result for the public was a hypercriticism of everything and a widespread doubt of what was read and said.

Although censorship was never extended to books, they could be and were (and still are) frequently withdrawn on police orders. In this case, authors and publishers may be punished. Again, this included both political and nonpolitical material. Foreign periodicals and books might be confiscated or prevented from entering the country, although the latter form of control almost never succeeded.

The political police, which went back to some timid forms in the pre-1926 days, was reorganized in the 1930's, apparently with the advice and training of German and Italian experts. First called P.V.D.E. (Polícia de Vigilância e Defesa do Estado), it had its name shortened into P.I.D.E. (Polícia Internacional e de Defesa do Estado) after 1945 when its powers were considerably increased.

Although less violent—and especially less well organized—than the German Gestapo or the Soviet Secret Police, the P.V.D.E.-P.I.D.E. record was good enough to make us think of the Inquisition in its golden days. As with the Inquisition the Portuguese Secret Police reached such extremes of power and pervasiveness under Salazar that it defied the authority of the state itself—including that of the Armed Forces—and gradually became a state within the state. And like the Inquisition, it had to justify its own existence and powers by often "inventing" nonexistent threats to the regime's security and "making" Communists and other opponents to the New State out of tenuous presumptions or hearsay. It is, of course, too early to try to analyze objectively an institution that goes on functioning (although under a different name) and on which so many partisan views have been expressed. But it may be said that neither P.V.D.E. nor P.I.D.E. belong in a civilized world and partake rather of pre-liberal prejudices and methods. The insistence of the Secret Police on the most sophisticated forms of torture, as well as other physical and psychological pressures (written and non-written testimonies on this subject are endless); their use of dismal civilian prisons and concentration camps (a major one was in operation in the Cape Verde Islands from 1936 to 1956, its name, Tarrafal, becoming a symbol of the New State methods of terror); their breaking into residences and seizure of personal belongings; their presence everywhere (so people believe and what people believe does make the general ambience)—all this cemented Salazar's power over the decades and helped explain the famous "order in the streets" he was so proud in claiming. It seems beyond doubt that the Secret Police killed hundreds (if not thousands), while keeping many others in jail for years and years. In 1956 a governmental act introduced the so-called "security measures," which enabled the Ministry of Justice under proposal of the Police to keep indefinitely under arrest (by three-year renewals of the term of sentence) all those who were believed to be dangerous to "society." It is true that such measures have rarely been applied; yet they created a dangerous principle, by overcoming the concept of individual rights and equating political prisoners with the worst delinquents. Also, the act of 1956 implicitly gave the Police the power of unilaterally deciding on how "dangerous" or "regenerated" a political prisoner was.

The main targets of the P.V.D.E.-P.I.D.E. were always the Communists or Communist sympathizers, whose martyrs far surpassed any other oppositionists. It also seems a fact that lower-class elements were generally treated worse than the middle or upper class. Nevertheless, all currents of opinion, including the Catholics and the Integralists, were victims of police persecutions.

Other police corps that acted as instruments of repression were the National Guard (Guarda Nacional Republicana), particularly active in rural areas, the ordinary Police Force (Polícia de Segurança Pública), used to break up meetings and demonstrations, and even the Fiscal Guard (Guarda Fiscal). None of them, however, was specifically related to the New State; their activities were traceable to the past when they sometimes had more strength and influence (as, for instance, the National Guard in the early 1920's).

The repressive mechanism did not stop here. On the contrary, other, less evident, forces were often more relevant in achieving the goals of the regime than the obvious censorship and police authority. This was true of the political pressures on civil servants, which lead to a complete taming of most elements, including instructors and army and navy forces. From time to time, selective purges got rid of the most dangerous and acted as examples to the others. Also, in a small country like Portugal, highly centralized, political pressures affected many "independent" professions, other than the civil servants. Sometimes, the real political reasons for persecution were carefully omitted, professional or moral motivations being invoked instead. Pressure was also put on firms to dismiss or deny admission to politically unreliable people. And a whole climate of "moderate" terror has been shrewdly established. Quoting Hermínio Martins,

> The Portuguese case provides an object lesson in the economy of terror. There can be an optimum coefficient of terror comprehensive in impact, embracing the totality of the population, without the extermination of large numbers, but with maximum visibility or publicity as well as cruelty. The

Portuguese régime has achieved such an optimum: with a small number of political murders and arrests (between 1948 and 1959 the annual rate of political "cases" registered by the P.I.D.E. with the political tribunals fluctuated between 700 and 2,000) it has succeeded in politically atomizing the underlying population and paralyzing the élite opposition. Part of its success lies in the unremitting character of the repression, with no wide swings between "excesses" and "liberalizations."

According to Salazar himself (speech of May 26, 1934), the "gospel" of the New State encompassed the Constitution, the Colonial Act, the Organic Charter of the Empire, the Statute of National Labor, and the program of the National Union. To this, the Concordat of 1940 should be added. Leaving the colonial texts to another chapter, and having already mentioned one of the other documents, let us now briefly analyze the Constitution of 1933.

Influenced by the Republican Constitution of 1911, the Constitutional Charter of the Monarchy, and the German Constitution of 1919, the new constitutional text reflected a clear compromise between the "demo-liberal" principles (which Salazar so sharply attacked) and the Integralist-Fascist tendencies, both theoretically and practically expressed in many governmental acts since 1926. It meant a further compromise between republic and monarchy. Because of this, it met with little real approval and actual enforcement, being an object of derision for most oppositionists and one of slight concern for the regime itself.

The Constitution defined the state as unitary and corporative. It classified power in four branches: the President of the Republic, the National Assembly, the government, and the tribunals. It gave the President extensive powers, comparable to those which the Constitutional Charter granted the king; moreover, it provided for the President to be elected by popular vote. A presidential regime might have resulted, yet Salazar's thirty-six-year-old premiership transferred power to the government and reduced the President to almost nothing.

The National Assembly (Assembleia Nacional) was formed by ninety representatives (*deputados*) elected by the people for a four-year term. Its functions were to supervise administration, and to vote the acts proposed by the government or the representatives. In practice, the latter rarely happened, most laws coming from the government, and the role of the National Assembly has always been minimal.

A Corporative Chamber (Câmara Corporativa), composed of representatives (*procuradores*) of the corporations, the municipalities, the
Church, the universities, the institutes of charity, and the bodies of
administration, assists the National Assembly and the government in
lawmaking. Its role has generally been negligible.

The government became the real source of power, and its head
(President of the Council of Ministers) the true and sole leader of the
country. Quoting Marcelo Caetano, one could define the Portuguese
system as a "presidentialism of the prime-minister."

The Constitution of 1933 also registered all kinds of freedoms for
the citizen (including freedom of speech, association, the right to
habeas corpus, etc.) but made the citizen dependent upon "special
laws" which must regulate him. In practice, such "special laws" often
overruled the Constitution itself and became the actual law of the
country.

Several amendments changed the Constitution now and then but
generally in secondary points only. Thus, the number of representatives to the National Assembly went up to 120 (1945), then to 130
(1959). The Colonial Act, considered a part of the Constitution, was
substantially altered in 1951. The only major change took place in
1959, by making the election of the President dependent upon an
electoral college (composed of the National Assembly, the Corporative
Chamber and representatives of the municipalities and the Overseas
provinces) rather than upon direct suffrage.

Despite the few practical implications of the electoral system,
mention should be made of its functioning. The size of the electorate,
to start with, did not significantly increase in forty years, although
college-graduated women and female heads of family were given voting
rights in the early 1930's: 1,300,000 in 1933, about 1,500,000 in the
1960's. In the same period, however, the population grew by two million and the illiteracy rate declined by 50 per cent. This means that a
considerable part of the people qualified to vote (and illiterates were
not) never did register, or rather that a good many others were written
off the balloting rolls. Both things did happen, maintenance on the
voting lists generally (but not consistently) depending upon actual
vote-casting in the previous election. Electoral registration was never
encouraged, a symptom of both governmental fear before a wide-

reaching election and doctrinal scorn of elections as such. As a rule, a high level of abstentions featured the electoral "farces" (as opposition-ists called them), although the official figures almost always gave over 80 or 90 per cent victory results.

Up to 1945, only the National Union might nominate the candi-dates to the National Assembly and the Presidency. Conceived by Salazar as a sort of "anti-party," uniting every Portuguese to a common goal, the National Union virtually became a government party from its very beginning. Indeed the New State differed in such a revolu-tionary way from demo-liberal or socialist tendencies that a real na-tional union in tune with its principles was utterly impossible. Also, Salazar deliberately closed the door to any possible union when say-ing: "We have a doctrine and are a force . . . under these circum-stances there are no possible agreements, nor transitions, nor com-promise" (speech of November 1932). Again, in 1940, he repeated words of condemnation to all his political foes and talked of them as having been "spurned" by the "Fatherland's justice." Thus, the National Union only encompassed the Right-wing, Fascist, or In-tegralist-oriented side of the nation. In terms of pre-1926 political currents, it gathered together most of the Constitutional Monarchists, Integralists, Legitimists, Catholics (namely the C.A.D.C. and the Cath-olic Center people), members of the Union of the Economic Interests, along with some "Liberals" (of Cunha Leal's party) and "Nation-alists." All the others stayed outside, with a few exceptions, their more than forty-year uncompromising opposition to what they always called "the Dictatorship" featuring a rare and exemplary, albeit useless, attitude in Portuguese history. The regime was never able to "in-tegrate" that opposition (although neutralizing it completely); it has remained a sort of permanent ghost haunting the regime's achieve-ments and victories. Unlike Spain and even Italy, where a significant part of the intelligentsia subscribed to Fascism, the great majority of the Portuguese intellectuals chose the hard road of opposing an au-thoritarian regime. (This was particularly true since the 1930's. Previ-ously, an older generation of intellectuals was somewhat more sym-pathetic to the dictatorship. Fernando Pessoa, the greatest Portuguese author of the twentieth century, openly applauded the revolution of May 1926 and its further steps, but he died in 1935.) Despite the several amnesties granted—incidentally never complete and often tricky—scores of distinguished writers, scientists, professors, politicians, as well as thousands of gifted persons, lived in forced exile a great part of their lives and died abroad. Others chose a voluntary exile rather than compromise or be persecuted at home. This happened, to cite a few instances, to men like old President Bernardino Machado (in exile from 1926 to 1940), former Premiers Afonso Costa (who died in Paris in 1937) and José Domingues dos Santos (1927 to the 1950's), essayist António Sérgio (1927 to 1936), and historian Jaime Cortesão (1927 to 1956). Professor Egas Moniz, Portugal's sole Nobel Prize winner (1949), was often harassed too.

The Catholic feature of the New State must be emphasized but not exaggerated, for Salazar's regime (unlike Franco's) never posed as an "apostolic" system engaged in some kind of crusade against anti-Catholic elements. The Premier's few public remarks on Catholicism and religion in general were always strikingly moderate and tolerant, in contrast to his strong beliefs and extremist attitudes on other subjects. His speech of 1940, when the Concordat with Rome was signed, showed a remarkably middle-of-the-way position, uncommitted to any all-pervasive Church influence and definitely opposed to Church meddling with politics. In this sense, one might conclude that the Maurrassist political standpoint prevailed over Salazar's own religious beliefs, and that the traditional Portuguese anticlerical policy did not entirely disappear from his handling of state affairs. His masters had probably been the clever bourgeois statesmen of the constitutional period prior to 1910, when the Church was more controlled by the state than in control of it.

Thus, no attempt was made to reunite Church and state. No one was ever persecuted or even discriminated against because of his religious faith or atheist principles. And the Concordat, while yielding to some Catholic requirements such as the abolition of divorce for couples married in church or the teaching of religion in schools, neither put an end to civil marriage and civil divorce nor gave back to the Church all the property confiscated since 1910. Cemeteries were not sacralized. Religious orders were accepted providing they indulged in some kind of charitable or educational work. Religious oaths were not reestablished. Classes on religion were not compulsory and no passing exams were required. Official schools of theology could never be reestablished at the universities. In short, if the Concordat meant a sort of compromise between the pre-1910 situation and the lay attitude of the Republican regime, it leaned more to the latter than to the former.

It is true that no anti-Catholic propaganda or writings were permitted and that the propagation of other religions was generally discouraged. This, however, derived more from subscribing to tradition and to the advantages of religious homogeneity than from intolerance. In the 1950's a certain revival of religious fanaticism led to the constitutional definition of the Catholic religion as the "religion of the Portuguese Nation," which the original text of the 1933 Constitution had carefully avoided.

More than any definite clerical attitude, Salazar rather emphasized his stand in defense of "Christian civilization" and the creating of a state well equipped for that purpose. Such a belief could be traced back to his speeches in the early 1930's and became a sort of obsession in his later years as premier. He often posed as a prophet of the world's tragedies because of the Western leaders' relinquishment of the true values of Western civilization, which he had always underlined, and because of their surrender to the forces of evil. Such forces were of course Communism, another of Salazar's and his regime's obsessions to the end. Salazar's public mention of Communism and its threats became more frequent after 1936 (because of the Spanish Civil War) and a favorite topic after the end of World War II. Neither the Soviet Union nor any of the Communist countries were ever recognized by the Portuguese government with the exception of Cuba (because with Cuba diplomatic relations were never broken). The foreign attacks on the Portuguese Overseas policy in the 1950's and 1960's gave Salazar and the regime a further reason to stress this anti-Communist attitude and discover a Communist conspiracy against the West.

PORTUGAL BY THE MIDDLE OF THE TWENTIETH CENTURY

When Salazar took power, in 1928, Portugal was obsessed with financial crisis. Balancing the budget was the top priority in every party program. Most countries of Europe (though by no means all) had balanced theirs a decade after the war, and Portugal wanted to be among them. Salazar's first budget, that of 1928–29, accomplished the miracle: revenues reached 2,175,000 contos, while expenditures were kept to 1,900,000 contos, i.e., a surplus of 275,000 contos. To achieve such a result, Salazar's policy had consisted in cutting back expenditures (by 270,000 contos) through strict economies, and in slightly increasing revenues (by 207,000 contos) by introducing some new taxes and better management of public monies (the so-called finance reforms).

From 1928–29 to the present Portuguese budgets have been balanced. This has become a sort of fetish of the New State and a cornerstone of its administration, a symbol of good management and continuous progress. To World War II revenues were practically stagnant, the 1939 figure showing not more than 50,000 contos over the 1928–29 figure. Expenditures declined a little, with the result that surpluses never went beyond the level of Salazar's first year in government. In 1936 a finance reform changed the fiscal year and made it coincide with the civil year.

World War II brought some prosperity to the country. Being neutral, Portugal could sell her products quite favorably without greatly disturbing expenditures for war material. Exports of wolfram made many people wealthy and helped the state too. By 1946 revenues had nearly doubled (in relation to the 1939 level), while currency debasement did not go beyond 10 per cent. Gold reserves reached high levels, creating monetary stability.

This trend continued after the war. In the late 1940's revenues surpassed 5 million contos, reaching 9 million in the following decade. The amazing increase of the 1960's brought revenues to almost 13 million in 1966, 20 million in 1967 and 22 million in 1968, double 1960 and ten times those of the prewar era. The taxation reforms of 1958–65 altered the basic rules followed until then, improving efficiency on behalf of the state. New taxes were created, particularly in 1965 (surplus value tax) and 1966 (transactions tax). Expenditures, of course, increased similarly. From the end of the war onward, the tendency was to reduce surpluses more and more, with only a few exceptional years. In the same period the escudo was debased only once (1949) by about 12 per cent.

The world's economic crises did affect Portugal but only moderately. The depression of 1929 had its impact on public revenues, which slightly decreased from 1929–30 to 1932–33, recovering slowly afterward. Prices went down (index 2272 in 1929, index 1960 in 1932), bank rates fell, and unemployment increased slightly. Yet Portugal's overwhelming economic dependency upon countries like England and France rather than the United States, as well as her small degree of industrialization, slowed down any catastrophic results. The public work policy actively carried on by the administration prevented generalized unemployment. Currency was tied to the British pound up to the 1930's: in June 1931 Salazar had completed his first finance reform and publicly announced the return to a gold standard (which England had done as early as 1925). Yet, when the gold standard was abandoned by Britain in September 1931, Portugal had to do likewise, with a few months between a return to gold and the final farewell to gold. With the outbreak of World War II (1939) Portugal tied her currency to both the dollar and the pound in order to keep its value with a minimum of change. The cost of living started increasing again, 1941 reaching the level of 1929. Only in the late 1940's was it possible to slow down the rise in prices. Inflation began again with the African rebellions (1961–64) and economic expansion. In 1968 the cost of living had gone up 31 per cent over that of 1958.

Comparable in so many ways to mid-nineteenth-century Fontism (see chapter 10), the New State embarked on an extensive program of public works. Beyond all the propaganda effects—constantly heralded at home and abroad—this policy aimed at a development and betterment of substructures considered instrumental in the shaping of the country's new economy. Public works became a sort of leitmotiv, a subject that revealed the new Portugal on the move, and indeed one of the great achievements of Salazar's administration. But while Fontism had mostly relied on private investments and private initiatives—a liberal state would not permit it otherwise—public works under the New State were fundamentally a government undertaking, and a way to avoid unemployment in epochs of economic depression or stagnation.

The railroads changed little. The railroad network of 3,300 km. of the mid-1920's increased only slightly, to 3,500 km. in 1935 and 3,600 km. in the 1940's, but then stopped increasing altogether as roads and motor cars developed instead. Rolling stock, however, improved, as well as service in general. Electrified railroads started in 1926, but for more than thirty years only 25 km. of railways were electrified. In the 1950's and 1960's electrification and equipment with Diesel locomotives speeded up (almost 900 km. were electrified in 1968). In 1951 the government granted a railroad monopoly to the largest operating private company (Companhia Portuguesa de Caminhos de Ferro), giving up its share in railroad ownership. Another important novelty was the opening of the Lisbon subway in 1959.

Road building and road repairing were for many years the proud symbol of a new administration. The total road network doubled in twenty-five years (13,000 km. in the mid-1920's, 26,000 by 1950) and surpassed 30,000 km. in 1968. The first—and for a long time the only —expressway was opened to traffic in the 1940's, modeled after Germany's. Road repairing was still more important, particularly in the late 1920's and the 1930's, large sums being allotted yearly for that purpose. To the late 1950's Portuguese roads could be regarded as good by European patterns. Yet traffic increase—particularly of trucks—and a gradual lack of concern with highway repair brought about a considerable deterioration in the 1960's and the obvious need for radically changing the entire road structure of the country. Road building was accompanied by bridge building, several outstanding and spectacular bridges being erected from the 1930's to the present (the arch-bridge over the Douro at Oporto, opened in 1963; the bridge over the Tagus in Lisbon, the longest suspension bridge in Europe, opened in 1966).

Telegraph and telephone networks expanded remarkably too (8,000 km. of cables by 1930, 100,000 in 1968; 300 km. of phone wires in 1930, nearly 60,000 in 1968), phones being totally nationalized in the mid-1960's.

Port facilities were considerably improved. In Lisbon, Leixões (the port of Oporto), and other places extensive works were carried on for the purpose of enlarging piers, deepening bottoms, erecting protective walls, and equipping harbors with modern facilities. The same happened with airports, although to a lesser degree.

A policy of land irrigation and electrification led to the building of numerous dams scattered all over the country (Castelo do Bode, Cabril, Paradela), a field in which Portuguese engineers excelled and became known worldwide. Yet Portugal was far from being totally electrified in the 1960's.

Public works encompassed many other aspects of life such as housing (houses for workers), health (hospitals), sports (stadiums), justice (courthouses and prisons), administration (government buildings), army and navy (barracks, shipyards), tourism and history (state-owned inns and restoration of monuments). State participation in most works undertaken by private initiative or by the municipalities became a matter of fact, a natural and indispensable condition, increasing everyone's dependency upon the administration.

The public works policy bore fruit, making possible—along with the general expansion of Europe—the rapid economic development of Portugal in the 1950's and the 1960's. In the balance of trade, for instance, exports rose ten times between 1926 and 1951 (mostly after World War II), then doubled to 1964, and reached more than twenty-eight times their former level in 1967 (722,000 contos in 1926; 7,563,000 contos in 1951; 14,814,000 contos in 1964; 19,685,000 contos in 1967). As imports increased only twelve times (2,342,000 contos in 1926; 29,135,000 contos in 1967), the usual deficit of the balance of trade—only avoided in 1941–43 because of the war—declined in relation to the trade volume. Exports, which were generally below the deficit level, showed a surplus for the first time in 1936–46, and then permanently after 1950 (with an exception only in 1961). The remaining deficit was largely made up with money sent by emigrants and with the profits of tourism, particularly since the 1950's.

The development of exports was a result of industrialization mainly, yet some agriculture and mining products (like cork, wine, fruit, and stone) also expanded or obtained better prices. Textiles constituted one-fourth of all exports in the mid-1960's, but only one-fifth in 1961, 5 per cent in 1934, and 6 per cent in 1926. Chemical products doubled in five years (1961–65) for export purposes, reaching 7 per cent of all exports in 1965. Paper machinery also doubled in the same period. The steel industry was introduced in the 1950's. Canned fish maintained its place as an important item in foreign markets. Altogether, the role of industry in exports rose from one-third (1926) to almost two-thirds by the late 1960's. Imports hardly changed in character. Portugal continued to order all kinds of manufactured items, like machinery and transport equipment, textiles, plastics, rubber, oil and coal, metals, grain, and the like.

Highly revealing for the political situation of Portugal in the world were the changes in export-import markets. To the 1920's Great Britain had by far the leading place in both. In the early 1930's one-third to one-fourth of all imports came from Britain. Germany, the United States, Belgium-Luxemburg, and France were far behind. The Overseas provinces were as important as Germany, with about one-ninth of imports. Exports went first to the colonial empire (one-fifth to one-fourth), followed closely by Great Britain. Much behind was Germany, France, Spain, and the United States.

World War II and world changes afterward modified this picture. The dependency upon the Overseas provinces constantly increased; they reached first place both in imports (17 per cent in 1954, 14.2 per cent in 1967) and exports (25.3 per cent in 1954, 24.3 per cent in 1967). The second place was irregularly held by Britain (imports—15 per cent in 1954, 13.7 per cent in 1967; exports—15 per cent in 1954, 21.5 per cent in 1967), closely followed by Germany (imports—13.7 per cent in 1954, 15 per cent in 1967; exports—6.9 per cent in 1954, 5.3 per cent in 1967) and the United States (imports—8.3 per cent in 1954, 6.9 per cent in 1967; exports—10.3 per cent in 1954, 10 per cent in 1967).

Despite the great changes and accomplishments which took place in most economic fields, particularly after World War II, the New State could not transform Portugal into a well-developed country. The main reason was that in other underdeveloped countries of Europe the rate of economic growth was faster than in Portugal, and was coupled with a wise policy of cultural development which Portugal lacked. In the 1950's the administration launched extensive plans of combined national development including the Overseas provinces, the Portuguese equivalent of the famous Soviet Five-Year Plans. A first Plano de Fomento covering the years 1953–58 was followed by a second (1959–64), then by a complementary one (Plano Intercalar, 1965–67) and finally by a third one (1968–73). It is still too early to appraise the value and impact of these plans but it seems beyond doubt that their contribution to the shaping of a developed country, halfway between capitalism and socialism, was a major one. In the mid-1960's Portugal's gross national product provided a yearly per capita revenue of $408.00 (Sweden—$2,740.00; Turkey—$275.00), placing her among the lowest-ranking European countries. The number of emigrants leaving Portugal in search of better salaries was a clear proof of poor conditions at home. The war in Africa, if it provided a stimulus for economic development and migration, also hampered prospects of a faster rate of growth at home, with 50 per cent of the national budget being applied to military expenses. Portugal's increasing dependency upon the Overseas provinces (see chapter 14) was another obstacle to a full development in the framework of a united Europe.

In the field of agriculture, one of the main concerns for many years was to achieve self-sufficiency in grain production. A direct result of the pre-1926 situation, this goal also reflected a general European tendency in the 1930's. Mussolini had launched his widely advertised "battle of wheat" or campaign for wheat production; it had a strong impact on Portugal. In 1929 the *campanha do trigo* (wheat campaign) was started, and throughout the thirties a vast effort was aimed at enlarging harvest areas, particularly in the South. Results looked promising at the beginning: wheat areas increased and wheat production grew from 284,000 tons to a maximum of 771,000 tons (1935). In 1934 and 1935 harvests were so bountiful that wheat was stored for export purposes. Final results, however, were poor. Most soils had not been conditioned for grain cultivation and became quickly exhausted. Problems arose as how to place wheat surpluses in international markets at a compensating price. Overproduction proved as harmful as underproduction had once been. Moreover, the population increase completely destroyed any prospects of making Portugal self-sufficient in grain. Despite some sporadic attitudes to the contrary, the wheat campaign was over by World War II, and wheat imports had to be resumed once more. Nonetheless, some of the early results remained, both harvest lands and wheat production (along with maize and other crops) continuing to increase to the 1960's.

Much more successful and useful was the tree-planting policy, which converted barren fields and mountain soil into green and productive lands. The total forest area increased from 23.1 per cent in 1920 to 27.8 per cent in 1939, and to 28.2 per cent in 1957. Irrigation also developed, with a growing number of dams and artificial lakes scattered over the country. A general campaign for agrarian production, launched in the 1930's and the 1940's, was coupled with a somewhat more successful effort for rational colonization inside Portugal (Junta de Colonização Interna), something being done in the field of land reclamation with enduring results.

Among the traditional cultures vineyards somewhat expanded to the 1940's, wine production increasing from 5 million to 14 million hectoliters but declining later on. Olive oil, cork, and fruit had their production substantially enlarged too. Fishing also developed, with important results for the canning industry, one of the most relevant in Portugal.

From 1930 to 1968 the population of Portugal increased more than one-third. The rate of growth was particularly high from 1930 to 1940. Figures, as shown by decennial censuses, were 6,825,883 in 1930, 7,722,152 in 1940, 8,441,312 in 1950, and 8,889,392 in 1960. By the late 1960's the number of Portuguese exceeded 9.5 million. The death rate declined by 50 per cent from 1926 (20.43 per thousand) to 1965 (10.72 per thousand) although child mortality was still high: 64.9 per thousand in 1965 (it was 126.1 per thousand in 1940). The birthrate declined too (32.82 per thousand in 1926; 23.74 per thousand in 1965).

An important factor explaining demographic changes was emigration. After the high figures of the post-1919 period, emigration declined during the 1930's and the 1940's because of restrictions adopted by American countries and because of the war. The return to normality brought about a new and ever-increasing wave of emigration to Brazil (1945 to 1963), the United States and Canada (in the late 1960's), and Europe (also in the 1960's). Official figures registered 20,000 emigrants in 1950, 30,000 in 1951, nearly 50,000 in 1952, a 30,000 average in 1953–63, 55,000 in 1964, 89,000 in 1965, 120,000 in 1966, and 95,000 in 1967. The last three figures surpassed the high levels of 1912–13 (see chapter 12) in absolute figures but not in proportion to the population. In the 1960's most emigrants went to France and Germany where they were offered salaries far higher than those at home. Regardless of the human aspects of the problem, emigration brought about a number of advantages, such as important amounts of foreign exchange credits regularly mailed to Portugal, as well as the need for a higher mechanization of agriculture, and the raising of rural salaries at home. Yet it deprived the country of hundreds of thousands of able men and women, posing difficult labor problems.

Urban growth continued, the areas of Lisbon and Oporto attracting a great influx from the rural and the more backward hinterland. In 1960, 25.1 per cent of all Portuguese lived in those two areas. Total urban population, however, did not go beyond 22.8 per cent. This means that a large percentage (49 per cent in 1950, 44 per cent in 1960, 40 per cent in the late 1960's) still depended upon agriculture, with less than a third (34 per cent in 1950, 29 per cent in 1960, 30 per cent in the late 1960's) occupied in industrial jobs.

Reforms in administration stand out among the main achievements of the New State governments. Concerned with "order" above all, Salazar and his ministers tried their best to improve public services in general. In all ministries internal reforms were carried on, particularly in the early 1930's, aiming at a more efficient and economic organization. Public services, such as the Post Office, also experienced important changes. The army and navy were several times reorganized. Extensive reforms took place in the field of justice too.

The number of ministers was successively increased, according to a higher specialization of functions: ten in 1926 (Interior, Justice, Finance, War, Navy, Foreign Affairs, Commerce and Communications, Colonies, Education, Agriculture; in 1932 Agriculture was put together with Commerce, but a Ministry for Public Works was created); eleven from 1933 to 1940 (Agriculture autonomous again); ten from 1940 to 1947 (Agriculture and Commerce reunited under the general title of Economy); eleven from 1947 to 1950 (Communications added); thirteen from 1950 to 1955 (National Defense and Presidency, a sort of Vice-Premiership, added); fourteen from 1955 to 1958 (a new Ministry of Health); fifteen from 1958 to 1965 (Corporations created); fourteen again from 1965 to 1969 (Presidency abolished). Many undersecretaries were also created, which increased the total figure of government members to nearly thirty in the mid-1960's.

Salazar also changed traditional methods of governing. Cabinet meetings were reduced to a minimum and replaced by frequent two- or three-person meetings between the Prime Minister and his ministers. Total Cabinet reshufflings came to an end in 1932. Up to his forced retirement, thirty-six years later, Salazar changed 50 per cent or more of his cabinet members all at once only five times: in 1936, 1944, 1947, 1958, and 1968. Periodic changes of ministers (once a year to 1936, once each three or four years afterward with few exceptions) generally affected no more than a third of his people. This practice brought about continuity in administration and perfect control by the Prime Minister, who never met a complete set of new faces at once. The average number of years in power for cabinet ministers from 1932 to 1968 reached four and a half. Yet there were much longer ministries, stretching for ten or more years: Navy Minister Américo Tomás (later elected President) ruled from 1944 to 1958; his successor, Fernando Quintanilha de Mendonça Dias, in 1958–68; Justice Minister João Antunes Varela was in power from 1954 to 1967 and his predecessor, Manuel Cavaleiro Ferreira, from 1944 to 1954; Finance Minister António Pinto Barbosa ruled in 1955–65; Public Works Minister Eduardo Arantes e Oliveira in 1954–67; Communications Ministers Manuel Gomes de Araújo and Carlos Ribeiro held power in 1947–58 and 1958–68. Permanence in power increased after the end of World War II, as Salazar grew older and less inclined to change.

The two administrative codes of 1936 and 1940 stressed centralization for all practical purposes. Yet the general administrative division of Portugal was basically unaltered. Besides the parishes (*freguesias*), municipalities (*concelhos*), and districts (*distritos*), the Constitution of 1933 officially reintroduced the provinces as units of administration. Eleven in number (Minho, Trás-os-Montes e Alto Douro, Douro Litoral, Beira Alta, Beira Baixa, Beira Litoral, Estremadura, Ribatejo, Alto Alentejo, Baixo Alentejo, and the Algarve), they were later eliminated again, according to the reform of 1959. A new district was also created in Setúbal (1926). The number of both *concelhos* and *freguesias* considerably increased after 1926, a result of the population growth. The ecclesiastical division was improved with the setting up of a new bishopric in Aveiro (1940). With the publication of a new Civil Code in 1966, the New State achieved one of its coveted aims. Most of the country's legislation from top to bottom was now its own.

A policy of mass education was never a top priority for the New State, despite periodical claims to the contrary by officials. The total rate of illiteracy went down slowly to the 1950's: 67.8 per cent in 1930, 55 per cent in 1940, 45 per cent in 1950. Primary schools numbered

some 7,000 in 1927, 10,000 in 1940, and 10,800 in 1950, with corresponding figures for teachers of 8,500 in 1927, 13,400 in 1940, and
14,000 in 1950. Plans for school building and effective erection of
schools were a feature of the New State era, yet they brought about a
replacement of the new for the old, rather than a significant increase
in total number. After 1950 some further steps were taken to promote
literacy: widespread campaigns for adult teaching and mass education
with considerable propaganda aims but also some real impact on illiteracy were conducted in 1953 and 1956. Primary schools reached
11,500 in 1960 and 18,000 in 1968. Illiteracy declined to 38.1 per cent
in 1960 but was still 30 per cent in 1968, which placed Portugal below
all other European countries. Elementary teaching, abolished in 1936,
again got some official support after the 1950's. Compulsory school
years increased from three to four in 1960 and then to six in 1967.
Yet the percentage of the national product applied to education was
only 1.9 per cent in 1963, indeed more than in Spain but less than in
countries like Cuba (5.8 per cent), Mexico (3 per cent) or Greece (2.1
per cent).

Secondary and technical education received comparatively more
attention from government. New high schools and technical schools
rose everywhere, school population increasing from 32,000 in 1926,
74,000 in 1940, 95,000 in 1950, 217,000 in 1960, and 350,000 in 1968,
ten times over. The number of teachers, however, did not grow proportionately, with the result that classes became larger and education
deteriorated. Nonetheless, Portuguese secondary education did retain
quality, despite the heavy political indoctrination in subjects like
history, philosophy, and "political and administrative organization of
the nation." The highly centralized education system led to the so-
called "sole books" (*livros únicos*), officially approved by the government and imposed on all schools as the only authorized textbooks. The
livro único policy was also adopted in primary schools. Several reforms
in secondary education, generally influenced by French methods, were
introduced to improve techniques and update the system with relative
success (1929–32, 1936, 1947–48, etc.).

Higher education generally declined, a result of political harassment and mistrust of instructors and students alike. Periodic purges
deprived the universities of some of their best talents, while political

reasons prevented recruiting of qualified staff, hindered promotions and shoved up mediocre but politically reliable people. In 1930 a government act created a Technical University in Lisbon encompassing the existing schools of Engineering, Business Administration, Agronomy, and Veterinary Science, but no new schools were ever established. On the contrary, the government closed down the School of Arts in Porto (1928) and the School of Pharmacy in Coimbra (1928, restored 1932), and envisioned doing the same for the Schools of Law and Arts of Lisbon. In 1933 the School of Commerce of Porto was also closed. It was only after the 1950's that the university system progressed a little, benefiting from the country's economic expansion and the enrollment of larger and larger numbers of young people (6,000 students in 1926; 9,000 in 1940; 14,000 in 1950; 20,000 in 1960; 35,000 in 1968). The School of Arts of Porto was reopened (1961), and a new School of Economics also in Porto, made its appearance (1953).

Successive reforms in each group of upper schools enhanced centralization but had very little impact on quality of education. Basically, and with a few exceptions in colleges of science and engineering, methods and subjects remained the same as before 1926, often with unchanged staffs and endowments. The public works policy led to the building of a new campus at Coimbra (started in 1948), then to the beginning of another one in Lisbon (started in 1953). In the fields of medicine and engineering, however, some real progress was achieved, with the creation of several excellent laboratories and other centers of research (Institute of Stomatology, Institutes of Climatology and Hydrology, etc.) and the development of existing ones (like the Cancer Institute). The National Laboratory for Civil Engineering, founded in 1946, quickly ranked among the best in the world.

Student organizations were either disbanded or strictly controlled by government acts. Contacts with international groups were forbidden. Official policies of enhancing the role of the Mocidade Portuguesa in the universities, however, failed utterly, and students always represented the most untamed and active focus of rebellion against the regime, particularly after 1960.

Government control of research activities led to the strengthening of the junta founded in 1924 (see chapter 12), which gradually became the only source of grants and the sole framework for post-graduate studies. Renamed Junta de Educação Nacional (1929), then Instituto para (later de) a Alta Cultura (1936), it evolved toward a highly bureaucratic organism, politically oriented and discriminatory.

Competition with the all-pervasive government control of education started only in the 1950's, with the establishment of the wealthy Gulbenkian Foundation and several other less important private groups with cultural and scientific purposes. The Church also managed to create a rudimentary Catholic University (1960's); and several private schools for less formal and more practical matters (business management, foreign languages, hotel management, tourism) opened their doors to a large audience.

Outside regular education the general development of culture was jeopardized by the growing interference of the government and its mistrust of progressive currents of thought. In the world of letters censorship operated again and again, erasing or mutilating articles, bringing periodicals to an abrupt end and preventing others from appearing. Countless book manuscripts could never be published because of editors' fears of possible consequences. Many others were confiscated shortly after publication. Similar things happened with theater plays and movies, as well as with radio and television broadcasts. Very few international movements of cultural renovation could enter Portugal on a wide basis or entered only when they were no longer new. Portuguese authors and other interested people had to travel abroad or depend upon foreign publications in order to get acquainted with the current world of culture and overcome the prevalent stagnation and backwardness at home. To their credit it must be emphasized that they always managed to keep up with what was going on in the world. Yet, curbed in their possibilities of addressing a broad audience, they had to hoard that knowledge or transmit it in a superficial and crippled way only. As a consequence, the up-to-date cultural elite contracted more and more, and became a sort of closed aristocracy whose contacts with the people tended to be narrower and narrower.

Major prose and poetry writers to the 1950's were Aquilino Ribeiro (1885–1963) and Miguel Torga (born in 1907), both Nobel prize candidates; Ferreira de Castro (born 1898) most of whose works were translated into numerous languages; José Régio (1901–69); Alves

Redol (1911–69), the greatest exponent of neo-realism; and António
Sérgio (1883–1969), the philosopher and essayist.

One of the great moments in the Portuguese cultural life in
modern times was undoubtedly the "discovery" of Fernando Pessoa's
work (see chapter 12). Unknown to most people up to the 1940's,
Pessoa quickly became one of the top Portuguese and world writers,
ranging immediately after Camões according to many critics. His
major books were all published in the 1940's and 1950's (since 1943),
and his strong impact on Portuguese literature is still hard to measure.
His works are currently being translated into English and French.

Journalism declined with the establishment of censorship and the
systematic harassment of the publication of new periodicals. The number of periodicals (some 500 in 1926) increased to 702 in 1933, then
went down to 497 in 1944. Although it went up again later (1,111 in
1967), it could never reach its former level in proportion to the literate
population of the country and in relation to its impact on public
opinion. Political reasons again were instrumental in discouraging all
kinds of literary activity, from poetry (the least hindered) to play-
writing, or in preventing the rise and development of new themes
(generally regarded as subversive). Nonetheless, the Portuguese were
able to survive and even to try some competition with foreign countries. By the mid-1960's Portugal ranked fourteenth in Europe in the
number of books published yearly (it had ranked eleventh in 1960),
which roughly corresponded to her demographic place in the continent—irrespective of her illiteracy rate—and seventeenth in the
world. In proportion to her total population this put her above countries like the United States. Translations from foreign books reached
one-fifth of the total number of books published altogether.

Political ideologies had a lesser impact on the arts, yet the trend
toward centralization in every field did influence the development of
architecture, sculpture, painting, and the other arts. Many artists were
forced into permanent exile or residence for long periods outside Portugal. The foundation of the National Secretariate of Propaganda—
later called National Secretariate for Information—in 1933 was instrumental in creating a fascist "national" style (very much influenced
by "traditional" forms), which pervaded the arts at least to the 1950's.
Under the direction of António Ferro (1895–1956), the S.N.P.-S.N.I.

undertook multiple efforts in every artistic field, mostly perhaps with typical political goals but some others with highly interesting features of art development. New trends, more liberated from official control, asserted themselves after World War II, accompanied by a younger generation of remarkable painters, sculptors, and architects. On the world scene, however, only painter Maria Helena Vieira da Silva (born 1908), who lived abroad after 1928, should be mentioned.

The Cinema declined after a brief period of timid flourishment in the thirties, when the vogue of musicals or song-based films was general throughout the world. Official insistence on old-fashioned or propaganda themes and discouragement of innovation harassed neo-realism and other modern trends, leading to the gradual vanishing of Portuguese cinema.

Science and technology developed unevenly. In some fields, such as medicine, Portugal's contribution was a major one. Professor Egas Moniz (1874–1955) received the Nobel prize in 1949 for his discoveries in brain angiography and leucothomy. He founded an important school of research in those and other fields. Tropical medicine, too, had a remarkable development in Portugal. Another good example of progress was civil engineering. Many sciences, however, stagnated or declined, for lack of funds devoted to equipment and research or because of political discrimination.

THE EVENTS

Cabeçadas' government, a compromise between the Republican public opinion and the Fascist-oriented army groups, had no basis to endure. It tried to conciliate what, by its very ideological principles, was irreconcilable. Backed by most of the Army, General Gomes da Costa staged a coup d'état (June 17) and imposed his full authority on the new cabinet. Yet his dubious reliability as a Rightist (he had belonged to the Radical Party) and his thorough ineptitude at political maneuvering led to his quick downfall. On July 9, 1926, another Army coup, directed by monarchist General Sinel de Cordes, ousted Gomes da Costa (who was arrested and deported to the Azores; he was later awarded the title of field marshal and allowed to return) and replaced him with General Oscar Carmona, a Rightist and a former foreign minister in a short-lived Nationalist government, who had little military prestige.

Up to 1928, Sinel de Cordes and Carmona ruled Portugal in a typical military dictatorship. Carmona kept the presidency but Cordes was the Finance Minister and the strong man of the new regime. He tried to reorganize finance and to balance the budget, as well as stimulate Portugal's economy. But he had no preparation for such an undertaking, and the results were disastrous. The deficit rose to an unheard-of amount and the government had to ask the League of Nations for a loan.

The dictatorship was obviously backed by a large number of people, at least in the beginning. As they were dissatisfied and united against the "status quo," they applauded the revolution, many because they were unable to understand it and many others because they thought they could take advantage of it. This was clearly true of the parties in opposition to the Democrats. But, as the Rightist elements began to take the lead and the Fascist and Monarchist trends began to assert themselves, more and more people began to regard the new regime with concern, even within the armed forces. Several groups claimed that Sinel de Cordes and Carmona had betrayed the revolution and its goals, that the Republic was in danger and the democratic institutions threatened. Indeed, the regime had established censorship of the press at the outset, along with several other repressive measures.

The growing opposition expressed itself in the usual way: force. In February 1927 a violent revolution broke out in Porto and in Lisbon, gathering together Army and Navy corps and thousands of civilians. It failed, with several hundreds dead or wounded. In July 1928 another though less serious army and civilian uprising took place in Lisbon, Setúbal, and elsewhere. This one also failed. In 1931 there were two revolts, the first one in Madeira, the Azores, and Portuguese Guinea (led by deported politicians and holding out for nearly a month); the second one in Lisbon. The government always won. Some abortive coups d'état within the leading elements themselves also took place but no essential change occurred in the regime except that it became increasingly Right-oriented. The consequences of such uprisings and conspiracies were the development and improvement of the repressive machine. Censorship was tightened up, thousands were arrested (many being deported to the Overseas), the secret police interfered more and more in everyone's daily life. Civil servants, army and navy officers, and schoolteachers were dismissed because of their hostility (or even suspicion of hostility) to the regime. Thousands fled the country and lived in exile. In this way, the dictatorship gradually got rid of its worst enemies, including most of the professional revolutionaries or conspiracy-trained elements, and was able to impose on the country a state of "peace and tranquility."

Late in 1927 it had become clear that Sinel de Cordes' financial policy led nowhere but to catastrophe. The government formally requested help from the League of Nations. Previously, it had tried to get money from foreign banks. But in Paris the main exiles, including ex-President Bernardino Machado, Afonso Costa, and several others, had warned the foreign governments that only Parliament might ask for loans of any kind, and that they would not acknowledge any loans if they ever returned to power. The League sent to Lisbon a committee of experts, who studied the Portuguese situation and set up a number of conditions for the loan involving practically international control of Portugal's finances. This the regime thought offensive to the country's independence, and the loan was rejected. It also meant the end for Sinel de Cordes. His prestige sunk to nothing; and he and his clique had to step back and be replaced by new and younger people.

Meanwhile, some dictatorial acts had changed the Constitution (which theoretically remained in force), providing for a popular presidential election. Carmona was the only candidate and was therefore elected President of the Republic. He entrusted Coronel Vicente de Freitas with the task of forming a new government (April 1928). This cabinet, totally different from the former one (the Foreign Minister excepted), included Professor Oliveira Salazar as its Finance Minister.

Less of a politician than his predecessor, Vicente de Freitas seemed to point toward a national conciliation policy within a Republican framework. Only three of the cabinet members were military, and emphasis was placed on technicians with little or no definite political affiliation. Carmona ceased to play any major role in politics. But this trend did not continue. A cabinet reshuffling in November opened the door to extreme Rightist elements in the portfolios of

Justice and Education. In July 1929 the Right wing obtained a victory
on a minor religious issue, which led to Vicente de Freitas' resignation and to the appointment of another moderate, General Ivens Fer-
raz, as premier. His intent to carry on a moderate policy of national
union failed too. In January 1930 Carmona accepted General Domingos de Oliveira, a more Right-oriented personality, as Prime Minister.
This meant Professor Salazar's nearly complete triumph.

Oliveira Salazar, a thirty-nine-year-old professor of economics at
the University of Coimbra (School of Law), was deeply involved in
politics when he accepted the Finance portfolio. He had organized
and developed the Catholic Party and had been proposed as Catholic
representative to Parliament several times, being elected once. In 1919,
he was suspected of plotting against the Republic, and dismissed from
his teaching position for several months. Far from being unknown, he
was regarded as a good deputy of the Right-wing, Catholic interests,
sympathetic to the Monarchy. Moreover, his books and articles on
economic and financial problems had made him praised and respected
by friends and foes. Cabeçadas accepted him as Finance Minister in
1926, but Gomes da Costa's coup d'état ousted him after some days in
office. In 1928 he accepted Vicente de Freitas' invitation on condition
that he would control all the private budgets of the ministries and
have the right of *veto* on every increase of expenditure.

His successful policy gained him immense prestige and made of
him the "saviour" of the country. The budget for 1928–29 envisaged a
surplus, the first one in fifteen years. His concise and quiet speech,
elegant and simple, in contrast to the usual vain rhetoric of politicians,
was pleasing to, and could be understood by, everybody. In June 1928,
for instance, he told the nation that a good policy of administration
must be "so clear and simple as any good housekeeper can make it—
a plain and modest policy, which consists in spending well what one
possesses and in not spending more than one's own resources."

Gradually, Salazar's control of the government reached the political and military. Already in 1929 he was addressing the nation on
nonfinancial problems and suggesting slogans of government in which
Right-wing nationalism was emphasized ("Nothing against the Nation,
all for the Nation"). In 1930 he made two famous speeches in which
the main points of the future organization of Portugal were clearly

defined. Behind Salazar, of course, were powerful forces: capital and banking, which wanted a free hand to expand without restrictions, protected from social claims, strikes and continuous unrest; the Church, proclaiming a new victory of the Christian ideals and morals over the Republican demo-liberal atheism, and exploiting the Fátima apparitions; the majority of the Army, constantly praised by Salazar himself, respected and granted increasing privileges; the Right-wing intellectuals with a high percentage of professors from Coimbra; and most Monarchists, firmly believing that Salazar's full control of power would give them back their king (Manuel II himself uttered explicit praise of Salazar).

The so-called "New State," as well as the National Union, or government party, were also defined throughout 1930 and 1931. The dictatorship policy regarding the Overseas also had a written expression, in a sort of code called the "Colonial Act" (see chapter 14). Opposing the regime in a legal way, a number of democrats, socialists, former 1926 revolutionaries (including Cabeçadas himself), and many others tried to organize a Republican Socialist Alliance, under the main leadership of General Norton de Matos. But the dictatorship would not tolerate it. As to the other parties, they were either disbanded or inactive. The growing repressive machine prevented every political activity outside the leading groups.

In July 1932 Domingos de Oliveira peacefully stepped down, and President Carmona formally entrusted Salazar with forming a government of his own. It included a number of young civilians, mostly belonging to Salazar's own generation or still younger, and devout admirers of his. The most promising personalities were Armindo Monteiro, a law professor and Minister of the Colonies; Duarte Pacheco, an engineer, Minister of the Public Works; and Sebastião Ramires, another engineer, Minister of Commerce, Industry and Agriculture.

Throughout 1932 and 1933, the final steps toward a Fascist state took place. Ex-king Manuel had died in England with no direct successors, and Salazar made it clear that he considered the monarchical question closed. He also proposed the dissolution of the Catholic Party, dismissed any agreements or compromises with the opposition groups, and called upon a national rally with the National Union, of which he became the leader. The draft of a new Constitution was published in February 1933 and a vote was held on March 19. According to the official figures, only 6,190 people dared to vote "No"; there were some 800,000 "Yes" and about 500,000 abstentions, which the government regarded as approving ballots according to the terms of a previously announced declaration. The Statute of the National Labor followed, along with other forms of the new corporate organization of the country. All political parties, secret societies, and labor unions were disbanded. Late in 1934 the first general elections brought to the new Parliament an all-National Union representativeness (no other candidates could be nominated). In 1935 Carmona was reelected President without opposition. Throughout 1936, two typically Fascist organizations, the Portuguese Legion, a body of volunteers for the defense of the regime, and the Portuguese Youth, a compulsory paramilitary framework for the young, made their appearance, rousing much enthusiasm and response. The "New State" seemed firmly established.

Yet dissension continued to assert itself, even within the ranks of the "Nationalists," as the partisans of the new order liked to be called. Former Premier Vicente de Freitas, the man who had called Salazar to the government, denounced the National Union as a totalitarian party and criticized the new Constitution; he was promptly dismissed from his office as President of the Lisbon municipality (1933). Reacting against the new labor organization, thousands of workers launched a general strike, partially successful (1934). In the same year, the National-Syndicalists, or Blue Shirts, a fascist group which had supported Salazar, tried a plot against his "non-revolutionary" trend. In 1935, some Right-wing and Monarchist elements were planning a military uprising in Lisbon, which was uncovered by the Secret Police. In 1936, the Spanish Civil War encouraged two battleships to revolt in Lisbon and led to a certain social unrest. The "last" effective attempt to knock out the regime happened a year later when a bomb, designed to kill the Prime Minister, failed to explode.

It was not too difficult for the dictatorship and the New State to be at ease with the foreign powers and to be accepted among them. England was very relieved to see the end of the political and social turmoil which might have endangered her economic interests and the security of the peninsula. As early as 1931 the Prince of Wales and his brother, the Duke of Kent, paid an official visit to Portugal. In France, the pressure of the exiles strained good relationships for a while but not for long. Italy, of course, had only praise for the new order. Spain, where General Primo de Rivera ruled, was the first country to welcome the new Portuguese order, modeled after that of Spain, Carmona visiting Madrid and other places in 1929, and meeting King Alfonso XIII with all his government. The proclamation of the Spanish Republic (1931) worried the Portuguese cabinet, particularly when many exiles moved from France to Spain and started benefiting from the Spanish system of freedom to organize conspiracies against the dictatorship. Yet the Spanish Republic quickly moved to the Right, and it was possible for Salazar to keep good diplomatic contacts. The Portuguese Foreign Minister, Armindo Monteiro, even paid an official visit to Madrid during 1935. The victory of the Popular Front and the outbreak of the Spanish Civil War undoubtedly worried Salazar and his partisans for some months. But as the Spanish Nationalists quickly took control of their country all along the Portuguese border, the regime felt safe again. Actually, Portugal had been a center of conspiracy against the Spanish Republic for some time, and was among the Nationalists' best friends immediately after the insurrection. During the fierce battles close to the border, Republican fugitives in Portugal were promptly turned over to the Nationalists. A privately owned broadcasting company in Portugal, fully supported by the government, decisively helped the Spanish insurgents with all kinds of information. Portuguese Fascist volunteers soon joined Franco in his struggle for Spain, estimated at 20,000 *viriatos* (volunteers), of whom 8,000 died. In October 1936 Salazar broke diplomatic relations with the Republican government, recognizing Franco as early as May 1938. Because of weapon deliveries to Nationalist Spain, Portugal even severed her diplomatic relations with weapon-producer Czechoslovakia, when that country demanded assurance that the weapons delivered to Portugal would not be sold to Spain. It should also be mentioned that within the League of Nations, Portugal always backed Italy in the Ethiopian affair.

What should be emphasized—and that to Salazar's credit—is that a new foreign policy for Portugal was in the making. While never re-

jecting the traditional alliance with England, the New State tried a
more independent and nationalist tack, which accounted for Portugal's
political sympathies. The rise of Nazi Germany, Fascist Italy, and
Nationalist Spain undoubtedly favored and conditioned that policy.
Economically, too, Salazar was trying to make Portugal less dependent
upon one country and more dependent upon several. The economic
features of the world in the 1930's and 1940's—World War II forcing
all neutral or non-occupied nations to face new choices—helped him in
that direction.

At home, Salazar's control of the regime increased as time passed.
He himself realized that a new era of consolidation had started by
1936. Besides the direction of the government, and the portfolio of
Finance, he took for himself those of War (after 1936) and Foreign
Affairs (after 1936), all of which he kept until World War II. He considered himself the guide of the nation, believed that there were things
which only he could do ("unfortunately there are a lot of things that
seemingly only I can do"—official note published in September 1935),
and convinced more and more of his countrymen of that too. His all-
pervasive interference in every field of administration even extended
to programs of celebration and festivities. In 1938, for instance, he
drafted a full program of the 1939 and 1940 commemorations of Portugal's eight hundred years of autonomy and three hundred years of
restoration of independence, down to the details of the kinds of books
to be officially published and the pageantry to be organized. He became more and more of a dictator, more and more inclined to deify
himself and to trust others less. As a result, his choice of able collaborators started to shrink, his grant of autonomy to his fellow-ministers
declined, and he relied more and more upon favorites and upon a
system of repression.

The outbreak of World War II gave him some five years of truce
at home. Most of his enemies agreed to stop any subversive action
until the end of the war. Portugal declared her neutrality from the
very beginning, and was able to enforce it because of a complex group
of motives. Salazar's cunning should not be dismissed, but Mussolini's
awkwardness in attacking Greece in the fall of 1940 and inability to
win that war without German help (the attack in the Balkans, April
1941), was the main factor that prevented Hitler from invading the

Iberian Peninsula and occupying Portugal at the right time. Franco's unwillingness to commit Spain to another war slowed down the German plans of capturing Gibraltar and later postponed them indefinitely.

Salazar's neutrality, however, had its price, and a heavy one. He swallowed his pride and tolerated the national humiliation of watching Portuguese Timor (in Indonesia) being invaded by Australia (1941), then by Japanese troops (1942), and fully occupied for three years with tens of thousands of lives lost and extensive destruction, without any response on his part, not even a break in diplomatic relations with Japan. He was also compelled to allow the Allies (Great Britain and the United States) to establish military bases in the Azores (1943) with little or no compensation. Despite a romantic eulogy to Poland, early in October 1939, Salazar's sympathies obviously were much more with Germany and Italy (so much of whose regimes he had copied at home) than with democratic Great Britain or the United States, allied to his obsessive foe, Soviet Russia. But luckily for him and the political situation he had built up in Portugal, Franco Spain remained neutral and survived the allied victory. With Franco, Salazar had signed a treaty of nonaggression and friendship as early as March 1939. Such a treaty was confirmed by a joint declaration of both countries in May 1940, followed by a protocol in July and by a meeting of Franco and Salazar in Seville, in February 1942. The so-called "Iberian Bloc" thus came into existence. This new bulwark of Portugal's external policy (a clear innovation in the country's external tradition) counterbalanced the alliance with England, which Salazar always carefully emphasized.

The year 1940 represented for the New State in all its purity the peak of glory. To commemorate the tricentennial of independence the regime organized a full set of ceremonies, expositions, congresses, and publications, of which the "Exposition of the Portuguese World" was the best example. Carefully prepared and brilliantly presented by some of the most competent architects, artists, and decorators of Portugal, the Exposition was in itself a typical Fascist display in its manner of interpreting the past and abusing it to herald the present. It could be regarded as a personal success for Salazar and for António Ferro, the able head of the National Secretariate of Propaganda, directly depending upon him.

Troubles started again with the end of the war. The allied victory in Europe (May 1945) was a pretext for pro-democratic and pro-socialist demonstrations throughout the country. For most people, and particularly for the opponents of the regime, the triumph of the democracies heralded drastic changes within the New State, if not the return to a fully democratic system. This conviction created widespread public opinion in the main cities, which questioned Salazar's achievements and continuance in power. Great Britain and the United States were also favorable to a political change in Portugal (as in Spain) and pressured Salazar about it. In September, the National Assembly was dissolved, and the government announced free elections for the coming November. Such an announcement aroused great agitation, both within and outside the regime. Tens of thousands gave their adherence to the newly created M.U.D. (Movimento de Unidade Democrática or Movement of Democratic Unity), a sort of Popular Front against the "New State." Censorship of the press was lifted during the electoral campaign, revealing widespread discontent and a wish for revolutionary changes.

The opposition soon realized, however, that the freedom granted was a very relative one, and that it had no time to promote a political organization of its own which could fight the regime at the polls. It asked for a postponement of the elections. When Salazar answered in the negative, it gave up and refused to participate. All of the National Union nominees were therefore elected without question, as before (in 1934, 1938, 1942). Shortly afterward, a vast purge aiming at those who had subscribed to the M.U.D. jailed several hundreds, dismissed many civil servants (including army and navy officials), and placed under surveillance a large number. The Secret Police was reorganized and its methods perfected; it even got a new name—P.I.D.E. (Polícia Internacional e de Defesa do Estado). All the repressive machinery was improved. Obviously, Salazar had not counted upon such a widespread movement against the regime and was both angered and worried. The same may be said of the major social and economic forces which backed him: the upper class, the Army, the Church. On the other hand, revolutionary action by the M.U.D. was discouraged by England and the United States, increasingly concerned about a Communist take-over of Europe.

From 1945 on, the existence of an opposition cannot be denied. It has expressed itself in many different ways, but it has existed as a permanent bogey to the government. In 1946, a military uprising took place in the North (from Porto to Mealhada, north of Coimbra), the first one in ten years. Although the regime put it down easily, it opened a new era of abortive plots and conspiracies. In 1947 one of the most important of these showed wide military participation, with the possible backing of President Carmona himself, who wished greater freedom of action and was tired of Salazar's leadership. The main reflex of the anti-Salazar movement, however, was shown every four years, when general elections took place, or whenever presidential elections called upon the popular vote. During the one-month electoral campaign, the government would reduce censorship to a minimum, allow open attacks on the institutions and enable the opposition to display its force and ability. Yet, as no changes took place in the electoral law and as no warrants of free balloting ever occurred, the opposition nominees either withdrew on the eve of election day or accepted competition on the uneven governmental terms and lost. This happened again and again, in 1949, 1953, 1957, 1961, and 1965. It became a matter of general strategy for the opposition and its very raison d'être; but it also became a clever safety valve for Salazar's control of the country, and a good propaganda weapon to tell the foreign countries that the Portuguese regime was not Fascist and depended upon popular support. It also hampered the opposition's legality and divided it as to the best methods for overthrowing the New State.

Until 1949 the regime undoubtedly faced a serious crisis. Many people expected the victorious Allies to adopt, in regard to Portugal, the boycott policy they were using in regard to Spain. The United Nations opposed Portugal's admission. At home there was uneasiness, many rumors, aborted conspiracies, and increasing repression. Schoolteachers and university professors were being fired. The concentration camp of Tarrafal (Cape Verde Islands) reopened its gates for the first political prisoners, most of them Communists or Communist-sympathizers. In the presidential elections of 1949 (Carmona had been reelected again in 1942, without opposition), the M.U.D. nominated aged General Norton de Matos, the former War Minister in Afonso Costa's time, and twice governor of Angola. Contrary to all forecasts,

Norton de Matos campaigned vigorously with the help of a remarkable group of advisers. He denounced all the failures and contradictions of Salazarism, pointed out the evils of repression and continuous censorship, and announced his intentions of restoring democracy to the country. Many Portuguese believed in Norton's possible victory, and Salazar may have feared it too. No guarantees of free elections were given, and when the M.U.D. nominee realized the unchanging situation, he withdrew from the race. The almost senile Carmona, despite his growing dislike of Salazar, was therefore reelected once again. Yet, in several parts of Angola, a province in which Norton de Matos enjoyed great popularity, and where electoral competition went on to the end, he won a majority.

The year 1949 was the high point for a united front against Salazar. Internal dissension, which had existed since 1945, became more and more threatening. Communists, socialists, moderates, and old democrats fought one another for preeminence, strategy, and goals. The memories of the "good old days" before 1926, and the fact that the old personalities, active in politics twenty-five years before, were the ones with prestige and political authority, plagued the Portuguese opposition with personal bitterness, rivalries, and old-fashioned ideals. This prevented the opposition from adjusting to modern times and proposing to the nation something definite, clear, and appealing. For many, to throw down the regime would mean to erase all of the Fascist legislation since 1926. But for many, benefits of all kinds had resulted from that legislation and from its practical achievements. It also became clear that the clandestine Communist Party, being the only opposition group with some cohesion and organization, tended to prove itself to the others and instill its doctrines. This further contributed to the split in the M.U.D. and provided excellent material for clever Fascist propaganda.

When President Carmona died, in April 1951, elections presented little danger to the government. The moderates nominated old Admiral Quintão Meireles, a former minister of the Vicente de Freitas' cabinet (1928–29), one of those who felt that Salazar and his partisans had betrayed the revolution. The Left campaigned for Rui Luis Gomes, a renowned mathematician and university professor. The Supreme Court denied its placet to him, on the accusation of Communism; Quintão Meireles withdrew as usual; and Salazar's candidate, General Craveiro Lopes, was elected without question.

By that time, the regime had undoubtedly overcome its first serious crisis and was gradually strengthening its position. Fearing a Communist takeover and not wanting to take risks, the Western Allies were now definitely backing Salazar. Portugal became a member of NATO from its very beginning (1949) and posed as a defender of the free world. To appease international public opinion and rising criticism of colonialism, an amendment to the Constitution repealed the Colonial Act of 1930 and introduced some changes in the status of the "natives" as well as in the official name for the colonies (from then on called "Overseas provinces"). The Soviet Union allowed Portugal to enter the United Nations, along with several other countries in 1955. At home, public works were intensified, industrialization fostered, and salaries raised. Governmental stability increased. Several foreign heads of state and cabinet members visited the country. At the same time, repression was the rule and repressive methods improved. Salazar's ivory tower had become more impregnable as he grew older; and contacts with the lower ranks of administration, as well as the people in general, altogether ceased, particularly after he dropped the ministries of Finance (1940), War (1944), and Foreign Affairs (1947), and simply remained as the head of the government. Thus, it became easier for a group of protégés and more clever advisers to surround him and make him listen to them almost exclusively. As a consequence, too, corruption within the administration seems to have grown. Coronel Fernando dos Santos Costa, the War Minister since 1944 and for a long time considered the "strong man" of the regime, gradually stood out as one of the premier's favorites and a possible successor. An extreme Rightist and Monarchist, he probably influenced Salazar to open the monarchical question again by calling to Portugal the pretender to the throne, Duarte Nuno (a grandson of King Miguel), allowing him and his family to dwell in the country, tolerating open monarchical organization and propaganda (in contrast to the Republican opposition groups), and even mentioning the possibility of a "monarchical solution" in one of his speeches. The tension between President Carmona and Salazar may have been one of the reasons behind the premier's decision to support the monarchists again.

In 1958 the second great political crisis for the regime began. Salazar's growing insensibility and unawareness of the world he was living in provoked extensive reaction, not only within the opposition ranks but among the regime's supporters. In the National Union a "liberal" wing had risen, which demanded a progressive opening up of the political structure to a larger group of persons. They required a change, or reform, in methods of administration, government policies (both at home and abroad, including the Overseas problem), and attitude toward the opposition. A younger generation of technicians and intellectuals had also matured, with no responsibilities or connections with the earlier times of the Salazar administration. They were willing to share government tasks and jobs, but they wanted up-to-date changes. Yet they deeply respected and admired Salazar, having little historical knowledge of the past and not questioning most of the regime statements in regard to the Democratic or pre-Republican period.

This "left"-wing group had been represented in government now and then. By the late 1950's, one of its leaders was Marcelo Caetano, a professor of law in Lisbon, a historian, and one of the ablest and most enlightened supporters of the regime. A former monarchist and extreme Fascist in his youth, he had gradually evolved toward a more moderate and "Center-Left" position within the National Union. He had worked with Salazar several times and been a part of his cabinet, as Minister of the Colonies in 1944–47. He returned to power in 1955 as Minister of the Presidency, a sort of vice-premiership.

The presidential elections of 1958 showed unmistakably the dissensions within the regime. President Craveiro Lopes, who had tried to be other than a puppet in Salazar's hands, was not renominated by the National Union. Instead, Admiral Américo Tomás, the Minister of Marine since 1944 and a docile admirer of the premier's, was chosen. The moderate opposition accepted Air Force General Humberto Delgado, a hot-blooded top civil servant and former partisan of Salazar's, as its leader. The extreme Left nominated Arlindo Vicente, a well-known lawyer.

Delgado proved to be the man fit for the situation. A demagogue, he easily got in close contact with the people and aroused widespread enthusiasm throughout Portugal, as never before. The Left soon re-

alized Delgado's charisma and dropped its separate candidacy, rally-
ing behind him. As in 1949 the regime feared for its survival and prepared military action in case of a possible takeover by the opposition.
Although no guarantees of electoral freedom were granted, and no
poll control by the opposition was accepted, Delgado decided to fight
to the end. Official figures gave him one-fourth of the votes (he won
in several places, including a number of towns in Mozambique), but
he always claimed to be the real winner.

Once the election was over, repression was intensified again. General Delgado was dismissed from his position, then forced to ask for
political asylum at the Brazilian Embassy. He later left Portugal for
Brazil and Algeria. Many of his partisans were fired, arrested, and
tried. The bishop of Porto, who wrote a letter to Salazar insisting
on a change of government methods and policies, had to leave the
country too. A cabinet reshuffling (August 1958), if it sacrificed Santos
Costa—who was becoming too much for the premier himself, also got
rid of Marcelo Caetano.

Political turmoil continued. A group of liberal Catholics were
now actively engaging in political activities and fighting against the
regime which, so they claimed, was jeopardizing the Church's position
with the people. In March 1959, a rebellion in Lisbon was uncovered
with the Catholics having a major role. In 1961 the general situation
worsened with the capture of the liner Santa Maria by political exiles,
in connection with the Angolan uprising in February (see chapter 14).
In April of the same year, the Minister of Defense, General Botelho
Moniz, attempted a coup d'état against Salazar, but failed. In December, the Portuguese possessions in India were invaded and lost, an
event that very much shook the prestige of the regime. All this led to
a new military uprising, on January 1, 1962, in Beja (Alentejo) where
the Under-Secretary of the Army lost his life. Finally, a widespread
student and faculty movement broke out in March (mostly in Lisbon)
and lasted through May. It included strikes, demonstrations, protests,
and massive arrests. At the beginning, Marcelo Caetano, who was then
the President of the University of Lisbon, resigned in a quarrel with
the government on university autonomy.

Yet it was still possible for Salazar to emerge victorious from this
crisis and start another period of stabilization (albeit short, and the

last one). Repressive measures hit both students and instructors. Many were expelled from the university and prevented from studying for several periods of time or altogether. Hundreds were arrested, tried, and condemned. Some teachers were dismissed and others forced to resign under several pretexts. The students did continue their fight for university autonomy and political freedom, but with much less vigor than before. Utterly divided, the opposition posed no great problems to the regime. The years after 1962 were marked by the rise of several petty groups of Chinese-oriented Communists, independent Communists, or other Marxists with different tendencies.

In 1965, Admiral Américo Tomás was reelected President. Deciding to run no more risks, Salazar had caused the Constitution to be amended (1959), providing for an election by a body of electors instead of by the people.

The main question had now shifted from Portugal to the Overseas where the African revolts, acts of terrorism, and foreign participation were worrying everyone. Guerrilla wars broke out in Portuguese Guinea (1963) and in Mozambique (1964). In Macao, the Communists imposed their authority (1966), while tolerating a theoretical Portuguese rule. The military draft was intensified and the number of years of conscription increased. Most draftees spent two years in one of the threatened Overseas provinces. Many never came back. The colonial problem helped to isolate Portugal from the other countries, particularly in the United Nations. Yet, once more the Portuguese foreign policy triumphed, by carefully exploring any dissensions among the Western powers and the African countries, granting economic privileges and interests to foreign initiatives and capital at home, as well as military bases to NATO fellow-members (Germany, France). At the same time, much more attention began to be paid to the colonies by increasingly investing money, developing local resources, and fostering economy and education. The Minister of the Overseas, Adriano Moreira, a former Leftist, played a relevant role in all this, and for a while (1961–62) he was regarded as a possible successor to Salazar. Emigration from Portugal to Angola and Mozambique soared in the 1960's, the number of white settlers doubling or trebling.

By the late 1960's, and despite the apparent maintenance of order and quiet, the regime was no longer what it had been. Division plagued its ranks; Salazar's obvious senility and inflexibility endangered administration and general policy. Control had almost completely passed on to the censorship services and the Secret Police. In February 1965, General Humberto Delgado was assassinated when trying to cross the Spanish-Portuguese border secretly. Most people attributed responsibility for this murder to the P.I.D.E. in complicity with the Spanish Secret Service (many also claimed that some Communist groups had played a part in preparing a trap for Delgado, who was threatening Communist control among the exiles). In 1968, opposition leader Mário Soares was deported to the Overseas, a fact without precedent since the 1930's. Repression haunted the late 1960's as in the days of triumphant Fascism. To many people, it became clear that something had to change in a short time.

The change came in a most unexpected way. Early in September 1968, a chair collapsed under Salazar, whose head hit the ground. The result was a blood clot in his brain. Following an operation to remove it, the premier suffered a brain hemorrhage (September 16), and his condition was soon considered hopeless for purposes of practical recovery. On September 26, President Américo Tomás, quite unwillingly, had to replace the seventy-nine-year-old head of the government and to appoint Marcelo Caetano instead. If the regime was not over, at least forty years of continuous, personal rule were.

CHAPTER FOURTEEN

THE OVERSEAS EMPIRE IN THE TWENTIETH CENTURY

POLICIES

As early as 1911 the Republic established a new ministry in the cabinet, that of "Colonies" (*Colónias*). It was a sign of the growing concern with the Overseas territories, the fulfillment of Republican promises, and a good beginning for more thorough development of Portuguese Africa and Asia. The word "colonies" meant little—a result of French influence (in France, a *ministère des colonies* existed since 1894) rather than any new doctrine in administration. From a constitutional standpoint the "colonies" were considered part of the nation as before, and the first Republican Foreign Minister, Bernardino Machado (1910–11), had clearly stated that the new government regarded the Portuguese Overseas dominions as a patrimony as sacred as the territory of the motherland itself. In the Constitution of 1911, as well as in many other official texts, the word "colony" appeared along with the word "province" with obviously the same meaning.

Nonetheless, the Republic did introduce essential changes in the Overseas administration. For at least a decade new principles of colonial government were employed to shape a more progressive Portuguese Africa and to foster its development decisively.

The "new look" was based on extensive decentralization, a trend quite characteristic of the Republican ideology since the old propaganda days (see chapter 12). Early in 1914 the Afonso Costa government (Almeida Ribeiro, Minister of Colonies) presented to Congress some basic rules of administration (Leis Orgânicas), sort of constitutional texts, which were approved in general (1914) and then in particular (1917) for each of the Overseas territories. They set up the bases for financial and administrative decentralization. They also established basic principles on how to deal with the indigenous populations. Accepting in general the doctrine espoused by António Enes and his followers (see chapter 11), the acts of 1914–17 set forth a sort of native law, totally different from the Portuguese one, and applicable to the African (and Timoran) stage of civilization. In each colony natives were to be tutored and protected by the governor and his subordinates under special legislation. Private law would follow their usages and traditions. No political rights were acknowledged to them except within their own tribal life.

The abnormal circumstances caused by Sidónio Pais' uprising (late 1917) and World War I prevented a complete enforcement of those acts. But as soon as victory came, along with the Democrats' return to power (1919), the Portuguese administration decided to carry on decentralization on a wide basis and to regulate the laws on native policy. The Constitution had to be amended to make room for the new principles. After a lengthy parliamentary debate, the bills of August 1920 introduced six new articles in the constitutional text and changed a seventh one. According to the adopted wording, the Portuguese colonies would have financial autonomy and decentralization (under supervision of the mother country), compatible with the development of each one. Special organic laws would apply to them. Functions of administration would belong to the governor of each colony, assisted by an executive council and supervised by the Portuguese Executive. When the latter thought it convenient, executive powers could be temporarily delegated to High Commissioners (a practice sporadically followed in the past), whose functions would be merged with those of governor. Indeed, the government appointed former Cabinet ministers Norton de Matos and Brito Camacho as the first High Commissioners to Angola and Mozambique. They left Portugal early in 1921.

The policy of colonial autonomy, better defined and corrected in the years following, came to an end with the gradual definition of the

New State (see chapter 13). The trend toward decentralization was reversed, and a more centralized system, similar to the one before 1914, restored. Successive laws enhanced control by Lisbon with the intent of curbing abuses and dictatorial tendencies (1926). Governors-general replaced High Commissioners again (1930). A new word, "Portuguese Colonial Empire" (Império Colonial Português), made its appearance in the official terminology. The acts of 1926 (João Belo) underlined the political unity of the colonial territories, although theoretically maintaining an administrative and financial autonomy for each of them. The policy regarding the natives changed little. In 1926 a Political, Civil, and Criminal Statute for the noncivilized Africans of Angola and Mozambique was enacted, regulating a number of principles already set forth and applied before. It was later (1927) extended to Portuguese Guinea too. Altered in 1929, the Native Statute underwent further changes a year later.

The "Colonial Act" (Acto Colonial) of 1930, in the conception and writing of which Salazar played a major role, enforced the basic principles of 1926. Conceived as a sort of Constitution for the Overseas territories (and therefore broader in scope than the Native Statute that was not suppressed by it), later appended to the Constitution of 1933, it introduced some ultra-nationalist tendencies, so dear to Salazar. Thus, its article 2 declared to belong "to the organic essence of the Portuguese Nation the historical mission of possessing and colonizing overseas dominions, as well as civilizing the native populations encompassed by them." Article 5 considered the Portuguese Colonial Empire as interdependent in its several parts and with the mother country. Article 12 forbade chartered companies but allowed the existing ones to subsist to the deadline of their contracts. Article 13 defended national interests against foreign capital. A number of other articles protected and defended the "natives of the colonies"—though no clear definition of "native" was given—with full guarantee to their property, free labor, and freedom of conscience. Yet article 20 gave the state the right to compel natives to work "in public works of general interest for the community, in occupations the result of which belongs to them, in execution of penal judiciary decisions, or for the fulfillment of fiscal obligations." Article 22 spoke of "special statutes" for the natives, according to their stage of evolution, and pledged to

respect (temporarily, one assumes) their current usages "which may not
be incompatible with morals and the admonitions of humanity."

As time passed, centralization was more and more enforced, to the
extent of condemning the pre-1926 regime as a-national. Writing in
the late 1930's, former Colonial Minister Armindo Monteiro sharply
accused the past Portuguese administrations of "renouncing its duties
to the Overseas territories" and High Commissioner Norton de Matos
of usurping powers belonging to Congress. In Armindo Monteiro's
words, "the idea of national solidarity was erased from Angola's law."

The principles of the New State concerning colonial administration were also embodied in the "Organic Charter of the Colonial Empire" and the Overseas administrative reform, both enacted in 1933.
A conference of all the colonial governors met in Lisbon in 1935 to re-
inforce the premise of solidarity. President Carmona paid a first visit
to São Tomé and Angola (1938), then to Cape Verde and Mozambique
(1939). His successors Craveiro Lopes and Américo Tomás visited all
the Overseas territories again and again. Other frequent visitors were
the Colonial Ministers.

All the legislation concerning natives defended principles traditional in Portuguese history. Its final purpose consisted in bringing
the "non-civilized" Africans and Timorans up into the European
civilization and the Portuguese nation, by means of a gradual change
in their usages and their moral and social values. Local cultures, social
organization, and law should be respected and maintained, but only on
a transitional basis. As soon as the natives were regarded as Europeanized—by learning Portuguese, going to school and becoming Chris-
tians—they received the status of "assimilated" (assimilados) and were
granted rights like any Portuguese citizen. The condition of native was
never imposed on Cape Verde, India, or Macao, where every inhabitant held the status of citizen.

The assimilado policy was logical from a European standpoint,
but it also had a number of dangers. It might tend to circumscribe the
native in a vast ghetto and make it hard for him to leave it. To state
when someone became "assimilated" was largely arbitrary and uncon-
trollable. Moreover, most of the assimilado practice took place in the
1930's and the 1940's, which were periods of stagnation for Portuguese Africa. As a result, the number of "assimilated" increased only

very slowly: some 30,000 in Angola and a little more than 4,000 in Mozambique in 1950. It is true that these figures are much behind the actuality, for thousands of "civilized" Africans refused, in their turn, to apply for an *assimilado* condition, which would force them to pay higher taxes. But it is also true that *assimilados* hardly became first-class citizens, being discriminated against both economically and socially.

After the end of World War II, anticolonialism gained a new dimension. Critics of the Portuguese colonial system arose, denouncing the serfdom of most Africans and the economic stagnation of the colonies. To appease this first wave of attacks, Salazar approved some changes in the early 1950's. The Constitution was amended, with the essence of the "Colonial Act" being inserted in its text as title 7, under the heading "On the Portuguese Overseas." The words "colony" and "colonial" altogether disappeared, giving way to "overseas province" and "overseas." The official designation of "Empire" faded away. The condition of "natives" was officially defined as transitory (1951). A new "Organic Law" (Lei Orgânica do Ultramar Português) appeared in 1953, followed by a more enlightened Statute of the Portuguese Natives of the Provinces of Guinea, Angola, and Mozambique (1954).

In this way, the Portuguese government could evade the Charter of the United Nations with all of its clauses on the responsibility and the duties of colonial countries regarding dependent territories. Portugal simply ignored resolutions like the one of November 1960, requiring her to report on her colonial management without delay. Similar resolutions have been passed again and again to the present, with the same fate. Addressing the National Press Club at Washington, in November 1967, the Portuguese Foreign Minister, A. Franco Nogueira, claimed that "we (the Portuguese) consider ourselves to be an African nation as well, through integration and multiracialism."

In 1961 the Statute of the Portuguese Natives came to an end, and all the inhabitants of Angola, Mozambique, and Guinea became full Portuguese citizens. The *assimilado* condition disappeared, and African populations were given "wider possibilities of looking after their interests and participating in the administration of their affairs." Colonial Minister Adriano Moreira (1961–62) tried to reintroduce ad-

ministrative and economic decentralization by establishing municipal
assemblies, commissions, and local committees, recognizing village
councils as local administrative bodies, granting land concessions, etc.
Although basic principles of converting the African into a European
did not change, greater attention was paid to tribal cultures and traditions, and to studying, analyzing, and even preserving traditional
practices and institutions.

The international campaign against the Portuguese colonial labor
system (see chapter 11) led to a new effort to change European-African
relationships, particularly in Angola and São Tomé. The Republican
ethic proclaimed liberty and equality for all. Republican propagandists had denounced all kinds of abuses practiced both at home and
in the Overseas provinces. No wonder that, once victorious, they tried
very hard to correct every fault in colonial administration and to introduce a new spirit of governing. On the other hand, the European
attitude toward the Africans at the time defended work as a moral and
legal obligation, a civilizing factor which every colonial power should
impose on the natives to make citizens out of them. From such a contradiction a narrow and difficult solution resulted, urging the indigenous populations to work with a minimum of force.

Governor Norton de Matos was the best-known exponent of the
Republican "new look" toward the Africans. As he clearly stated, he
found slavery in Angola "hidden, disguised, deceitful." This was indeed the situation in several other non-Portuguese colonies too, where
some form of slavery had been maintained because of labor shortages
and powerful world economic forces.

Norton de Matos curbed, as much as he could, the compulsory recruitment of African labor. The labor code of 1911 was suspended
during his governorship. He forbade corporal punishment, published
an abundant set of decrees providing official protection to the African,
curbed alcoholism, and instituted committees for assistance to the
natives. He also tried, and often succeeded, in repatriating Angolan
workers living in São Tomé. At the same time, a plan to convert many
Africans into permanent farmers was drafted and partly executed.
Norton de Matos' idea was to grant each African farmer full ownership of his plot, and to organize land cadaster, where every inhabitant,
or community, could have his name permanently registered. In this

way, he argued, a new Angola would be built, and the African need for offering their labor to the white planters would, if not altogether disappear, at least be considerably reduced.

Norton de Matos' first period as governor (1912–15) virtually changed the traditional methods of labor hiring. Free hiring contracts replaced the disguised forms of slavery. Salaries were fixed and often raised, while official surveyors inspected native conditions of life, particularly in nourishment, housing, dressing, and medical assistance. From 1915 to 1921 administrative control of these and other matters somewhat slackened, mostly because of government instability (nine governors in six years), but Norton de Matos' return with higher powers confirmed the Republican policy to the late 1920's, even after his second resignation (1924).

The 1930's and the 1940's were regressive or stagnant periods in regard to protection for the African. The Republican program required a permanent struggle against tradition, prejudice, and vested interests. Many acts had never been enforced or were just starting to be. With the change of policies in Lisbon, however, the white settlers were given a much freer hand than before. The fight against capitalist interests and their consequent exploitation of native labor slowed down. Much progressive legislation of Norton de Matos (and other governors) was forgotten or neglected. Disguised forms of slavery reappeared. A number of decrees further restricted freedom of Africans to choose where to work. Only the assistance provided by missionaries increased because of the New State's open protection of the Church.

In more recent times Mozambique, rather than Angola, became the main target of all attacks regarding forced labor hiring. Indeed, the development of South Africa as a major economic power required cheap workers from the neighboring countries, Mozambique being the obvious and easiest place to find them. The long-established emigration to the South African mines became better organized and regulated with the passage of time. An annual contingent of 50,000 African workers was regularly supplied by the Portuguese government to Transvaal throughout the whole Republican period. Many others passed the border clandestinely. An agreement signed in 1928 allowed for the recruitment of at least 65,000 and at most 100,000 Mozambicans by the Transvaal mining corporation, but such figures have rarely been reached. Export of labor, also to Rhodesia, accounted for a considerable sum in the colony's receipts. Despite an increasing concern with health assistance, and the repatriation of most workers after a period of two to three years, hiring conditions were never perfect and death rates were often high among such emigrants (4 per cent to 5 per cent in the 1920's).

Several laws (1953, 1960, 1961, 1962) have forbidden all forms of nonremunerated work and obligatory labor. Although labor conditions considerably improved from 1910 to the present (particularly after 1961), exploitation of the Africans went on, because of economic needs and long-established traditions. One form or another of compulsory labor was always present, because of "economic ills," "emergency," or similar arguments.

What must be emphasized is that economic motivations, rather than racial attitudes, generally were behind the Portuguese-African relationships. Only in Mozambique, and by no means consistently, was there some racist bias against the blacks, by Rhodesian or South African influence, and despite official efforts to the contrary. Exploitation of the native, actual (and illegal) discrimination, negligence in fostering literacy, and most other signs of a typical "colonial" regime could also be found in Portugal, where the lower classes were similarly exploited, discriminated against, and neglected in their illiteracy. The history of the Portuguese Overseas territories and the policy of Portugal in Africa in the twentieth century have to be understood as a magnified replica of the history of Portugal, with all of her slow economic development, defects in social structure, and cultural backwardness. Failure to recognize this has led to all kinds of misunderstandings and erroneous interpretations.

FROM PACIFICATION TO THE PROSPECTS OF INDEPENDENCE

By 1910 Portuguese authority was more or less respected by the native populations of Angola, Mozambique, Guinea, and Timor. The Republican administration, putting its emphasis on the civilian rather than the military, tried to avoid as much as possible "subjugation" campaigns in the traditional manner. Instead, governors were instructed to devote their energies to peaceful, yet firm and consistent, contacts with the indigenous peoples that might substitute a useful, paternalistic, and appealing image of the Portuguese for the destructive, authoritarian, and hateful image of the conqueror. Even when military force was found necessary, methods and practices of pacification were to have less violence and hero worship than before.

Military campaigns did occur in North Mozambique to 1913, in West Timor in 1912–13, in Northwest Angola to 1914, and especially in Guinea (see chapter 11) to 1915. World War I fostered some rebellions against the Portuguese by German influence, both in Angola and in Mozambique. German forces raided the border of the two Portuguese colonies as early as 1914, inflicting some casualties on the local garrisons. Lisbon sent two expeditions to Angola (1914–15) and four to Mozambique (1914–17). In Angola the fight with the Germans did not last long and was limited to border skirmishes, marches, and countermarches. South African and British troops completely occupied German Southwest Africa by the summer of 1915, which put an end to the war. Yet an African rebellion south of the Cunene River (southern Angola) late in 1914 forced the Portuguese to a lengthy and extensive campaign of subjugation to the summer of 1915 against three main tribes (the Cuanhamas, the Cuamatos, and the Evales) under the command of Lieutenant-Colonel Alves Roçadas, then of General Pereira de Eça. In Mozambique war brought about worse results. After a brief period of success (spring-summer 1916), when the Portuguese troops reoccupied Kionga and invaded Tanganyika, German counteroffensives under Von Lettow-Vorbeck pushed the Portuguese south nearly to Quelimane (summer 1918) and then retreated peacefully north again.

Summing up, World War I cost Portugal in Africa about 15,000 casualties, with some 5,000 dead and more than 10,000 wounded, among Europeans and Africans. Total effectives had reached 57,000 (32,000 Europeans and 25,000 African troops).

A few native uprisings still happened here and there in the 1920's, but with minor participation of tribes and still less impact on the colonies' general life. In the 1930's Guinea registered some agitation

too. Police operations were enough to put them down. Later, urban
rioting and protests did occur, as in Portugal, for economic reasons,
but without involving any sort of resistance to the Portuguese rule.

World War II meant a fight in Timor only. Late in 1941, Austral-
ian troops landed on the island and occupied it, despite the official
protests of Lisbon. The Japanese came next to oust the Australians,
and occupied the island in their turn, this time with open violence
and intensive destruction. Guerrilla warfare between them and small
groups of Australians and Portuguese Timorans did last to the end of
the war. When the Japanese left, in 1945, thousands of Timorans had
died in combat and in concentration camps, Dili and other towns had
been burned out, and crops were destroyed.

Although independence movements in Portuguese Africa began
only in the 1960's, their roots can be traced back to the time of the
first Republic. Unrestricted freedom of press and association encouraged several groups of Europeanized blacks and half-breeds, living
both in the colonies and in Portugal proper, to form societies and
start newspapers where they denounced the abuses of the administration. In 1920 an African League (*Liga Africana*), established in Lisbon,
tried to gather together the blacks and mulattoes who were studying
in Portugal. The League participated in the third Pan African Conference held in London and organized the second session of the
Conference in Lisbon (1923). Other societies arose in Angola and
Mozambique, all demanding more rapid development of the colonies
and equal rights for the Africans. But by the early 1930's authoritarian
repression spreading from Portugal to the Overseas muzzled open
protests and confined the African societies and newspapers to more
harmless activities. From then on, African consciousness, revolt against
Portugal, or resistance to the assimilation policy could only be expressed in literature—poetry and short stories.

After World War II the general awakening of Africa and the
widespread independence movements had their impact on the Portuguese colonies too. Several more or less clandestine groups appeared
both in Africa and in Portugal uniting Africans. By 1950, some black
and mulatto students of the University of Lisbon met and drafted a
precise program of independence under an African framework. Among
them were men like Eduardo Mondlane from Mozambique and Mário

de Andrade from Angola. Harassed by the police, they had to leave Portugal and went into exile. Later they returned to Africa and started organizing rebellions in Angola, Mozambique, and Guinea.

Theirs was a typical intellectual movement with very few contacts with the local populations. Submerged in a primitive, tribal way of life, the overwhelming majority of the Africans did not respond to intellectual activists and could not understand their goals. They had no national feeling whatsoever for "Angola" or "Mozambique," artificial creations of the late nineteenth century, which could only have meaning for the Portuguese settlers or the few Europeanized blacks and mulattoes. The peoples of Portuguese Africa, thoroughly divided by tribal (and language) differences, could hardly reach beyond their narrow horizons of local agriculture and cattle raising. Therefore, the only possible way of promoting rebellion was to foster racial hatred (black versus white) and/or to exploit discontent against physical violence on the part of the settlers.

Another possibility was to join forces with the anti-Salazar movement, launching a general rebellion against Fascism as a first step toward a subsequent revolt against colonialism. This seems to have been accepted by some Portuguese opposition groups—particularly among exiles—although one wonders to what extent they thought of it just as a political strategy to overthrow the New State. In any case, a former adviser and protégé of Salazar's, exiled Captain Henrique Galvão, was instrumental in organizing a timed revolution of both anti-Fascist and black independent activists in Angola. His plans were still broader, for they included a Portuguese-Spanish union of anti-Fascists, who would raise the banner of free Spain and free Portugal in the Spanish colonies of Fernando Po and Rio Muni (equatorial Africa) and thence proceed to Angola. For this purpose the liner Santa Maria was hijacked in Caribbean waters in the extraordinary adventure of January 1961.

Yet, if Galvão's plans failed, the Angolan uprising did not. In February 1961 some hundreds of members of the M.P.L.A. (Movimento Popular de Libertação de Angola), headed by Mário de Andrade, attacked several prisons, barracks, and the broadcasting station of Luanda. The government, however, was aware of potential rebellion and had sent troops to Angola beforehand (besides arresting hundreds of suspects and indulging in other acts of precaution), and could control the situation and rout the attackers. A widespread feeling of fear among the settlers led to the slaughtering of scores of blacks and the flight of hundreds of others, many of whom joined the insurgents. In March, tribes in northern Angola rebelled with Congolese backing and massacred several hundred settlers (including children) in a most savage way. All this brought about increasing repression from the side of authorities and whites alike, with the support of many natives as well. Hundreds were killed and retaliation was drastic, with African villages entirely wiped out and blacks hastily fleeing Angola toward the Congo. It seems that the Northern uprising was predominantly organized by another Angolan group, the U.P.A. (União das Populações de Angola), headed by Holden Roberto, a rival of Mário de Andrade's.

The rebellions of 1961 made many people, inside and outside Portugal, think that the days of Portuguese colonialism were numbered and that the granting of independence to all or most of Portugal's colonies would happen in the near future. A guerrilla war started in northern Angola, with some territory actually occupied throughout 1961. Reports of alleged Portuguese atrocities were widely publicized, and international focus on the Portuguese case attracted world attention. Yet the insurgents, like the foreign countries in general, underestimated Portugal's tenacity and capacity to deal with the war by military and other means. Relatively well-trained and well-equipped troops were sent in larger and larger numbers. The P.I.D.E. displayed no less activity, their agents in Africa outnumbering those active in Portugal. Force and terror controlled Angola in the times after the first uprising. The administration realized, however, that other means were necessary. The government's funds poured in as never before. Attention was finally paid to long-lasting claims. Africans were granted all rights, better jobs, and higher salaries. Public education and welfare were improved. Public works were intensified. In less than ten years more was done to foster the development of the colonies than in the three decades before. Quoting Douglas Wheeler, "the atmosphere of 1966–67 in Luanda is reflected in half-serious proposals that Portugal should erect a monument to the *catana,* the African field machete used as a weapon in the 1961 attacks, to honor the instrument of what many consider an economic 'miracle' in Angola." At the same time, Salazar's foreign policy aimed at getting NATO support for the Portuguese position—which could be obtained only indirectly—convincing the Western world of the advantages of Portuguese survival in Africa, welcoming foreign capital, and tightening relations with south and central African countries. Salazar succeeded remarkably well in most points. South Africa and Rhodesia became Portugal's best allies in the South, but some new black states, like Malawi and even Zambia, also accepted collaboration with Portugal because of economic advantages and technical assistance. A major power in Africa, with the second highest number of whites south of the Sahara, Portugal developed a cunning foreign policy which prevented much help to the independence cause.

Nonetheless, guerrilla warfare did not fade away. On the contrary, it increased with the outbreak of rebellions in Guinea (1963) and north Mozambique (1964). Unlike Angola, where internal dissension plagued the rebels (five major groups could be counted in 1967, subdivided in more than a dozen party units), both Guinea and Mozambique held on under nearly unified organizations. In Guinea the P.A.I.G.C. (Partido Africano da Independência da Guiné e Cabo Verde), with Amílcar Cabral as secretary-general and headquarters in Conacry (Republic of Guinea) controlled the situation on the side of the insurgents. Partly because of this, partly because of sparse European settlement, the guerrillas progressed rapidly and claimed effective control of one-third to one-half of the colony (but of no cities) by the late 1960's. In Mozambique, unity was achieved under the able leadership of Eduardo Mondlane and his FRELIMO (Frente de Libertação de Moçambique), with headquarters in Dar-es-Salaam (Tanzania). FRELIMO developed its activity in the north of the colony, claiming effective control of a small area between the rivers Rovuma and Lúrio (exactly where the Portuguese occupation was more reduced). Yet Mondlane's assassination in 1969 inflicted a terrible blow to the independence cause.

By 1968 more than 100,000 Portuguese troops were active in the three territories, yet actual confrontation only rarely happened and the great majority of soldiers went back home without having ever seen or heard the enemy. The result was that casualties were relatively few: 1,653 dead in combat to December 31, 1968. Casualties by accidents were perhaps twice as high, which raised total figures to about 5,000, i.e., as many in eight years as during World War I in Portuguese Africa. Thus the impact from actual fighting in both colonies (Guinea excepted) and in Portugal was slight, except as a source of political agitation. On the contrary, war brought about prosperity and a better way of life for thousands of soldiers, who got a higher payment than in their daily jobs at home. Coupled with an intensive nationalist propaganda carried on by the government and with brain washing at the barracks, this fact made the war, if not popular, at least not thoroughly abhorred.

The smaller colonies were not free from agitation. In São Tomé an uprising of African workers (1953), because of labor conditions, led to violent repression but also to some attempts at meeting the demands of labor. On the Gulf of Guinea coast armed forces of the newly created Republic of Dahomey ousted the few Portuguese officials from the fortress of Ajudá, after a romantic gesture on the part of their commander of setting fire to the building before surrendering (1961). In India, Nehru's administration vainly tried for years to induce a voluntary withdrawal of the Portuguese from Goa, Damão, and Diu, as the French had done with their smaller enclaves. Lisbon, however, stuck to the doctrine that such territories were part of the fatherland and could not be surrendered. Several peaceful "invasions" of the three districts by Indian volunteers began in the 1950's. The Portuguese responded by shooting and by putting many in jail. In 1954 two tiny enclaves near Damão were permanently occupied by India. Portugal filed a complaint to the United Nations (1955). At last Nehru realized that only force could make the Portuguese leave. In December 1961 Indian troops invaded Goa, Damão, and Diu. Greatly outnumbered, the Portuguese offered a symbolic resistance only, Governor-General Vassalo e Silva surrendering without further question. After a few months, all the Portuguese and thousands of Goans were repatriated. Once in Lisbon, Vassalo e Silva and his military staff were court-martialed and expelled from the army.

In Macao, the political opposition between Fascist Portugal and Communist China led to intervention by China and quasi-occupation of the town. Chinese pressures began in the early 1950's; in 1955–57 they prevented official celebrations of four hundred years of "Portuguese" Macao, alleging that Macao had always been a part of China. In the 1960's, Maoist propaganda flooded the tiny colony. When the authorities tried to resist, China fostered an uprising (1966), which compelled the governor and Lisbon to yield to every demand the Chinese asked. From then on, Macao virtually came under Communist control.

Summing up, the Portuguese Empire faced serious problems in the 1960's, with the loss of one colony, the acceptance of a sort of protectorate of another, and a guerrilla war in three more. Yet the Portuguese were able to survive, and by 1968 they controlled the situation better than they had since 1961.

THE "EMPIRE" BY THE MIDDLE OF THE CENTURY

A history of Portuguese Africa in the twentieth century should consider three principal periods: one, from the end of the military campaigns to about 1930, featured by decentralization and unbalanced development; a second one, from 1930 to the 1950's, characterized by stagnation or little growth; and a third period to the present, displaying an immense leap forward. This three-period theory more or less applies to the several aspects one might envisage.

The demographic analysis shows it clearly. In Angola the number of white settlers increased from less than 10,000 in 1910 to about 50,000 in 1930, a 500 per cent growth; after a decade of stagnation or even decline (44,000 in 1940), the white population reached some 100,000 in the mid-1950's, double the 1930 figure; yet, by the end of the 1960's, there were more than 300,000 whites, treble the preceding decade. In Mozambique white population jumped from a little more than 5,000 at the time of the proclamation of the Republic to nearly 28,000 in 1930; in 1945 it barely passed 31,000, in 1950 nearly 50,000, but it doubled in 1960 and doubled again at the end of the decade. This was the result of canalizing to both territories a part of the usually high Portuguese emigration, particularly after 1960, when the economic expansion of Angola and Mozambique started offering emigrants conditions and facilities similar to those they expected to find in foreign countries.

Changes in the number of blacks showed a possible decline in
Angola, from about 4 million in 1910 to about 3 million in 1930, although statistics are not reliable for this period. By 1950, however,
they had reached the level of 1910 again, were near 5 million ten years
later and surpassed that number by the late 1960's. In Mozambique,
black population evolved from a little more than 3 million in 1910 to
3.5 million in 1920, 4 million in 1930, 5 million in 1940, then 5,600,000
in 1950, 6,600,000 in 1960, and over 7 million at the end of the decade.

White settlers and native blacks were not the only population
groups of Portuguese Africa. Mulattoes were an important category
at the beginning of the century, their number matching or even sur-
passing that of whites in either Angola or Mozambique. As time went
by, the percentage of mulattoes declined because of increasing white
immigration from Europe. There were about 15,000 in Angola in 1930,
and only 30,000 in the mid-1950's. In East Africa they increased from
some 12,000 in 1930 to double that number in 1950. Nearly as important was the group of Indians and Orientals in Mozambique
(15,000 in 1950), a result of emigration from Goa, Macao, and other
Asian countries.

Opposition of cities and countryside increased both in Angola and
in Mozambique. While most whites, mulattoes, Asians and Europeanized blacks lived in towns, the overwhelming majority of non-Europe-
anized Africans continued to dwell in the countryside, devoted to their
traditional agricultural way of life. As in the motherland, cities totally
controlled the rest of the country, Luanda and Lourenço Marques (to
the 1950's) containing at least half of the Europeanized population
and centralizing the colony's life, exactly like Lisbon in Portugal. The
development of the Portuguese white settlement led to the foundation
of new towns or the quick growth of many others. Thus, in Angola,
Lobito rose from nothing in 1910 to the second most important town,
immediately after Luanda (50,000 inhabitants) in 1960; Nova Lisboa
(formerly Huambo), practically founded by Norton de Matos in 1912
and officially nominated as capital of Angola (act of 1928), was the
second city of the colony in 1950 and the third ten years later (40,000
people); Malanje, Sá da Bandeira, and Carmona, almost nonexistent at
the beginning of the century, had risen to fifth, sixth, and seventh
places in the 1960's. Luanda, however, became the great metropolis of

Portuguese West Africa, the second Portuguese town immediately after Lisbon and a large city on the continent: 15,000 inhabitants in 1910, 30,000 in 1923, 60,000 in 1940, 140,000 in 1950, 225,000 in 1960, nearly 500,000 in 1968, with an ever-increasing proportion of whites. In Mozambique the urban structure was somewhat different; Lourenço Marques being located too far south, there was a quick development of other towns scattered all over the country, the growth pace of which it was unable to match. Thus, being five times larger than the second city in 1910 (some 15,000 people against 3,000 for Beira), Lourenço Marques' lead declined to less than double in 1928 (37,000 and 20,000 for Beira), and it was narrowed considerably by Quelimane in 1960 (64,000 against 78,000 for Lourenço Marques), closely followed by João Belo (49,000), Beira (45,000), Tete (38,000), Vila Cabral (28,000), and Porto Amélia (21,000). João Belo and Vila Cabral were insignificant villages at the end of World War II.

The government tried to attract Portuguese colonization to the countryside by fostering rural settlement in several places such as Cela in Angola, where settlers were forbidden to hire African labor. Mixed settlements also appeared (Cunene in Angola, Médio Limpopo in Mozambique) as well as a few for African families only (Caconda in Angola, Inhamissa in Mozambique). At the time massive emigration from Portugal was eased after the end of World War II, with the result that thousands of families started leaving Portugal for Africa year after year. Emigration of non-Portuguese to Portuguese Africa as a rule was not encouraged.

In the late 1960's, areas of higher density of population in both Angola and Mozambique encompassed the traditional coast line and plateau regions plus a number of new lands where railroad tracks passed or highways had been built. The spreading of guerrilla warfare and the consequent setting up of Portuguese garrisons all over the vast territories of the two colonies have contributed to a better knowledge of remote zones and the opening of new roads in recent years.

In the smaller colonies population patterns followed entirely different trends. Continuous growth occurred only in Guinea (343,000 in 1926, 350,000 in 1940, 510,000 in 1950, 544,000 in 1960) but at a very low rate. In the other provinces the number of people varied. In Cape Verde there were almost as many inhabitants in 1950 as fifty years before (less than 150,000) with fluctuations in the intervening years. The 1960 census registered a little more than 200,000 people. Overpopulated for its resources, Cape Verde sent emigrants in large numbers to the United States, Brazil, and other countries. In São Tomé, population declined to the 1950's (68,000 in 1910, 56,000 in 1950), then went up a little (63,000 in 1960). Again, the two small islands had reached their demographic limit. Portuguese India's population declined, then went up (like all of India) to the 1950's: 550,000 by 1910, 432,000 in 1926, 580,000 in 1930, 624,000 in 1940, 637,000 in 1950; the troubled political situation afterward led to a decline again, thousands having migrated to the Indian Union as well as to Mozambique and British East Africa (a traditional trend). On the eve of its loss by Portugal, Goa had only 626,000 inhabitants. Macao's population varied widely, due to immigrants from neighboring China. During World War II it may have reached 400,000 or more. Again, the Communist takeover flooded Macao with fleeing Chinese. The 1950 census registered 188,000 inhabitants, that of 1960 only 169,000, a figure already too high for the small size of the colony (16 square kilometers). In Timor the population grew up to the war, then declined because of killings and migrations: 440,000 in 1926, 460,000 in 1940, 442,000 in 1950, 517,000 in 1960. Consequently, and with the exception of Macao, no large towns have risen in any of these territories, where urbanism has been slow to develop. Provincial capitals varied between a few thousand (Dili in Timor) and the 20,000 reached by Pangim (Portuguese India) and Bissau (Guinea) in modern times. The latter gradually surpassed Bolama, Portuguese Guinea's former capital, and became the seat of administration.

Percentages of whites and half-breeds did not undergo essential changes. In Cape Verde mulattoes always predominated, in Portuguese India and Macao there were considerable numbers of mixed natives. In Guinea, São Tomé, and Timor the overwhelming majority were pure natives. In all cases (Cape Verde excepted) whites and half-breeds lived in towns, engaging in trade and administration rather than agriculture.

An important step in the regular organization of Angola, Mozambique, and Guinea consisted in substituting the civil for the military administration. At the time of the proclamation of the Republic, each of the two big colonies was generally divided in a certain number of districts (*distritos*), subdivided into captaincies-major (*capitanias-mores*), which further comprised administrative posts (*postos adminis-trativos*). In Guinea there were no districts, and captaincies-major were called residencies (*residências*). There were also a few municipalities (*concelhos*) in some districts where European density was greater. In every case the military prevailed over the civilian, and military organization characterized the three levels of the administrative system.

In 1911 a first attempt was made in Mozambique to introduce civil units in some areas. But it was in Angola that Governor-General Norton de Matos systematically fostered the new principle by creating in 1912 thirty-five administrative circumscriptions (*circunscrições ad-ministrativas*) at the second level, coexisting with the captaincies-major (twenty-five), the number of which significantly decreased. Eleven municipalities also came into existence. Gradually, the new civil units prevailed over the military, which altogether disappeared in 1921. The Angolan administrative reform of that year (Norton de Matos' second government) created eleven districts, sixty-five circumscriptions and 287 posts, besides thirteen municipalities. Progress in Angola's occupation had increased the number of districts to fourteen and the circumscriptions to eighty-two when Norton de Matos quit, in 1924. There were no significant changes to 1936 (though the number of circumscriptions declined), when a new administrative reform introduced larger units known as provinces (as in Portugal) and increased the municipalities to thirty, facing thirty-six circumscriptions. The reform of 1954 abolished the provinces, reduced the districts to thirteen, and registered fifty-five municipalities against only twenty circumscriptions, a step forward in the Europeanization of Angola's administrative system. In Mozambique the trend toward civil circumscriptions, later replaced by municipalities, followed a similar, if slower, pace. From the beginning of the century to 1936, there were five districts (a military territory, still existing in 1910, was shortly afterward annexed to Lourenço Marques), plus the areas administered by the two chartered companies. After 1935 the district of Mozambique absorbed the Nyasa Company territory. The reform of 1936 created three provinces, six districts—a fourth province and a seventh district appeared in 1941 with the territory of the Mozambique Company (the

UPPER LEFT: *Norton de Matos*. LOWER LEFT: *Marcelo Caetano*. BELOW: *Cambambe Dam, Angola.*

company charter ended in that year)—sixty-six circumscriptions and twelve municipalities. Districts were later increased to nine. In 1963 provinces disappeared, districts remained the same, but the number of municipalities increased to thirty-two against sixty-one circumscriptions. The greater backwardness of Mozambique in contrast to Angola is easily perceived by comparing such figures.

In Guinea, São Tomé, Macao, and Timor no districts or provinces were ever created. Guinea had two full municipalities in 1910, the same two in the 1920's and the 1930's, three in the late 1950's and nine in 1968. Timor kept its sole *concelho* to the present. Both colonies also had circumscriptions. In São Tomé, Macao, Cape Verde, and India full municipal organization was achieved very soon, no circumscriptions having ever been established. Two districts were set up for Cape Verde (1963) and three for Portuguese India, which dated from monarchical times.

General administration in each colony included local organs, such as the Legislative Council created in 1920 and several times reformed, an Economic and Social Council for Angola and Mozambique; and a Council of Government for the smaller colonies. Their powers varied according to circumstances but generally had little impact on the highly centralized colonial system.

The economic development of all the Portuguese Overseas provinces, but particularly Angola and Mozambique, was irregular and uneven. In most of the period 1910–68 the colonies—Guinea excepted—depended upon foreign markets and foreign capital more than on Portugal's. The wide fluctuations in the demand for tropical and equatorial products have had tragic consequences for colonial economies.

But the development of backward territories is also an outcome of good administration and of able statesmen. An exceptional leader like Norton de Matos (1912–15; 1921–24) followed, to a certain extent, by Vicente Ferreira (1926–28), was able to give Angola the impetus to put her ahead of Mozambique in European penetration and (later) economic development. Yet, by 1910 Mozambique's revenues and expenditures were double those of the West Coast colony, and its total volume of trade was also double Angolan trade. It was only in the late twenties and the thirties that Mozambique began to lag.

Until the first years of the twentieth century, rubber was the chief product exported by Angola and the main source of its revenues. Wax, coffee, fish, and hides followed, but at a great distance. This was still the situation in 1910, although the decline in demand for rubber—a consequence of the world's rubber crisis—was noticeable. From 1911 on, rubber exports fell sharply and Angola faced a difficult period of adjustment till World War I. Governor Norton de Matos succeeded in developing a number of cultures, namely those related to improved European settlement and traditional African agriculture: maize and beans, for example. He also fostered cotton, coffee, and sugar production. In the 1920's both coffee and cotton were on their way up, while coconut, palm oil, and wax provided important revenues too. Sugar faced a general crisis. After 1921 diamonds started giving Angola a new source of wealth.

Norton de Matos' second government, which elevated Angola and made of it the most important Portuguese colony to the present, brought about a difficult crisis (economic and financial) further aggravated by the High Commissioner's forced resignation in 1924. His successors were unable to slow down the crisis, which worsened with the beginnings of the world depression. Angola's development came to an end and stagnated up to World War II.

In the 1930's coffee had become number one in the colony's exports, followed by diamonds, fish meal, maize, cotton, and sisal. When coffee went down, again because of the world crisis, diamonds replaced it, maize took second place, and sugar and cotton came next. By the late 1940's coffee was back as Angola's main wealth, and so it has remained to the present. Diamonds, sisal (a prosperous culture because of World War II, the Korea war, the Vietnam war and all wars in general), maize, sugar, and cotton followed. In the 1950's iron ore was discovered and quickly ranked among Angola's sources of income. So did oil, actively explored in the 1960's.

Foreign investments were encouraged, and extensive economic concessions were granted to a few powerful companies. The *Diamang* (Angola Diamond Company), with Portuguese, Belgian, French, English, and American capital, founded in 1917 and given the first important privileges under Norton de Matos in 1921, saw its concessions further enlarged and confirmed. It became a true state within Angola, a sort of new Mozambique-type company, with exclusive rights to diamond extraction all over the colony and extensive authority over several thousand square miles. It organized its own police system, built its own road system, and created its own towns (e.g., Henrique de Carvalho, Portugália). It also patronized some interesting cultural activities shown by the establishment of a museum and the annual publication of monographs on African ethnography, geology, botany, zoology, and history.

Figures for external trade clearly show the several periods of Angola's economic development. To the early 1920's, the colony progressed little. Exports and imports displayed few variations and even indicated some decline during World War II if one recalls the debasement of the escudo. Yet surpluses in the balance of trade happened now and then, and deficits were generally small. In the 1920's both imports and exports increased, a result of Norton de Matos' policy. Angola's crisis and the depression put them down again. In 1936 Angola exported scarcely more than in 1924 and imported far less. World War II unleashed a continuous leap forward in both exports and imports: export figures for 1945 were almost double those of 1938, but figures for 1948 were more than double those of 1945. Expansion slowed down from 1954 to 1961 but from then on it reached levels unheard of, export figures for 1967 doubling those of ten years before. As to the balance of trade, it was consistently positive from the early 1930's on, to the 1950's. Portugal always was Angola's main partner, both for imports and exports, yet her position as a buyer generally declined to the late 1950's, as colonial trade with foreign countries developed. Exports to Portugal declined from 90 per cent (by 1910), to 77 per cent (1913), 53 per cent (1923), 57 per cent (1933), 39 per cent (1943), 21 per cent (1953), 25 per cent (1963), and 36 per cent (1967). As to imports, the figures were about 90 per cent (1910), 77 per cent (1920), 54 per cent (1922), 51 per cent (1933), 74 per cent (1943), 48 per cent (1953), 48 per cent (1963), and 38 per cent (1967).

Government plans for general economic development began in Angola prior to those in the motherland. A first Plano de Fomento started in 1938, followed by a second in 1945 and a third in 1951. In 1953 the launching of the first of such plans in Portugal brought the Angolan ones to an end, because it encompassed all the Portuguese economic area, including the Overseas provinces.

A public works policy, actively carried on since 1912 (initiated by Norton de Matos), helped in the development of Angola. There were at the time 100 km. of roads and less than 1,000 km. of railways. Twelve years later the road network reached 25,000 km. (nine-tenths of which were built in 1912–15 and 1921–23), while railroads covered more than 1,500 km. Afterward the growth slowed down: to 1933, 10,000 km. more of roads were built, but from then on, to 1960, the road network stagnated. A new leap forward only began in the 1960's: 35,500 km. in 1960, 72,000 in 1967. Railroads progressed to the late 1920's: the Moçâmedes line was continued to Sá da Bandeira (1923); the Benguela line reached Huambo (now Nova Lisboa) in 1912, then Silva Porto (1922), and finally the border with Congo (1929), more than half of its whole course being built in 1926–29; a new track was built from Porto Amboim inland (1923–25) in central Angola. The total network exceeded 2,000 km. at the time of World War II. Since then several small branches of the main lines have been opened to traffic, while the Amboim and the Moçâmedes ones progressed a little longer. The total network encompassed 3,200 km. in 1965–67. Air transport services came into existence in 1938, planes reaching most of Angola during the 1950's and enlarging their flights afterward. Sea communications with Portugal and other countries improved considerably, as more and better ships were acquired by Portuguese maritime companies, and port facilities were improved. Lobito became the first port of Angola after the extensive works carried on since 1922 and the completion of the Benguela railroad. Luanda came second, then Moçâmedes and many others. As in Portugal several big dams were begun, particularly in the 1940's and the 1950's, with the main purpose of supplying electric power and irrigating vast areas.

The economic development of Mozambique followed a different pattern. More than half of the colony belonged to three private companies (see chapter 11), two of which were chartered. Their lands were among the oldest colonized by the Portuguese and where European settlement was most developed. This means that the Lisbon government had to invest much less in Mozambique than in Angola to obtain similar results but also that sheer economic problems, such as international economic conjunctures, would have a much greater impact than in Angola.

Up to the 1960's public revenues of the colony were consistently

higher than in Angola. So was external trade, if one added the values
of exports (or imports) from the Lourenço Marques–administered part
to those from the chartered companies. Yet Mozambique had fewer
Europeans, a more irregular distribution of white population, and a
smaller road and railroad network.

Altogether, Mozambique's main production and sources of wealth
did not change much in fifty years. As in Angola rubber played a major
role at the beginning of the century, but not so exclusively as on the
West Coast. Oleaginous products (copra, sesame, peanuts) actually
held first place, and kept it to the present. Sugar came third. When
rubber declined and finally disappeared, sugar held second place,
followed by sisal and cotton. Such was the situation in the mid-1920's
and the mid-1960's the only difference being that cotton and sugar
changed places. Tea also became a major source of wealth.

The Mozambique Company prospered and contributed to the
colony's development to the mid-1920's. Its exports generally surpassed those of the rest of the province (Nyasa Company included),
despite the fact that it encompassed only one-sixth of Mozambique's
territory and one-tenth of the colony's population. The Beira railroad
and the Beira port permitted an ever-increasing international traffic.
Beira had become the second town of Mozambique (20,000 in 1928),
much ahead of any other. The Company had proportionally opened
more schools and could register a higher attendance than the govern-
ment-administered sector (1930: 6,402 grammar-school pupils against
42,868; 1940: 8,408 against 72,154). It built new railroads, opened a
substantial road network, and made several other improvements.

An economic and financial crisis began to affect the Mozambique
Company by 1923–24 with dramatic results. Exports went down
sharply (figures for 1927 were one-third of 1922). A slight recovery in
1928 was negated by the outbreak of the depression, which thoroughly
ruined the Company's external trade and main source of prosperity.
In 1933 exports had declined to 0.7 thousand gold contos in contrast to
2.6 thousand in 1927 and the peak of 8.7 thousand in 1922. Although
the situation improved in the following years, exports were still at the
1.3 thousand level by 1940, the eve of the Company's last days.

Completely different was the Nyasa Company's troubled existence.
It never had the means, nor perhaps the able administration, to carry

on the development of a vast region with little European penetration and settlement. It never built any railroads, and only a few roads resulted from its action. Its capital cities, Ibo, then Porto Amélia, never went beyond the level of tiny villages (Porto Amélia had 1,633 inhabitants in 1928, of which only 67 were whites). It suffered from World War I, being invaded by the German forces from Tanganyika, which ravaged a part of the territory and were expelled only in 1918. Its trade movement was relatively small, stagnant, or in decline, with a few years of prosperity (1911–12; 1926–29). When it ended its days, in 1929, exports reached one-fourteenth of the colony's and one-fourth of the Mozambique Company's. Yet it encompassed one-fourth of Portuguese East Africa, with one-eighth of its total population. For the Lisbon government the inheritance of the Nyasa Company was a heavy burden.

The Republican decentralization system and the High Commissioner regime failed to foster Mozambique's development as it did Angola's. Governor Alvaro de Castro (1915–18) and High Commissioner Brito Camacho (1921–23), probably the two most energetic leaders appointed by Lisbon, were in no way comparable to Norton de Matos. Mozambique somewhat stagnated to the late 1930's, when public revenues started increasing. From 1935 to 1945 revenues doubled, then doubled again in five years, and again to 1955. From 1955 to 1967 they doubled once more, yet the pace of growth was lagging behind that of Angola. From 1965 on, Mozambique's revenues were below those of the West Coast. In trade, World War II again was a major stimulating factor, but surpluses were lacking and the total trade volume was below that of the other coast. The balance of trade showed a consistent deficit, although exports very much increased; in 1967 they were double the value of ten years before. However, receipts from transit trade, migrant earnings, and tourism resulted in a satisfactory balance of payments. All this means that Mozambique paid more to the government (because it possessed a tighter and more developed capitalist structure and a larger population) but was actually poorer in economic resources.

The Republican period meant for Mozambique a considerable development of substructures, namely port equipment and railroads. Lourenço Marques and Beira, due to their international importance, were equipped with modern facilities and therefore attracted most of Transvaal's and Rhodesia's traffic. New railroads were built in the South (Goba line, reaching the border with Swaziland, opened 1912; Limpopo line, connecting Lourenço Marques with Rhodesia, opened 1914; and other smaller ones); the Center (Tete and Quelimane lines); and the North (Mozambique line connecting the coast with Vila Cabral, started 1924). Therefore, the railroad network jumped from 500 km. in 1910, to almost 1,000 in 1920, and 2,000 in 1925. Growth continued in the 1930's, with 2,500 km. in 1935. A period of stagnation followed, but enlargement of the railway network was resumed from the 1950's onward: 2,700 km. in 1955, 3,200 in 1960, more than 3,500 in 1967.

Other public works included roads: 14,000 km. in 1928, 24,000 in 1940, 37,000 in 1955, 38,000 in 1967; dams; schools; and the usual public works also displayed in the mother country as a token of the New State administration.

Industrial development in both colonies drew comparatively much less attention. To the 1960's Portugal followed a typical colonial policy of fostering the production of raw materials but discouraging industrial activities in the Overseas provinces. Only the rubber and textile industries had some significance by the late 1950's. The outbreak of the guerrilla war changed the whole picture and brought about a quick industrial rise, which it is still too early to appraise from a historical standpoint.

The existence of the smaller colonies, Macao excepted, was not an easy one. Efforts to develop Angola and Mozambique often led the Lisbon administration to forget or neglect the other ones. Their economies and financial situation were far from brilliant, despite the fact that they frequently displayed surpluses in the balance of trade and the budget. The usual deficits found in Portugal or in Angola and Mozambique, up to the time of the New State, did not often exist in the smaller Overseas territories. In Cape Verde, for instance, budgets were balanced in difficult years such as 1916, 1917, 1919, and 1920. São Tomé's relative importance declined, yet the colony continued to be the largest or one of the largest producers of cacao and to prosper economically. Since the 1930's, the policy of "solidarity" among the mother country and all the colonies, coupled with the absolute re-

quirement of presenting balanced budgets every year (not always accomplished), has meant that the most prosperous territories paid for
the least prosperous ones, and all "re-paid" the mother country her
"loans."

In general one can say that the smaller colonies stagnated to the
1950's, when their economic expansion followed world prosperity, Portugal's, and that of their two big partners, Angola and Mozambique.
Public revenues doubled or more than doubled in Cape Verde,
Guinea, Macao, and Timor in 1958–67, while in São Tomé revenues
increased more than 50 per cent. In Portuguese India public revenues
had expanded six times since the late 1940's when Indian soldiers cut
it off from the Portuguese. In Guinea, exports sharply declined after
the beginning of the guerrilla war and the occupation of vast areas by
independence supporters.

From the 1950's onward, the New State administration envisaged
a common market (escudo zone) area for Portugal and the Overseas
territories. For that purpose tariffs were to be gradually reduced to
complete extinction over a ten-year period starting with 1962. The
partial execution of such an ambitious plan brought about closer
contacts between Portugal and all of her colonies.

Well aware of the importance of Catholic missions to Europeanize the Africans, the first Republic did not impose on the Overseas the
anticlerical policy followed at home (see chapter 12). Nonetheless the
Separation Law of 1911 foresaw a complete withdrawal of all religious
orders and their replacement by secular clerics. At the same time it
provided for the establishment of lay missions (called "civilization
missions") with teaching purposes void of any religious ideology.
Their missionaries (male and female) were to be properly educated at
home and possess a minimum training as instructors in Portugal. Even-
tually the lay missions would entirely replace the Christian ones.

None of these projects could be fully enforced. Few missionaries
belonging to orders ever left because of the Republican legislation.
Local circumstances justified their permanence and required a provisional suspension of the law. Persecutions were few and did not last.
Yet, as Catholic missions were not encouraged by the authorities,
competition by Protestant and even Moslem centers developed, arousing some protest and fear of "denationalization." After 1919 the Lis-

bon government decided to interfere and curb the free establishment
of foreign or non-Catholic missions, forcing them to comply with a
certain number of rules. Catholic missions recovered some support in
the early 1920's. On the other hand, the lay missions had little time
to develop and prosper, notwithstanding the important subsidies
which the law granted them. Only nine had been created in Angola
and five in Mozambique, when they were abolished in 1926 after the
Rightist takeover in Portugal. Full protection to the Catholic missionaries was restored again.

The new Organic Statute of the Portuguese Catholic Missions
(1926) enforced the nationalist spirit so dear to the "new order." It
repressed foreign and non-Catholic missions, increased subsidies, and
openly favored the Catholic priests. The Church was given a free hand
to operate in all Portuguese colonies under a highly privileged situation. The Concordat of 1940 (see chapter 13) and the Missionary
Agreement of the same year, both signed with the Vatican, further enhanced the possibilities of the Church in Christianizing and civilizing
the natives.

The number and equipment of missions, however, always failed to
meet the requirements of mass evangelization. In Angola, statistics
showed only 24 missions in 1910, 49 in the mid-1930's, 93 in the
1950's, and more than 200 by the early 1960's; in Mozambique there
were some 25 missions in 1910, 30 in 1930, 60 in 1940, double that
number in the 1950's and double again in the 1960's. Religious missions also maintained rudimentary and elementary schools. But with so
few effectives, their action had to be a limited one. Both in evangelization and education, results were far from brilliant. In the mid-1950's
the official number of Catholics (an estimate many considered too
optimistic) slightly surpassed one million in Angola (i.e., one-fourth of
the total population, facing more than half a million Protestants),
350,000 in Mozambique (one-fifteenth of the population against
500,000 Muslims), 66,000 in Timor, and 19,000 in Guinea.

An important result of the agreements between Church and state
after 1940 was the thorough reorganization of the ecclesiastical structure in the Portuguese Empire. In that year Angola and Mozambique
were raised to archbishoprics (with seats in each colony's capital), two
other dioceses being created in Angola—Nova Lisboa and Silva Porto

—and two in Mozambique—Beira and Nampula. Guinea was also separated from Cape Verde in 1940 and in 1955 it was made an apostolic prefecture. In Timor another diocese came into existence (1940). In this way ecclesiastical organization did coincide with the political shape of the Portuguese Empire, as in the sixteenth through the eighteenth centuries. Later development of both Angola and Mozambique led to new dioceses: Sá da Bandeira (1956), Malanje (1957), and Luso (1963) in West Africa, and Quelimane (1954), Porto Amélia (1957), Inhambane (1962), and Tete (1963) in East Africa. Ecclesiastical and civil districts were made almost coincident. In the East, the relative decline of the Portuguese influence put an end to the right of Patronage, which the Holy See practically abolished under agreement with the government of Portugal (1950), after considerable limitations since 1928.

Cultural development lagged much behind the economic. For many years, only Cape Verde, Macao, and Portuguese India had some educational framework worth mentioning. At the time of the proclamation of the Republic there was no secondary teaching whatsoever in the remaining five Overseas provinces.

Primary schools were ridiculously few for the total population. Angola had some fifty of them only in 1910, Mozambique perhaps double that number. For Guinea, São Tomé and Timor the figures were proportionately lower. In contrast, Cape Verde could boast ninety grammar schools, with Macao and India not too far behind. Aside from these three colonies school attendance was overwhelmingly restricted to the European or half-breed population.

Emigration increase and the Republican policy of fostering education brought about the need for more primary schools and the beginnings of a somewhat higher education. In Angola, grammar schools rose to eighty-four in 1923 plus half a dozen technical schools. The first *liceu* (high school) opened its doors in Luanda in 1918. Most of the rise had taken place during Norton de Matos' two administrations. In Mozambique education developed at a more rapid pace: 129 grammar schools in 1918 and 225 in 1926 (of which more than a half belonged to Catholic missions). High school teaching was carried on in two different places and there were several technical schools as well.

To the end of World War II education stagnated, or advanced

very slowly. In 1945 Angola had 129 primary schools with 8,000 pupils, Mozambique 822 with 120,000 (statistics in this case follow a different method, for they refer to the pre-primary teaching of African students as well), Guinea 44 with 870, São Tomé 14 with 1,700. Timor, just emerging from a destructive Japanese occupation, was reorganizing its educational system. The better-developed colonies displayed 100 schools with almost 6,000 pupils (Cape Verde), still surpassed by India (more than 10,000), and Macao. Secondary teaching showed higher figures in proportion, with 32 high schools and technical schools in Angola and 45 in Mozambique.

The great leap forward happened in the 1950's and the 1960's in all the Overseas provinces but especially in Angola and Mozambique. Figures for the school year 1966–67 showed 3,171 primary schools in Angola with an enrollment of 264,836. Mozambique's growth was still larger, both in schools (3,667) and pupils (468,983). Educational reforms in the 1960's created a unified governmental system for both rural and Europeanized Africans (together with the children of white settlers), all mission schools being officialized and instructed to offer the same kind of instruction everywhere. Methods of teaching Portuguese to the African pupils ranged among the most advanced in Africa. Textbooks—illustrated with pictures and stories from Angolan and Mozambican life—were of higher quality than those used in Portugal. Secondary education revealed a smaller, yet important, increase: 95 high schools in Portuguese West Africa, 84 in East Africa with student contingents more than ten times higher (Angola) and nearly four times higher (Mozambique) than in 1945. The need to respond to autonomist tendencies led the government to create universities in both colonies (1963), which developed rapidly.

In the other territories growth was less spectacular yet thoroughly positive. Secondary education was introduced in Guinea, São Tomé, and Timor. By the late 1960's the educational system in the Portuguese Overseas provinces, although far from being the best in Africa, showed an undeniable capacity for quick growth and could compare favorably with many others on the Continent.

The great question, undoubtedly, was how to provide mass education to the African rural populations. Christian missions had been making remarkable efforts in that direction, but they were never enough. Rates of illiteracy were still over 90 per cent in Guinea, Mozambique, and Angola (in 1950 they were, respectively, 98.85 per cent, 97.8 per cent and 96.4 per cent), over 80 per cent in São Tomé, and over 70 per cent in Cape Verde. In Angola and Mozambique hundreds of thousands, even millions, of remote Africans had no contact whatsoever with the Portuguese culture and were unable to speak Portuguese. In Macao constant migrations and countermigrations made percentages meaningless. In India, when the Portuguese left in 1961, the rate of illiteracy was above 70 per cent (78.3 per cent in 1950).

CONCLUSION

The appointment of Marcelo Caetano as Prime Minister was received with a mixture of hope, skepticism, and fear. Many people naively expected a radical change in policies, a practical end to the New State, with a gradual return to a regime of freedom and democracy. Others, who saw in both Salazar and his successor only symbols, thought the well-woven fabric of government had not been destroyed or even touched. Consequently, they expected little or no change. Many others were afraid of a troubled period following Salazar's retirement—either a Leftist takeover or the seizure of power by ultra-Rightist elements.

Marcelo Caetano's policy was extremely cautious. Well aware of the difficult situation he had inherited, he tried to keep things stable, making only slight and barely perceptible changes. He knew that powerful forces (the Army, the Navy, the police bodies, the top capitalists and bureaucrats, and a part of the Church hierarchy) were watching him closely and that he would have their support only if they were sure that "stability" and their vested interests would prevail. On the other hand, being in close contact with many opposition intellectuals and an intellectual himself, and fully realizing that times had changed, he felt he could not entirely shun a policy based upon some opening to the left and some appeal to the various opposition groups. Thus, as people said jokingly and as he himself quipped, he signaled "Left" and turned "Right."

To signal "Left" meant that he compromised on some minor, harmless points. He recalled opposition leader Mário Soares from his São Tomé exile and welcomed back many others, including the bishop of Porto, who had been forced to leave in 1958. He curbed the activities of the P.I.D.E., and he eased press censorship. He allowed a congress of opposition elements to meet in Aveiro under cover of being a historical "Republican Congress." Bookstores started to display all kinds of "subversive" works, which would have been immediately confiscated before. Theaters exhibited much more daring movies and plays. In public places people felt they breathed easier and talked more freely.

The turn "Right" was to maintain the New State structure. Salazar-appointed cabinet ministers were replaced only gradually by Marcelo Caetano's men, four of the Salazar men still ruling by the summer of 1970. Portuguese troops continued to be sent to Africa to fight the rebels. Political parties were not allowed. No amnesty was granted. Freedom of association was denied. There were no changes in foreign policy. The corporative framework was not touched. No press law appeared. Nothing in essence had really changed two years after Salazar's downfall.

The general elections of November 1969 may have been a turning point in Portugal's political life. For the first time in forty-four years the opposition went to the polls in almost all the districts of Portugal. And for the first time, too, free elections were held in several places though by no means in all. Women were allowed to vote. Opposition candidates belonged to several groups, officially designated as "electoral committees." In most of Portugal unity of opposition forces could be achieved, but in Lisbon and Porto the Communist-oriented and the Socialist-oriented factions broke apart. There were also Monarchists and even dissidents from the National Union. Yet, as no political parties were permitted and as electoral activity could only develop in the month prior to the elections, the opposition had no chance to break through the National Union's powerful machine. Many of the eligible voters had not registered and many others had been removed from the balloting lists. Trusting neither government nor opposition many people decided to stay home and await the outcome, with the result that the number of abstentions, particularly in large towns, surpassed the number of votes. Moreover, the law provided for election only if a candidate obtained 50 per cent of the ballots. With no representation allotted to minorities, the opposition lost everywhere, and once more the National Assembly was composed of one-party representatives. Nonetheless, dissent within the official party became somewhat more common. A group of young people believed in opposing the regime within its own framework. In the new National Assembly one-fourth to one-third of the representatives displayed some "heretic" tendencies and angry voices rose against the "immobility" of the administration. The official party itself changed its name to Popular National Action (Acção Nacional Popular).

With the electoral period coming to an end, the honeymoon between Marcelo Caetano and the opposition came to an end too. Bitter reproaches came from both sides, and opposition leaders started denouncing the Prime Minister's alleged hypocrisy and contradictions. The war in Africa was ·the main point of dissent, the government tolerating no questions whatsoever about Portugal's permanence in the Overseas or how it was dealing with these affairs. By the spring of 1970 Mário Soares was forced into exile again, while several other opposition leaders were arrested or persecuted.

Hostility of college students toward the regime and demands for thorough reforms in education prevented regular instruction in both 1969 and 1970. Early in 1970 the Premier appointed a new Education Minister, who made some compromises on student demands, possibly heralding fundamental changes in the system of instruction.

In any case, on balance Marcelo Caetano's two-year administration had some positive aspects from a non-Salazarist standpoint. However minor the progress, it still presented a contrast to Salazar's immobility. The all-pervasive atmosphere of fear had vanished, the P.I.D.E. (renamed General Direction of Security) appeared less harmful, only a few political prisoners were kept in jail, and censorship was milder. Salazar's death, in July 1970, was regarded by many as an end to one period of Portuguese history and the removal of an important obstacle to the country's moving in another direction.

BIBLIOGRAPHY

Chapter Ten: Constitutional Monarchy

Old Structures and New Order, pages 1–41

Among the general histories, only the *História de Portugal,* directed by Damião Peres, vol. VII, Barcelos, Portucalense Editora, 1935, is relevant for the analysis of structures. There is a school handbook by Fortunato de Almeida, *História das Instituições em Portugal,* 2nd ed., Porto, Magalhães e Moniz, 1903, which is quite useful as a survey. The *Dicionário de História de Portugal* once again deserves serious attention.

On the general economic—as well as social—aspects, see Armando Castro, *Introdução ao Estudo da Economia Portuguesa (Fins do séc. XVIII a princípios do séc. XX),* Lisbon, Cosmos, 1947; Vitorino Magalhães Godinho, *Prix et Monnaies au Portugal, 1750–1850,* Paris, SEVPEN, 1955; and Ezequiel de Campos, *O Enquadramento Geo-Económico da População Portuguesa através dos séculos,* 2nd ed., Lisbon, Ocidente, 1943. Joel Serrão provides some useful material on more specific subjects (including cultural matters) in his *Temas Oitocentistas, Para a História de Portugal no Século Passado,* vol. I, Lisbon, Ática, 1959, and vol. II, Lisbon, Portugália, 1962.

On currency see A. C. Teixeira de Aragão, *Descrição Geral e Histórica das Moedas cunhadas em nome dos Reis, Regentes e Governadores de Portugal,* vol. II, 2nd ed., Porto, Fernando Machado, n.d. The budget was studied by Armindo Monteiro, *Do Orçamento Português,* vol. I, Lisbon, 1921.

On the Church, see Fortunato de Almeida, *História da Igreja em Portugal,* vols. III and IV, 2nd ed., Porto, Civilização, 1970–72.

On cultural aspects see António José Saraiva and Óscar Lopes, *História da Literatura Portuguesa,* 2nd ed., Porto, Porto Editora, n.d., as well as José Tengarrinha, *História da Imprensa Periódica Portuguesa,* Lisbon, Portugália, 1965. On the arts there is a comprehensive monograph by José Augusto

França, *A Arte em Portugal no século XIX,* vols. I and II, Lisbon, Bertrand, 1966.

Among the nineteenth-century authors who wrote on contemporary history, Alexandre Herculano and Oliveira Martins are indispensable for today's historian, particularly Oliveira Martins' *Portugal Contemporâneo* (covering the period 1826–68), 3 vols., 7th ed., Lisbon, Guimarães, 1953.

The Political Life, pages 41–53

On the Liberal ideology and its early introduction in Portugal, there are good articles in the *Dicionário de História de Portugal,* directed by Joel Serrão, vol. II ("Liberalismo," "Maçonaria," "Imprensa," etc.). See also Joel Serrão's recent work, *Do Sebastianismo ao Socialismo em Portugal,* Lisbon, Livros Horizonte, 1969. All these articles and books include good bibliographies.

The Constitutions were studied by Marcelo Caetano, in a short, clear book, *História Breve das Constituições Portuguesas,* 2nd ed., Lisbon, Verbo, 1968.

There is no general work on the elections and the electoral systems. Marcelo Caetano gives some indications in the aforementioned book. A good source continues to be the *Manual Parlamentar para uso dos Senhores Deputados da Nação Portugueza,* edited by José Marcelino de Almeida Bessa, Lisbon, Imprensa Nacional, 1901.

On the parties and the party system, see the articles on each party and its leaders in the *Dicionário,* as well as M. Caetano's work, and the short article by A. H. de Oliveira Marques, "Revolution and Counterrevolution in Portugal—Problems of Portuguese History, 1900–1930," offprint of *Studien über die Revolution,* Berlin, Akademie-Verlag, 1969, pp. 403–418.

The general histories of Portugal also give information on the political life of the country in this period.

Main Events, pages 54–75

Damião Peres' edition of *História de Portugal,* vol. VII, Barcelos, Portucalense Editora, 1935, gives the best account of the facts. The *Dicionário de História de Portugal,* edited by Joel Serrão, includes, as usual, several excellent articles on persons and events. Joaquim Pedro de Oliveira Martins' *Portugal Contemporâneo,* 7th ed., 3 vols., Lisbon, Guimarães ed., 1953, covers the period to 1868, but should be used with extreme caution, for the author tends to adopt a too pessimistic view of his country's history.

Fortunato de Almeida's *História de Portugal,* vol. VI, Coimbra, 1929, is of little use except for the religious problems. It includes, however, good bibliographical references.

Chapter Eleven: Africa

Travels and Colonization, pages 77–91

On travels in Portuguese Africa, the best accounts are still the explorers' own reports, most of which were published in Lisbon throughout the nineteenth century. Gamito, Brochado, Silva Porto, Welwitsch, Serpa Pinto, Capelo, Ivens, Henrique de Carvalho, and others left complete descriptions of their deeds of which no English translations are available. There is no good history of the Portuguese expeditions in general, but accurate references can be found in the general works on Portugal and on Portuguese Africa, namely the *História da Expansão Portuguesa no Mundo,* edited by António Baião, Hernâni Cidade, and Manuel Múrias, vol. III, Lisbon, Ática, 1940, as well as under each explorer's entry in the *Dicionário de História de Portugal,* edited by Joel Serrão. Both works contain bibliographies. Another first-rate source for the scientific study of nineteenth-century Portuguese Africa is the *Boletim da Sociedade de Geografia de Lisboa,* published since the 1870's.

On other aspects see the general works mentioned, which provide much of the extremely scattered bibliography. On slavery see, among other sources, Sá da Bandeira's *O Trabalho Rural Africano e a Administração Colonial,* Lisbon, 1873, and Luciano Cordeiro's *Questões Histórico-Coloniais,* Lisbon, 1936. James Duffy's *A Question of Slavery,* Cambridge, Mass., 1967, must be used with caution because of the author's anti-Portuguese bias.

On the Christian missions and the Church policy see, besides the general histories and Fortunato de Almeida's *História da Igreja em Portugal,* Eduardo dos Santos, *L'Etat Portugais et le Problème Missionaire,* Lisbon, 1964.

Organization, pages 91–107

Besides the general works already mentioned (particularly the *História da Expansão Portuguesa no Mundo,* vol. III), Angel Marvaud's report on Portugal and her colonies (*Le Portugal et ses Colonies: Etude politique et économique,* Paris, Félix Alcan, 1912) is of immense value, especially for the economic and financial questions. The classic book by Pinheiro Chagas,

As Colonias Portuguezas no seculo XIX (1811 a 1890), Lisbon, A. M. Pereira, 1890, still renders good service. The chaotic *Historia das Colonias Portuguesas,* by Rocha Martins, Lisbon, Empresa Nacional de Publicidade, 1933, is useful but must be used with caution. A good general history restricted to the Overseas affairs is clearly lacking.

Political Events, pages 107–118

Although the bibliography on the political and military history of the Portuguese Overseas during the nineteenth century is a vast one, there is hardly a good, recommended, general survey. The best works available are the *História de Portugal,* edited by Damião Peres, vol. VII, Barcelos, Portucalense, 1935, and the *História da Expansão Portuguesa no Mundo,* edited by António Baião, Hernâni Cidade and Manuel Múrias, Vol. III, Lisbon, Ática, 1940.

In English there are at least two good and up-to-date monographs which cover the international aspects of the Portuguese African policy: Richard J. Hammond, *Portugal and Africa, 1815–1910: A Study in Uneconomic Imperialism,* Stanford, Calif., Stanford University Press, 1966, and Eric Axelson, *Portugal and the Scramble for Africa, 1875–1891,* Johannesburg, Witwatersrand University Press, 1967. See also Mabel V. Jackson Haight, *European Powers and South-East Africa: A Study of International Relations on the South-East Coast of Africa, 1796–1856,* New York and Washington, Praeger, 1967, and Philip R. Warhurst, *Anglo-Portuguese Relations in South-Central Africa, 1890–1900,* London, Longmans, 1962.

Chapter Twelve: The First Republic

The Main Problems to Be Solved, pages 119–149

There are extremely few syntheses on this period and on its special aspects that can be recommended. Damião Peres' *História de Portugal,* vol. VII, Barcelos, Portucalense, 1935, and "Suplemento," Porto, Portucalense, 1954, do cover the whole period but emphasize the factual and political elements. For a short survey see A. H. de Oliveira Marques, *Portugal no século XX: Problemas de história portuguesa 1900–1930,* offprint of *Ocidente,* vol. LXXVI, Lisbon, 1969, pp. 253–272 and especially his *A 1ᵃ República Portuguesa (para uma visão estrutural),* Lisbon, Livros Horizonte, n.d. [1971]. The *Dicionário de História de Portugal,* directed by Joel Serrão, contains some useful and up-to-date studies, all with bibliography.

There is more for literature and the arts: António José Saraiva and Óscar Lopes (*História da Literatura Portuguesa*, 2nd ed., Porto, Porto Editora, n.d.) explain the literary currents, while José Augusto França (*A Arte em Portugal no século XIX*, vol. II, Lisbon, Bertrand, 1966) gives a clear picture of the trends followed in the arts to the 1920's. For music, see João de Freitas Branco, *História da Música Portuguesa*, Lisbon, Europa-América, 1959.

There is nothing in English to recommend.

Ideologies and Political Structure, pages 149–164

On the Republican general ideology, the best account is from Joel Serrão (J.S.) in his article "Republicanismo," in the *Dicionário de História de Portugal*, III, 587–595, which also gives the most important bibliographical references. The party system has not been studied yet: see some remarks in Marcelo Caetano, *História Breve das Constituições Portuguesas*, 2nd ed., Lisbon, Verbo, 1968, in A. H. de Oliveira Marques, "Revolution and Counterrevolution in Portugal—Problems of Portuguese History, 1900–1930," offprint of *Studien über die Revolution*, Berlin, Akademie-Verlag, 1969, pp. 403–418, and especially in Damião Peres, *História de Portugal, Suplemento*, Porto, Portucalense, 1954. On the role played by Seara Nova there is a good article by Gerald Moser, "The Campaign of *Seara Nova* and Its Impact on Portuguese Literature, 1921–61" in *Luso-Brazilian Review*, II, 1 (June, 1965), 15–42, besides the survey by David Ferreira, "Seara Nova" in *Dicionário de História de Portugal*, III, Lisbon, 1968, 805–810. See also the articles included in this same Dictionary on each party and secret association.

The Constitution of 1911 was studied by several authors, as for instance, M. Caetano in the aforementioned book. There is no work on elections or electoral geography.

The Events, pages 164–175

The only work that gives a factual account of the Republican period is the *História de Portugal*, directed by Damião Peres, vol. VII, Barcelos, Portucalense, 1935 (chapters written by Ângelo Ribeiro and Hernâni Cidade), and particularly its *Suplemento*, Barcelos, Portucalense, 1954, written by Damião Peres himself. It covers the period to 1933. In English see A. H. de Oliveira Marques, "Revolution and Counterrevolution in Portugal—Problems of Portuguese History, 1900–1930," offprint of *Studien über die Revolution*, Berlin, Akademie-Verlag, 1969, pp. 403–418.

Chapter Thirteen: The "New State"

Portuguese Fascism, pages 177–194

The only recommended study of the New State is Hermínio Martins'
outstanding, if short, analysis, *Portugal,* an offprint from *European Fascism,*
edited by S. J. Woolf, London, Weidenfeld and Nicolson, 1968, pp. 302–336
(American edition, New York, Random House, 1969).

On Integralism, besides H. Martins, see Raul Proença, *Páginas de
Política,* vols. I and II, Lisbon, Seara Nova, 1938–39; Carlos Ferrão, *O
Integralismo e a República* (*Autópsia de um mito*), 3 vols., Lisbon, Século,
1964–66; David Ferreira's (D.F.) article "Integralismo Lusitano," in
Dicionário de História de Portugal, edited by Joel Serrão, II, 556–560; and
A Questão Ibérica (collection of lectures by leading Integralists), Lisbon,
1916.

On Italian and other foreign influences on the Portuguese regime, see
the long-forgotten, yet useful, small book, *Origine e caratteri dello "Stato
Nuovo" Portoghese,* edited by Aldo Bigarri, Milan, Instituto per gli studi di
Politica Internazionale, 1941.

The best source for the study of the essential New State principles and
evolution, as well as Salazar's thought, is of course Salazar himself: see his
Discursos e Notas Políticas, 5 vols., Coimbra, Coimbra Editora, 1935–68.
António Ferro's classic, *Salazar: Portugal and Her Leader,* Lisbon, 1939,
continues to be the best study on the Dictator, done by one of his followers.
Recommended biographies by non-Portuguese authors are Hugh Kay's
Salazar and Modern Portugal, London, Eyre & Spottiswoode, 1970, and
particularly Christian Rudel, *Salazar,* Paris, Mercure de France, 1969.
On Corporatism see Marcelo Caetano, *O sistema corporativo,* Lisbon,
1937. His short, excellent *História Breve das Constituições Portuguesas,* 2nd
ed. (important because of the author's rise to premiership and his authoritative remarks on Salazar's rule), Lisbon, Verbo, 1968, gives a summary of
the regime's constitutional framework.

I strongly advise anyone interested in the Portuguese political and
economic structure to consult any of the *liceu* (high-school) "political organization" textbooks for the upper grades, as for instance, A. Martins
Afonso, *Princípios Fundamentais de Organização Política e Administrativa
da Nação,* 14th ed., Lisbon, Papelaria Fernandes, n.d. [1966].

On repression see, for instance, among scores of passionate, yet valid,
testimonies, Fernando Queiroga, *Portugal Oprimido* (*Subsídios para a história do fascismo em Portugal*), Rio de Janeiro, Editora Germinal, 1958, or

P. Fryer and P. MacGowan Pinheiro, *Oldest Ally: A Portrait of Salazar's Portugal*, London, 1961, or the judiciary proceedings edited by lawyer Francisco Salgado Zenha, *Quatro Causas*, Lisbon, 1969.

Hermínio Martins is also the author of a short but penetrating analysis of the Portuguese opposition: *Opposition in Portugal*, reprint from *Government and Opposition*, vol. IV, No. 2 (Spring, 1969), pp. 250–263.

Portugal by the Middle of the Twentieth Century, pages 194–208

The use of yearly books such as the *Encyclopaedia Britannica Book of the Year*, the United Nations publications, and the Portuguese annual statistics (*Anuário Estatístico*) must make up for the lack of general histories or even detailed monographs on the New State as a whole. Ezequiel de Campos, *O Enquadramento Geo-Económico da População Portuguesa através dos Séculos*, 2nd ed., Lisbon, Ocidente, 1943, and Orlando Ribeiro, *Portugal*, vol. V of Manuel de Terán's *Geografía de España y Portugal*, Barcelona, Montaner y Simón, 1955, give interesting surveys on economic and demographic questions to the 1950's.

On Salazar's financial reforms, see Salazar himself, *A reorganização financeira, Dois anos no Ministério das Finanças, 1928–1930*, Coimbra, Coimbra Editora, 1930, followed by several of his speeches and notes, namely in *Discursos e Notas Políticas*, vol. II, *1935–1937*, Coimbra, Coimbra, Editora, 1937 ("Questões Financeiras," pp. 351–395). José Joaquim Teixeira Ribeiro in his textbook *Introdução ao Estudo da Moeda*, Coimbra, Atlântida, 1949, devotes one chapter to the Portuguese monetary evolution to 1948. See also Marcelo Caetano, *A obra financeira de Salazar*, Lisbon, 1934.

On public works there is an official publication called *Quinze Anos de Obras Públicas (1932–1947)*, Comissão Executiva da Exposição de Obras Públicas, 2 vols., Lisbon, 1949, covering the period to 1947. Among the many books and pamphlets on economic subjects, see Araújo Correia, *Portugal Económico e Financeiro*, Lisbon, 1938; Ezequiel de Campos, *Problemas Fundamentais Portugueses*, Lisbon, 1946; Pereira de Moura and Luis Maria Teixeira Pinto, *Problemas do crescimento económico português*, Lisbon, 1958; V. Xavier Pintado, *Structure and Growth of the Portuguese Economy*, Geneva, 1964; and Vitorino Magalhães Godinho, *O Socialismo e o Futuro da Península*, Lisbon, Horizonte, 1969. There is a good summary report on internal colonization by Henrique de Barros, *Economia Agrária*, vol. III, Lisbon, Sá da Costa, 1954. On other aspects of agriculture, see

Mário de Azevedo Gomes, Henrique de Barros, and Eugénio de Castro Caldas, "Traços principais da evolução da agricultura portuguesa entre as duas guerras mundiais," in *Revista do Centro de Estudos Económicos,* nos. 1 and 2 (1945), pp. 21–203 and 49–86; Álvaro Cunhal, *A Questão Agrária em Portugal,* Rio de Janeiro, Ed. Civilização Brasileira, 1968 (the communist standpoint), and others.

Population changes were studied by J. T. Montalvão Machado, *Como nascem e morrem os Portugueses,* Lisbon, Gomes e Rodrigues, n.d., and more recently, by Alberto de Alarcão, *Mobilidade Geográfica da População de Portugal (Continente e Ilhas Adjacentes): Migrações internas 1921– 1960,* Lisbon, Fundação Calouste Gulbenkian, 1969.

On administration, the best report is Marcelo Caetano's textbook, *Manual de Direito Administrativo,* 8th ed., 2 vols., Lisbon, Coimbra Editora, 1969. Educational problems were studied by scores of people. See, for instance, Rogério Fernandes, *Ensino: Sector em Crise,* Lisbon, Prelo, 1967; *Análise Quantitativa da Estrutura Escolar Portuguesa, 1950–1959,* Lisbon, Centro de Estudos de Estatística Económica do Instituto de Alta Cultura, 1960; or the two volumes of periodical *Análise Social,* vol. V and VI, 1967–68, devoted to "A Universidade na Vida Portuguesa."

For the general panorama of literature, see António José Saraiva and Óscar Lopes, *História da Literatura Portuguesa,* Porto, Porto Editora, n.d.

The Events, pages 208–224

Damião Peres' *História de Portugal: Suplemento,* Porto, Portucalense, 1954, stops in 1934. To 1945 there is a list of the main events (from the government standpoint) in the *Anais da Revolução Nacional,* ed. by João Ameal and Domingos Mascarenhas, 5 vols., Lisbon, 1948–56. For later times, as for the whole period, see the *Encyclopaedia Britannica Book of the Year* or any other good Encyclopedia.

Chapter Fourteen: The Overseas Empire in the Twentieth Century

Policies, pages 225–232

Damião Peres' *História de Portugal: Suplemento,* Porto, Portucalense, 1954, provides the main information for the period 1914–33. Further elements are contained in the António Baião, Hernâni Cidade, and Manuel Múrias edition of *História da Expansão Portuguesa no Mundo,* vol. III, Lisbon, Ática, 1940. See also Henrique Galvão and Carlos Selvagem, *Im-*

pério Ultramarino Português, 4 vols., Lisbon, Empresa Nacional de Publicidade, 1950–53.

For the period after 1945 the bibliography is large but scattered and uneven in objectivity. There are acceptable historical data in Ronald H. Chilcote, *Portuguese Africa,* Englewood Cliffs, Prentice Hall, Inc., 1967, and in Eduardo Mondlane's *The Struggle for Mozambique,* Penguin Books, 1969. From the other side see, for instance, Adriano Moreira's *Portugal's Stand in Africa,* New York, 1962, and *The Road for the Future,* Lisbon, 1963, along with many of his speeches and interviews translated into English. See also Marcelo Caetano, *Portugal e a internacionalização dos problemas africanos,* Lisbon, 1963, and A. Franco Nogueira, *The United Nations and Portugal: A Study of Anti-Colonialism,* London, 1963.

On specific labor problems and the Portuguese labor policy, see José Norton de Matos, *Memórias e Trabalhos da Minha Vida,* 4 vols., Lisbon, 1945–46 (particularly vol. 3), and his *A Província de Angola,* Porto, Maranus, 1926. For a general survey, see Joaquim M. da Silva Cunha, *O sistema português de política indígena: Princípios gerais,* Lisbon, Agência Geral do Ultramar, 1952, and his *O trabalho indígena: estudo de direito colonial,* Lisbon, 1954. On the problem to 1920, see James Duffy, *A Question of Slavery,* Oxford, Clarendon Press, 1967.

From Pacification to the Prospects of Independence, pages 232–239

On the last pacification campaigns and World War I in Portuguese Africa the bibliography is vast. See general surveys in *História da Expansão Portuguesa no Mundo,* edited by António Baião, Hernâni Cidade, and Manuel Múrias, vol. III, Lisbon, Ática, 1940, and in *História de Portugal,* edited by Damião Peres, vol. VII, and *Suplemento,* Barcelos and Porto, Portucalense, 1935 and 1954. See also the authoritative monograph by General M. Gomes da Costa, *A Guerra nas Colonias, 1914–1918,* Lisbon Portugal/Brasil, n.d.

Bibliography on the African uprisings is also vast. Most of it is unreliable because of partisanship.

On the side of the independence movements, see, among many others:

(a) General works—James Duffy, *Portugal in Africa,* Penguin Books, 1963; Ronald H. Chilcote, *Portuguese Africa,* Prentice-Hall, Englewood Cliffs, N.J., 1967; "Three Revolutions," special issue of *Africa Report* on Portuguese Africa, vol. 12, No. 8 (November, 1967).

(b) On Angola: *Angola: A Symposium: Views of a Revolt,* Oxford University Press, 1962; *Les Angolais,* edited by Robert Davezies, Paris, Editions de Minuit, 1965; Pierre Moser, *La Révolution Angolaise,* Tunis, Société d'Action, d'Édition et de Presse, 1966; John Marcum, *The Angolan Revolution,* vol. I, *The Anatomy of an Explosion* (*1950– 1962*), M.I.T. Press, Cambridge, Mass., 1969.

(c) On Mozambique: Eduardo Mondlane, *The Struggle for Mozambique,* Penguin Books, 1969.

(d) On Guinea: Gérard Chaliand, *Lutte armée en Afrique,* Paris, François Maspéro, 1967.

On the side of the Portuguese Government:
Angola: Curso de extensão universitária, Lisbon, 1963; Amândio César, *Angola 1961,* Lisbon, Verbo, 1962; Artur Maciel, *Angola Heroica,* Lisbon, Bertrand, 1963.

The "Empire" by the Middle of the Century, pages 239–257

There is no recommendable history of the Portuguese Empire in the twentieth century. Henrique Galvão's and Carlos Selvagem's four-volume work, *O Império Ultramarino Português,* Lisbon, Empresa Nacional de Publicidade, 1950–53, contains much useful information. Official statistics appear in *Anuário Estatístico do Império Colonial Português* (later called *Anuário Estatístico do Ultramar*), Lisbon, 1943–59 and in the general *Anuário Estatístico* for all of Portugal after 1960. Portuguese and general encyclopaedias must also be consulted. There are local *Anuários* in each colony. In English there is nothing really commendable, but both James Duffy's works (*Portuguese Africa,* Cambridge, Mass. and London, 1959; and *Portugal in Africa,* Penguin Books, 1963) and Ronald Chilcote's (*Portuguese Africa,* Englewood Cliffs, 1967) may be useful, if used with caution.

Bibliography on specific problems is endless. Chilcote gives a quite extensive and reliable list of books which can be used for the study of the Portuguese twentieth-century Empire.

INDEX

Abação, I, 51

Aboim, João Peres de, I, 119

Abrantes, Marquis of, I, 428

Abrilada, II, 58

Absolutism, II, 54-55, 58-59

Absolutists, political party, II, 49

Abū Ya'qub Yūsuf I (al-Shahid), I, 64

Abū Ya'qub Yūsuf II (al-Mansūr), I, 27, 64

Aden, I, 220, 234

Administration, local, I, 128: pre-Portugal, I, 13-19; Christian North, I, 58-59; al-Gharb al-Andalus, I, 70-71; Renaissance, I, 186-87; late 16th and 17th centuries, I, 295-96; colonial, I, 341-42, 364-66, II, 93-98, 242-46; late 17th and 18th centuries, I, 394-95; 19th century, II, 16; 20th century, II, 203

Aesuris, I, 20

Afonso I (Henriques) (1128-1185), I, 39, 41-44, 47, 57, 61-64

Afonso II (1211-1223), I, 45, 52, 53, 55, 65, 87, 88, 91

Afonso III (1248-1279), I, 45, 65, 78, 88, 96, 97, 101; reign of, I, 119-20

Afonso IV (1325-1357), I, 92, 97, 99, 113, 115, 117; reign of, I, 122-24, 140-41, 145

Afonso V (1438-1481), I, 88, 100, 115; regency of, 131-32, 144; reign of, I, 153, 161, 174, 175, 178, 180, 187, 189, 198, 207, 209, 214, 217; education of, I, 191

Afonso VI (1656-1683), I, 331; regency of, I, 331, 333, 395; reign of, I, 332-33, 395; coup d'état, I, 332, 333

Afonso I (Nzinga Mvemba), King of Congo, I, 247

Afonso, Duke of Bragança, I, 132, 207

Afonso, Prince, son of Afonso III, I, 120

Afonso, Prince, son of John I, I, 130, 138; Count of Barcelos, I, 88, 131

Afonso, Prince, son of John II, I, 181, 210

Afonso, Prince, son of Manuel I, I, 182

Afonso, Jorge, I, 203

Africa: East, I, 135, 229-31, 233, 248-49, 235, 277-85 passim, 338-40, 463, 472-74; North, I, 130-31, 135, 143, 161, 163, 214-15, 217-28; South, I, 220, 223, 277-85 passim; West, I, 135, 145, 149-51, 158, 217-20, 223-24, 230, 242-48, 269, 277-85 passim, 463-64

African League, II, 234

Agriculture, I, 4, 126, II, 2; Christian North, I, 22, 56; al-Gharb al-Andalus, I, 22, 67; 15th and 16th centuries, I, 108, 110-12, 168-70; Portuguese colonies, I, 153-54, 239, 240, II, 101-2; prices, I, 178, 273; 16th and 17th centuries, I, 272-73; 18th century, I, 381-82; 19th century, II, 3-4; 20th century, II, 121-22, 198, 200-1

Aguiar, Joaquim António de, minister, II, 23

Agulhas, Cape, I, 220

Fortunate, island of, I, 135
Francavila, Duke of, I, 320
France: relations with Portugal, I, 92, 125, 145, 148, 209, 329-30, 418-19, 424-25, 427, 448-49, II, 61, 70, 90; trade with Portugal, I, 92-93, II, 125, 199; cultural ties with Portugal, I, 193, 194; attacks on Portuguese ships and possessions, I, 215, 254, 310, 315, 357, 364, 370, 372, 424, 467, 474, II, 70; treaty of alliance with Portugal, I, 332; invasions of Portugal, I, 384, 387, 423, 425, 427-29, 455; Brazil border dispute, I, 448-49; intrusions into Portuguese colonies, II, 108-11
Franciscan order, I, 52, 82, 116, 286, 447, II, 24, 130; churches, I, 106-7; missionaries, I, 253, 350, 367
Franco, Gen. Francisco, II, 214, 216
Franco, João, minister, II, 18, 32, 73; premier, II, 74, 75
Freemasonry, II, 42, 51, 159-60
Freire, Filipe dos Santos, I, 452
Freitas, Barjona de, minister, II, 18, 19
Freitas, Col. Vicente de, II, 213; premier, II, 210-11
Freixo, I, 47, 173
Frio, I, 57
Fromariz, I, 51
Fronteira, Marquis of, I, 382, 383, 418
Funchal, I, 153-54, 238, 368-70, 464-65; bishopric, I, 238, 285
Fuschini, Augusto, minister, II, 72

Gabon, I, 219
Galhardo, Col. Eduardo, II, 117
Galicia, I, 6, 8, 10, 46, 58, 93, 315; Moslem conquest of, I, 25, 27-28
Gallaecia, Roman province, I, 8, 10, 13, 16, 18-20; Suevi in, I, 23, 24, 25
Galvão, Duarte, I, 230
Galvão, Capt. Henrique, II, 235
Gama, Arnaldo, II, 38
Gama, Basílio da, I, 454
Gama, Cristóvão da, I, 230-31
Gama, Vasco da, I, 214, 221, 223, 226, 229, 232, 251, 268-70

Gambia, I, 257, 259
Gambia River, I, 150, 230
Gamito, Capt. António Pedroso, II, 77-78
Garção, Correia, I, 412
Garcia, Elias, II, 150, 153
García, King of Galicia, I, 29
García, King of Leon, I, 28
Garrett, Almeida, II, 27; minister, II, 68
Gato, Manuel de Borba, I, 436-47
Geba River, I, 463; II, 81
"Generation of 1870," II, 39-40
Geography, I, 1-5, 46; knowledge of, I, 134-38, 204-5; Lisbon Geographical Society, II, 79, 107-8
Geraldes, Geraldo, I, 63-64
Geraldo, Archbishop, I, 43, 44
Germany: intrusions into Portuguese colonies, II, 109-10, 111-12, 115, 233; declaration of war, II, 167
Ghana, I, 246, 374; II, 218
Gibraltar, I, 162
Gilbert, bishop of Lisbon, I, 74-76
Glass industry, I, 382-83, II, 7
Goa, I, 220, 233-35, 249-50, 258, 320, 337-38, 343, 345-47, 351, 354-55, 463, 474-77, II, 101, 105, 114, 242; bishopric, I, 250, 347, II, 90, 91; population, I, 339-40; government, I, 342, 476-77
Godinho, Vitorino Magalhães, I, 280; quoted, I, 307
Godoy, Manuel de, I, 427
Goiás, province of, I, 432-33, 436-37, 459; diocese, I, 433
Góis, Bento de, I, 353
Góis, Damião de, I, 198
Goitacazes, Campo dos, I, 254
Gold: trade in, I, 93, 139, 159, 170, 175, 252, 257, 259-60, 261, 277, 324, 345, 355, 375, 383, 389-90, 437-39; importance of obtaining, I, 139-40; discovery of in Brazil, I, 437, 452; see also Monetary structure, coinage and currency
Gomes, Diogo, I, 150
Gomes, Estêvão, I, 228

Silveira, João Fernandez da, I, 184, 235
Silveira, José Xavier Mousinho da, minister, II, 2, 16, 61, 64
Silver, trade in, I, 69, 93, 96, 159, 174, 277, 308, 324, 345, 355, 376, 389, 449; see also Monetary structure, coinage and currency
Silves, Diogo de, I, 148
Silves, I, 12, 65, 74, 89, 90, 109; Christian reconquest of, I, 77; cathedral, I, 106; archbishop, I, 182; bishopric, I, 182, 187
Sintra, Pedro de, I, 150
Sintra, I, 174; palace, I, 202
Sixtus, IV, Pope, I, 206
Slavery: in Portugal, I, 55, 80, 167, 294-95; in colonies, I, 154, 238, 240, 242, 256-57, 260, ·360-62, 369, 373, 375, 435-37, 439-40, 444-45, 453, II, 86-90, 98-99; Casa dos Escravos, I, 262; abolition of, I, 405, II, 88
Slave trade, I, 140, 154, 158-59, 167, 170, 186, 246, 248, 259-60, 295, 361, 363, 373, 377-78, 385, 439-41, 467-69, II, 86-90, 98-99
Soares, Mário, II, 224, 259
Socialist party, II, 50, 151, 156, 170, 212
Social structure: Christian North, I, 53-56; al-Gharb al-Andalus, I, 68-70; after Reconquista, I, 80-81, 109-10; 15th century, I, 114-15, 179-86; decline of bourgeoisie, I, 293-94; Brazil, I, 364, 444-45; 17th and 18th centuries, I, 395-98, 403-6; under José I, I, 421-23; 19th century, II, 26-29; 182-83; class unrest, 20th century, II, 136-40
Society of Jesus, see Jesuits
Socotra, I, 229, 233, 234
Sofala, I, 233, 248, 249, 262, 339, 473, II, 79, 81
Soils, I, 4, 46, II, 3
Solis, João Dias de, I, 227, 264
Solor, I, 478, II, 115
Soult, Marshal, Duke of Dalmatia, I, 429

Sousa, Alberto de, II, 148
Sousa, António Caetano de, I, 410
Sousa, Francisco de, I, 356, 365
Sousa, Luis de, I, 304, 323
Sousa, Manuel de Faria e, I, 354
Sousa, Martim Afonso de, I, 231-32, 254-55, 364
Sousa, Tomé de, I, 364, 365
South America, I, 135-36, 221, 227-28; see also Brazil
Soveral, Marquis of, II, 116
Spain: trade with Portugal, I, 92-93, 274-75, 308-9; voyages of discovery, I, 227-28, 264; union with Portugal, I, 275, 283-84, 306-22; invasions of Portugal, I, 314-15, 384, 387, 423, 425, 427-29, 455; kings as rulers of Portugal, I, 315-22; war against Portugal, I, 332; alliance with France, I, 418-19, 424-25, 427, 429; Brazil border dispute, I, 449-50; in revolution of 1846, II, 67; treaties with Portugal (1940), II, 216
Spanish Armada, I, 316-17
Spanish Succession, War of (1702-1713), 384, 386n, 419, 448-49
Spice trade, I, 232, 257, 259-61, 274, 311, 324, 344, 346, 375, 385
Stefano of Naples, I, 191
Suevi (Swaefs), I, 11, 23-25
Sufism, I, 62, 72
Sugar: colonial sources of, I, 140, 154, 158, 170, 256, 361-62, 369, 375, 385; trade in, I, 154, 159, 238, 240, 253, 255, 257, 261, 274, 355, 362, 363, 369, 371, 375, 383, 385, 439, II, 123, 247, 250
Sumatra, I, 229, 231, 234, 235, 259, 260
Swabians, see Suevi

Tabīra, I, 63, 66; see also Tavira
Tagus River Basin, I, 5, 8, 12, 13, 20, 22, 31, 33, 61, 63, 64, 66-68, 89, 166, 429, II, 197; boundary of Al-Gharb al-Andalus, I, 77, 81
Taifa kingdoms, I, 31-34, 38, 62-64, 68, 77